RENEWALS 458-4574

LEGISLATIVE STAFFING

LEGISLATIVE STAFFING

A
Comparative
Perspective

Edited by

JAMES J. HEAPHEY
State University of New York at Albany

and

ALAN P. BALUTIS
State University of New York at Buffalo

SAGE Publications

Halsted Press Division
JOHN WILEY & SONS
New York — London — Sydney — Toronto

Distributed by Halsted Press, a Division of
John Wiley & Sons, Inc., New York

Printed in the United States of America

Library of Congress Cataloging in Publication Data
Main entry under title:

Legislative staffing.

    1. Legislative bodies–Officials and employees. 2. Legislative bodies–United States–States–Officials and employees. 3. United States. Congress–Officials and employees. I. Heaphey, James J., 1930- II. Balutis, Alan P.
JF540.5.L43   328.73   75-16413
ISBN 0-470-36671-0

FIRST PRINTING

CONTENTS

PREFACE

Why, one might ask, a book on legislative staff? And the editors of this volume might respond, why *not?* While not wishing to precipitate a Socratic dialogue, the simple point of the question-response is to emphasize that the need for this book, in our judgment, is evidenced in the question. Though legislative staffs have burgeoned in recent years and are generally considered by those familiar with legislatures to be tremendously important to the legislative process, they are not being discussed in the literature. Considerations of professional staffing in texts on the legislative process, both state and national, consist primarily of a recitation of figures and a prescriptive plea for larger staffs. This point, it might be noted, begs the question. Admittedly, the workload of legislatures is increasing annually. However, a mere increase in the size of staffs is not going to meet those problems which may exist.

This volume grows from the interests of its individual authors and from the institutional concerns of the Comparative Development Studies Center (CDSC) at the State University of New York at Albany. As an outcome of the Center's research/service programs and projects with legislatures throughout the United States and around the world, a book on legislative staff seemed eminently logical. For, in all its endeavors, the Center has stressed the perspectives and actions of the people involved in legislative development efforts and staffs, as the following chapters indicate, certainly figure significantly in these efforts. Wherever the Center has been involved, the questions and issues of this increasing commodity—legislative staff—have emerged. In Ethiopia as well as New York, Korea as well as Illinois, Brazil as well as California, staffing is a central concern.

A second question one might raise is why a comparative study of staff? Again, the logical answer is, why not? Although American staffing patterns begin at a point different from that of other countries (for example, most foreign legislative staff have permanent civil service status), similar problems and issues arise amid the differences. For example, information needs are a universal question, as are professionalism, recruitment, organization according to political or nonpolitical criteria, relationships are a part of (and reflect) the political system in which they operate. The structuring of the legislative staff, the nature of the services it performs, and the extent to which it plays an important policy role will differ to some degree with each polity and its functioning legislature. Thus, it is illuminating to consider and analyze different emergent patterns of staffing in different political systems—as are found in California, Florida, Michigan, New York, Virginia, the U.S. Congress, Lebanon, and Brazil, for example.

And a third question one might raise is who the authors regard as their audience for this book. The first audience, of course, is legislative staffers themselves. They will probably find much to bemoan by way of what is not covered in this volume; we ask their forbearance on the basis that this is an initial foray into previously unexplored territory. Second, we believe that executive staffers will find this volume relevant to their interests and concerns. The third audience is composed of scholars and students in academia who are searching for a better understanding of the legislative process. And, finally, we hope that the growing number of private citizens who are forming public interest groups will benefit from the labors that brought this volume to print.

J.J.H.
A.P.B.

ACKNOWLEDGEMENTS

Many people have helped directly or indirectly in the development of this book and several deserve a special word of appreciation. Daron K. Butler, Edgar Crane, and John Worthley offered helpful suggestions on several chapters. Rhoda Blecker of Sage Publications followed the manuscript through publication with great patience and helpful editorial advice. The finished manuscript would not have been possible without the dedicated typing assistance of Cynthia Breeden, Diane Biggins, Roslyn Capsico, Ann Bateman, and Barbara Rodriguez.

Editing a book can be a major strain on the entire family, and we are thankful for the patience and help of our wives, Lenore and Miriam. Finally, we note that this book is a joint venture and as such the authors are solely and equally responsible.

Albany, New York   J.J.H.
Buffalo, New York   A.P.B.

LEGISLATIVE STAFFING: ORGANIZATIONAL AND PHILOSOPHICAL CONSIDERATIONS

JAMES J. HEAPHEY

My purpose in this chapter is to attempt to provide a general introduction to the study of legislative staffing. My subjects are: legislative workload and organization; the role of legislative staff; distinctive organizational traits of legislatures; and metaphysics of legislative process.

These subjects are inextricably intertwined, in my judgment. Staff are appearing in increasing numbers in legislatures because the workload of legislatures requires their presence. As this increased workload and staffing are shaped into workable parameters, organizational patterns emerge within which staff find their roles. Some of these organizational patterns are familiar to any organization; others appear to be more distinctive to the legislature. For example, legislative organizations must be considerably more attuned to the needs of bargaining and quick decisions than must their executive agency counterparts.

There is and will continue to be a pressure toward "rationalizing" and "bureaucratizing" legislative organizations, which could be a drastic mistake. We need a philosophy of purpose if we are to deal meaningfully with questions of legislative staffing. This philosophy must begin with the function of a legislature in its societal setting, not with the question of what is a rational organization, and/or what will bring about the most efficient form of organizational action. The metaphysics of legislatures is a metaphysics of creative and changing reality rather than a metaphysics of permanence and routinized reality. The former requires organizational traits that maximize the capacity for the process to be realized in terms of the visions of the political actors within the process; the latter calls more for organizational traits that maximize the capacity to carry out routinized tasks rationally and efficiently.

Legislative staffers have distinctive and important roles which should be conceptualized and actualized with a broad metaphysics that encompasses the organizations in which they find their roles. What must be avoided in these early stages of understanding the legislative staff role is an itch to "solve" the legislature's problems by ridding it of its essence, which is that it is a political process.

LEGISLATIVE WORKLOAD AND ORGANIZATION

In 1934, W. F. Willoughby observed that "two of the most important developments of recent years affecting the work of legislative bodies are: the constant augmentation in the volume of work that they are called upon to perform; and the increasing complexity and technicality of the subjects with which they have to deal."[1] Legislatures, he said, are seen as staggering under the load thrown upon them. Due to lack of time, he went on to report, congresses and state legislators are adjourning with many matters of vital significance left undone. He added that it is the complex technical content of the workload that presents the greatest difficulties:

> Many of these measures, if they are to be properly handled, call for expert knowledge in such fields as law, economics, political science, the technology of public administration, business organization and finance, and branches of knowledge of a still more special character, a knowledge which but few of the members of our legislative bodies are likely to possess.[2]

Delegation of authority to other agencies to deal with technical aspects of legislation and to make decisions, Willoughby said, is the most effective means of dealing with technical complexity. Notwithstanding the well-established principle of American constitutional law that legislative authority may not be delegated, he also noted that "little legal difficulty is encountered by our legislative bodies in delegating to other agencies the rule-making power ... due to the liberal position taken by our courts whenever such action has been questioned."[3] By 1934, our legislative bodies had made wide usage of lessening work and taking care of technical details by delegating "rule-making powers to the executive and to administrative agencies and in the creation of special tribunals having as one of their chief functions the exercise of such power."[4]

Another way that legislatures had, by 1934, approached the workload and complexity problem, Willoughby said, was by establishing legislative reference and bill-drafting services within the legislative institution. In recent years increases in such legislative staffs have been mounting. Central staffs, staffs for party leadership, committee staffs, individual legislator staffs—these are some of the growing areas of legislative reform. It is now commonly accepted that legislators left to themselves have no way to cope with the complexities of the process they are elected to determine. In many states, the legislature is supposed to review an intricate and profoundly complex executive appropriations bill in a matter of weeks; with their own hands, legislators drown themselves in proposed bills; overseeing executive implementation of legislative acts is a dizzying experience. And so it goes. What Willoughby observed in 1934 as a workload and technical problem has become a nightmare. But legislatures are coping; they are organizing to perform their work. *It is within these organizations that the staff role emerges.*

The organizations formed by legislatures have jurisdictions, stages of action, procedures, and workflows working within these divisions. While it is perfectly coherent to describe a legislature as a political arena pitting interests against interests, coalitions against coalitions, party against party, etc., it is equally coherent to describe a legislature as an organized working process with work inputs and product outputs, with structured and timetabled ways of proceeding, with recognized expertise and division of labor principles. To do research in terms of one of these two descriptions is not to deny the validity and importance of the other. Indeed, as will be pointed out in a number of places in the following chapters, the ability of legislative staffers to contribute to the organizational features of the legislature depends in some measure, and often in very large measure, on their recognition of the legislature as a political process.

By viewing legislatures as organizations, we are not trying to suggest that the proper way for a legislature to proceed is solely in terms of technical and/or scientific rationality. Rather, the stress is on organization as a way of enabling the political process to reach outputs and products. The legislative process must be political, not expert-dominated, if it is to serve the legislative function. Of course, this is a difficult balance; as numerous studies of organizations have demonstrated it is no easy thing to "keep the experts on tap, not on top." The balance must always be struck in favor of the political purpose of a legislature. To abhor the politics of the legislative process is fatuous.

As organizations, legislatures confront organizational kinds of operating difficulties and issues. For example, the purpose of organization is to divide labor, specialize, and coordinate. This creates for all organizations a dialectic of centralization/decentralization. The need for rational, centralized decisions leads to the necessity of decentralizing information-gathering and processing activities which, in turn, create a challenge to the centralized authority.

Throughout the history of organizations, no one has fashioned the formula revealing the optimum amount of centralization/decentralization. Some observers, for example, believe that decentralization is a significant factor in the importance of Congress. John F. Bibby, for one, says that "one of the reasons for Congress' unique vitality among national legislatures is that its power is decentralized. In significant degree, this decentralization is caused by the standing committee system which has created numerous subject matter domains of great influence." [5]

While not denying the logic of Bibby's argument, it is important for us to point out that there are numerous critics of Congressional decentralization; it has been argued that this decentralization leads to "czarism" on committees, ineffective potential for action, and a lack of institutional accountability and responsibility. Of course, decentralization provides committee chairmen with more autonomy from party leadership in the House and, in turn, this leads to happy and unhappy results, depending upon what it is we expect from Congress. Centralization and decentralization remain as mixed blessings in organization theory.

Organizations Are Tools of Power

This is a message emphasized by Charles Perrow in *Complex Organizations.* [6] A decentralized organization places more power throughout the organization; a centralized organization places more power at its top. In organization theory, it is really impossible to argue the merits of one over the other without first declaring who should have power over what because that is essentially what centralization/decentralization is all about.

There are other organizational issues affecting legislatures which should be analyzed in terms of seeing organizations as tools; for example, the issue of rules and regulations. As Perrow puts it:

> "There ought to be a rule" is as valid as saying "there are too damn many rules around here." Rules do a lot of things in organizations: they protect as well as restrict; coordinate as well as block; channel effort as well as limit it; permit universalism as well as provide sanctuary for the inept; maintain stability as well as retard change; permit diversity as well as restrict it. They constitute the organizational memory and the means for change. As such, rules themselves are neither good nor bad, nor even that important.[7]

The number and character of desirable rules are strictly a question of what one hopes to accomplish with an organization (a tool). And it is no longer acceptable in organization theory to say that "efficiency and effectivenss," per se, are the goals of an organization. We cannot reach any intelligent and rational decisions on how to structure an organization unless we are prepared to discuss the question of *whose* efficiency and effectiveness we are trying to enhance.[8] Later in this chapter, an argument will be proposed that the efficiency and effectiveness of legislators-politicians are the most logical goals of a legislative organization.

Information-processing is another vital characteristic of organizations. According to a report prepared for the Joint Committee on Congressional Operations regarding modern information technology in the state legislatures, all legislatures share the following information needs:

> Assembly of salient facts and data, independently developed, accurate, as complete as possible, of maximum currency, and readily available for use.

> Access to and an understanding of the executive branch planning, budgeting, and program performance data required for effective review of governmental operations.

> Assistance in analysis of policy problems, which requires the additional capability to assess and apply policy-relevant information.[9]

An important organizational aspect of this area is that information gathered in government agencies is often not usable by the legislature, as is. There are two reasons for this: "data pollution" and "agency mission bias."

"Data pollution" is a situation in which data is so plentiful that its sheer volume prevents its usage. Partly, this has to do with organization, and partly with inability of information programmers to set reasonable limits on data input. As persons who have experience with data processing often note,

> Data is the raw material from which information is derived. . . . The significant characteristic that separates data from information is usefulness. Thus a compilation of data may, in itself, be of little value unless it provides knowledge leading to the achievement of some objective. Although any collection of data may have potential informational value, what constitutes information for one individual in a specific instance may lack significance for another or even for the same individual at a different time or under different circumstances. Specifically, information consists of *selected data*—data selected and organized with respect to user, problem, time, place and function.[10]

As Richard Nunez points out, executive agencies collect data vertically on a departmental or program base—in terms of education (or adult education), health (or prevalent children's diseases), etc.—whereas the legislature often needs data that cut horizontally across the agencies' missions and programs. Further, Nunez observes, it is the function of the legislature "to capture and express the people's social concerns. And often social problems arise, demanding attention, definition, and solution before adequate data are collected to aid legislators in their decision making." At these crucial points of decision-making, "the computer stands silent, without data to offer. Data generated by the executive branch are often of small help on crucial points, because the executive collected the data on known, previously debated problems and the data [were] collected for purposes of administration, not for policy or legislative decision making."[11]

This points to a need for legislatures to have their own independent sources of information.

It would appear that legislatures have more of an informal organizational component than their sisters and brothers in the executive branch. Most sociologists agree that informal organizational components spring up because (1) sometimes that is the only way work can be done, (2) in the process of performing roles in the formal organization individuals establish informal bases of cooperation such as friendship, and (3) the search for power over his environment leads the individual in an organization to form alliances that become informal components of organization.

Legislatures are probably more susceptible to the growth of informal components as a result of response to these three needs than organizations in the executive branch. It would seem that the continuing need to be thinking of the next election on the part of the legislators and the day-to-day instability of the staffers' positions would lead to widespread formation of informal groupings within legislative institutions.

All aspects of legislative organization have the potential for being of extreme importance. Even something which seems as politically irrelevant as meeting times of committees can have vital significance. For example, the historian Wallace Notestein, in his searching volume on the House of Commons during the years 1604-1610, says that procedures of the House during that time dictated a need to accept decisions of committees. Nine times out of ten, Notestein records, members of Parliament voted to sustain committee decisions. It was also part of the procedure to afford committees wide latitude to alter and even change the legislation sent to them for their consideration. The committees usually met in the early afternoon, and by that hour, Notestein says, the more easygoing members found their way back to their lodgings or offices, whereas members having strongly held beliefs at odds with the Crown went to the committee meetings and articulated their beliefs into law that had a ninety percent chance of survival on the floor. Thus, a great deal of legislation in opposition to expressed wishes of the Crown was passed.[12]

This example illustrates "systems politics" of organizations. Legislatures, like all organizations, are systems of decision-making which provide processes through which decisions must be made. There is a pervasive struggle for power over these processes as well as over the substantive aspects of the decisions. Usually, there are some systems in an organization with which a member of the organization will be concerned. A legislative staffer might be concerned, for example, with his or her relationship to leadership decision-making, with the legislative budget and fiscal process, with a particular policy area, and, perhaps, with budget-making and particular policy area processes of the executive. How these processes overlap will vary from situation to situation and over time in any one situation.

THE ROLE OF LEGISLATIVE STAFF

We know very little about legislative staff. We should know much more because the staff role is the point at which the legislature meets its "moment of truth" as an organization. By no means is it the case that one can be certain that adding legislative staff adds to the improvement of legislative decisions. That is only the hope. By no means is it the case that one knows that staffing, in general, increases the effectiveness of legislatures. Again, this is the hope.

It might seem surprising to some readers that there is a lacuna in the literature on legislative staff. It is certainly surprising to anyone who observes the workings of a legislature that the literature should neglect this vital component of the process. Indeed, a young Harvard man named Eric Redman went to work for the U.S. Senate, and the experience—Harvard cum Senate—inspired him to produce a book entitled *The Dance of Legislation,* in which he wrote:

> I found in the literature two major misconceptions. The first was that the President had eclipsed the Senate, and Congress as a whole, in the performance of the legislative function. . . . The second shortcoming of the literature related directly to the first, I felt. It lay in the implicit assumption that the Senate as an institution is made up solely of the one hundred men and women who are Senators. In the post-war era, however, the Senate staff has grown to approximately 3,000 individuals—a fact the literature rarely noted, and less often examined . . . anyone who knew the Senate would know that to ignore the role of staff is to ignore not only Senate reality but the key reason why the Senate is still capable of vying with the President for legislative leadership.[13]

Most of the literature on staff that does exist assumes a positive role for it to play, proceeds to praise its existence, and calls for a removal of obstacles to its unfettered operations. There are notable exceptions, such as Norman Meller's well-known caveat that staffing can lead to legislative captivity by the staffers. If legislatures need help, and if staff can provide some of that help, we need to examine the staff role critically to see where it helps, where it hurts, and, of course, we need to learn more about what must be double-edged swords of staff contributions.

Legislative staffing is considerably more complex than one might think. For example, in the fifty American states, program evaluation and performance auditing by legislative bodies is staff organized in six different ways: by legislative program evaluation agencies; by legislative audit agencies; by fiscal agencies and appropriations committees; by standing committees; by general legislative research agencies; and by hybrid agencies. No one of these organizational modes operates the same way in any of the states where it exists. The legislative institutional framework (political, social, and economic) shapes the operations of the agency and the reasonable parameters of action by the staff.[14]

The role of staff is not, in my judgment, a matter of *supplying* technical information; rather, it is one of *applying* technical information to complex decisions. Aristotle said that there are ten relevant aspects of a situation in which men make complex decisions affecting themselves and others: quality, quantity, relations, action, passion, place, time, situation, condition, and substance. In legislatures, men are facing very complex situations. The kind of knowledge staff persons usually bring to a situation from their formal education does not enable them to participate meaningfully in a legislative process. They need insights gained from experience with that process to find ways of relating what they know, and what they know how to do, to the process.

For example, a staffer educated and trained to seek and find precision and clarity in expression may find it necessary to seek and find a vague way of expressing the legislature's intent because vague language is sometimes the only acceptable outcome of a bargaining and negotiation process. As Nunez observed in an analysis of "legislative intent," the

> essential nature of the legislative process is compromise, bargain and consensus. Legislatures often resort to vagueness in language in order to obtain agreement among the widest number of legislators, or to avoid the thorny issues that would be exposed *were* exactness demanded.[15]

The relationship of scientific decision-making to the legislative process is, in scientific terms and logic, limited. Perhaps the best way to make this point is by referring to an example drawn by the political economist Vilfredo Pareto, who himself was a mathematical economist. Imagine, Pareto said, a community of 100 persons who have 700 products for exchange. Under absurdly oversimplified assumptions, he said, he calculated that 70,699 simultaneous equations were required to determine the prices equalizing demand and supply. He noted further that for a society of 40,000,000 people and several thousand products, the number of equations would be fabulous. In such a situation, Pareto concluded, practicable solutions should be made by the market, not by the mathematician.[16]

A legislature is a marketplace in which society, through its representatives, reaches bargains, deals, and agreements. For a staff person, or a university professor, to attempt to abstractly systematize this process into a rational model of exchange would be foolish and irrelevant. The more proper role of the staffer, or university professor, is to facilitate the workings of the marketplace. Of course, marketplaces differ—some are more monopolistic than others. It is not, in my judgment, the role of the staffer, or university professor, to change the nature of the market that the legislature establishes.

DISTINCTIVE ORGANIZATIONAL TRAITS OF LEGISLATURES

Legislative markets have three interrelated organizational traits especially important to legislative staff. First, they are more *lateral* than *scalar*. Second, they are collective choice forms of decision-making. Third, they are forums and instruments of politicians whose purposes and roles are different from the purposes and roles of administrative officials in the executive branch of government. The lateral aspects of legislative organizations require examination in some depth.

Chester Barnard developed the distinction between lateral and scalar organizations in a paper he delivered on the possibility of a world government organization. The lateral type is what he referred to as a political-type organization, whereas the scalar is what we usually think of as a bureaucratic, rational, efficient organization established to carry out certain circumscribed tasks.[17]

Lateral organizations are formed by mutual agreements and understandings, and they are entered into freely. Scalar organizations are vertical, articulated, and hierarchical. As James P. Mooney and Alan C. Reiley defined it in their classical treatise on organizations, "A scale means a series of steps; hence, something graduated. In organization, it means the graduation of duties, not according to differentiated functions, for this involves another and distinct principle of organization, but simply according to degrees of authority and corresponding responsibility."[18] In lateral organizations, the duty of command and the need to obey are not prerequisites to effective functioning. It is nonauthoritarian. Integration takes place horizontally, laterally. People working "side by side" are the basis of cooperation, as opposed to, in the scalar organization, cooperation resulting from "commands from above." Lateral organizations are usually established for short periods of time and limited to specific purposes. The purposes are personal to the people involved, not inherent in the organization created by the agreement. Because of this, the agreement is not the end or purpose of the organization. Pursuit of the agreement—that is, formulation of a set of programs to pursue the agreement—is not what holds the organization together or provides a system of priorities. Rather, the lateral organization is held together by the persons who formed it, and the maintenance of the organization depends upon the ability of the organization to satisfy the individual and particularized interests of its formers. At no time in the life of a lateral organization does the agreement supersede the individual interests of the parties to it as the animus for maintenance of the organization.

In scalar organizations, every part except the highest is clearly and wholly dependent upon a higher part; and every part except the lowest rests upon a foundation of lower parts. Relations between parts on the same level are determined by higher levels, not by agreements between those parts. Common purpose, organizationally established, forms the basis for participation of all persons. This participation is highly formalized; there are no aspects of personal choice on the part of the participants. An injury to one part is an injury to the entire organization. There is an unspoken assumption about the life of a scalar organization; it is assumed to be set up for an indefinite period of time.

Lateral organizations are usually unable to deal with long-range problems because it is difficult for members of them to foresee their own interests in the long term. Scalar organizations are prone to think in terms of five-year-type planning because prolongation serves the interests of their members, who are mainly concerned with prolonging their jobs.

Lateral organizations are often simpler than the agreement and understandings that bring them together, whereas scalar organizations are the opposite. The former are also usually less expensive than the latter, in terms of human resources, talents, and leadership needs, except when they turn into battlegrounds for power. Decisions in lateral organizations are more narrow and concrete than in the latter; therefore, they can be reached faster.

Lateral organizations are also more flexible and adaptable; change can take place through simple agreement to do so. In scalar organizations, change can come about only after long periods of abstraction, "planning," rationalizing, etc. One major reason for this is that the former organization is not valued for its own sake. Leaders of scalar organizations have to ask themselves, "What will this do to the organization, per se," as well as question the desirability of the object of change itself. Students of scalar organizations generally and consistently have found that leaders of scalar organizations are more concerned with maintaining the organization as it is than with change. Their individual motives and interests are apparently better served that way.

Loyalty to the organization is necessary in the scalar organization. Authority and discipline depend upon it because no system of authority and discipline can be enforced in an organization that lacks a large degree of loyalty. A primary function of leadership is to secure and maintain such loyalty. In the lateral organization, loyalty is highly personalized. Persons who work for those who form such an organization give their personal loyalty to the person(s) for whom they work and whose interest is being served by the organization and definitely not to the organization. For reasons stated above, it would not make sense for them to do so; it would be irrelevant loyalty. It may be that for reasons of self-esteem they may speak in terms of loyalty to the organization itself; but operationalization of that notion will lead to trouble. This means that there can be an easy, free flow into and out of the organization. In a scalar organization, a threat by an executive to leave it creates a problem of major proportions; in a lateral organization, there is no such problem.

There are different and important tendencies to self-destruction in the two organizations. In the lateral, there are no internal and formal means of preventing disruptive frictions and fights. Moral, traditional, cultural controls are at work; they either are or are not sufficient. There is usually a very high value placed on following these traditions, moralities, etc., though there is no way to formally enforce them. Scalar organizations are controlled by coordination through centralized authority. There is little freedom; therefore, strife and friction are relatively curtailed.

I have never seen or read about an organization that is entirely lateral or entirely scalar; rather, organizations appear to be mixtures of the two forms. Most executive agencies are predominantly scalar; however, entire collections of executive agencies—say, like the New York State government—are more lateral than scalar in many important ways. Legislatures are predominantly lateral, though they vary. We cannot develop here a detailed statement on the implications of this for legislative staffers. Hopefully—indeed, intendedly—this book is a step in that direction. For the present, we will "satisfice" with some inconclusive and nondefinitive remarks. Certainly, the major conclusion we would come to is that legislative staffers must be better able to relate to the self-interest of the people immediately around them than their colleagues in the executive branch of government. Of course, the executive staffer must be sensitive to people and know how to work with them; but the level and type of awareness is quite different, we believe. For the executive staffer, success is most likely if he or she first thinks of the formal system and conforms to its norms, and then tries to adapt interpersonal relationships as well as possible. For the legislative staffer, there is not such a formal system to conform to; the world begins and ends with the persons he or she works for and with. He or she may have to adapt some rules and regulations—such as, for example, payroll systems, bill-drafting facilities, etc.—to the preferences of the legislator or committee; but that adaptation is simply that—an adaptation.

There will undoubtedly be an attempt on the part of some staffers to decrease the flexibility of the lateral organization in order to achieve greater predictability and the kind of rationality predictability facilitates. These staffers will propose more formal institutionalization in the name of better (i.e., more "rationality from predictability") processes "for the legislature." These proposals will have their legislator who champions them, and there will be good reasons, both in terms of the champions' self-interest and the products of legislatures, for such support. Nonetheless, the potential irrelevancy of such "reforms" should not be overlooked.

We have said that legislative staffers work within lateral, not scalar organizations. For some staffers, this is not consistent with their immediate work situation, because while the legislature as a whole is a lateral organization, there are within it scalar suborganizations, such as are often found in legislative reference libraries, bill-drafting operations, personnel and management sections, and so forth. It is my experience that the extent to which such scalar organizations function nonpolitically and unresponsively to the needs of the legislature as a lateral organization, they will be irrelevant to the more important aspects of legislative process.

The explanation for this, as I see it, is that lateral organization is necessary, inter alia, when almost every aspect of a decision is relevant to the politics of the decision, where there can be very little delegation to technicians of aspects that are nonpolitical. Scalar organizations are based on division of labor and delegation of routinized, technical aspects of decisions that are governed by regulations. The less a legislator feels personal control over just about all aspects of decisions, the more will he or she try to increase the control. Thus, if a scalar organizational unit within the legislature has succeeded in isolating itself from the political-legislative process, in becoming a nonpolitical, professional, highly technical operation, the legislator will not turn to it for information and assistance. This is so simply because the legislator wants information from persons who *are* politically involved.

Another way to make this point is by considering something Barnard said about these forms of organization:

> Scalar organization is greatly superior to that of free agreement in respect to coordination and power of accomplishment. [However]

activities of great complexity seem susceptible of large-size scalar organization only if these activities are capable of being segregated into relatively simple groups in space or in time and if the relation between the segregations is relatively simple, even though the interdependence between them is complete. . . . When there are innumerable interactions not isolatable into small groups having simple interrelations, but on the contrary having a large number of simultaneous interdependencies, scalar organization may be impossible, whereas organization by free agreement has been . . . successful.[19]

The legislative process is a situation in which "there are innumerable interactions not isolatable into small groups, etc." If scalar organizations are established in situations requiring lateral organization, they will be potentially irrelevant to the situation.

Obviously, some staffers have no choice in the matter; they are assigned into a scalar organization and told to act like bureaucrats. In such cases, leadership of those organizations is of vital importance, for the leader is the interface between the legislature's needs as a lateral organization and the scalar organization he heads.

My generalization about scalar organizational behavior being potentially irrelevant to legislative needs is one of the most important generalizations that should be studied, in my judgment. Legislative reformers usually recommend increased usage of scalar organization; they do so not directly, but indirectly by recommending that the legislative process be made more technical and more formalized. To the extent that my generalization is an accurate description of the state of affairs in legislatures, we are confronted with the need to apply reformers' prescriptions cautiously. In a number of foreign legislatures I have studied, I find the scalar organization to be predominant for staffing patterns. The normal pattern is to provide civil service status for all legislative staff, under a political "secretary general," or his equivalent, and to organize the staff in hierarchical slots quite similar to the organization of executive agencies. Abdo I. Baaklini and I have analyzed such organizations in the legislatures of Brazil, Costa Rica, and Lebanon; our conclusion is that it is important for staffers in such organizations to avoid the notion that theirs is a nonpolitical, neutral role within the legislative process.[20]

The second organizational characteristic of legislatures distinguishing them from executive agencies is that they are collective-choice forms of decision-making. Of course, this characteristic of legislative organizations is complementary to that of lateral organizations. The opposite of collective choice is unilateral choice. Collective choice is the only possibility for a lateral organization.

Furthermore, legislatures are unique kinds of collective choice organizations. A common assumption of collective choice models is that preferences between any two alternatives are not affected by other alternatives; it is known as "the principle of the independence of irrelevant alternatives."[21] The rationality of legislative decisions, from the individual legislator's perspective, includes alternatives other than the apparent two. Each legislative decision has "yes" and "no" components. But individual legislators consider alternatives other than the two apparent ones, and these considerations affect their vote.

For example, a legislator may, in contemplating his vote on school busing, consider the following kinds of other alternative thoughts:

—If this bill goes through, there will be further demands for racial integration in the schools.

—If this bill goes through, there will be no further demands for racial integration.

—If this bill is passed, the executive will fail to properly implement it; therefore, this bill will embarrass the executive.

—The executive can use this bill to enhance its prestige.

Legislators know that public policy-making is like Heraclitean reality; it is always in a state of *becoming,* rather than of *being.* A choice made today is a steppingstone to a new set of events. The legislator is aware of being a creator, an author of events. Therefore, he tries to understand what he augurs. One of the truly admirable aspects of this is that the legislator *qua* politician looks into the future implications of today's legislative action because he, the politician, must take responsibility for those implications in the voting booths.

It may be difficult for a legislative staffer to accept situations in which issues are being decided not on their intrinsic merits, but on interpretations of expected repercussions. It is undoubtedly frustrating to be a staffer working assiduously on an immediate issue in a context where the issue is subordinate to political predictions of its ramifications. But, as the political sociologist Karl Mannheim, the Austrian statesman Albert Schaffle, and others have argued, the essence of political activity in legislatures is to make decisions that generate new and unique situations.[22] Again, this is the function of a lateral organization, to give birth to the unborn, whereas scalar organizations deal with routinized operations, or, as Mannheim, Schaffle, and others put it, political organizations provide a structure for "conduct," whereas bureaucratic agencies provide a structure for "reproductive behavior." "Conduct" requires personal decisions; "reproductive behavior" does not. "Conduct" does not begin "until we reach the area where rationalization has not yet penetrated, and where we are forced to make decisions in situations which have as yet not been subjected to regulation."[23]

It is interesting to note that Aristotle pointed out how little was known in his time about the wisdom that best informs legislation. He noted that legislators did not write about it and the intellectuals (at the time, the sophists) wrote and preached about it without knowing anything about it.[24] My discussions with legislators and legislative staffers working at the cutting edges of policy-making lead me to the observation that, like Napoleon, *"on s'engage, puis on voit"*–that is, one *sees* only after getting engaged in the battle. Or, to put it another way, one develops a sense of proportion, guidelines to "conduct," only within the din of decision-making. We are, I believe, slightly better off with regard to understanding the nature of "conduct" than the Athenians were, but not very much so.

The third organizational characteristic of legislatures is related to the other two. Legislatures serve the purposes of politicians, not bureaucrats. Mannheim said that bureaucrats have a "fundamental tendency ... to turn all problems of politics into problems of administration."[25] I would add that legislators have a fundamental tendency to turn all problems of administration into problems of politics.

The premier expert on bureaucracy and politics, Max Weber, offered some interesting and relevant commentary on differences between bureaucrats and politicians. Politicians prove themselves in the electoral and legislative processes, he noted, whereas administrative officials prove themselves in the performance of administrative work. The administrative official strives for an image of impartiality, devotion to duty, decisiveness within a framework of rules provided by others, and trained competence in carrying out official assignments. A personal opinion is of little consequence and is subordinated to the demands of supervisors.

The political leader is first, foremost, and always engaged in a struggle for power. He rises through battle with others; he survives by the skin of his competitors' nonsurvival and his ability to gain support. The politician could be no more than a party official if he had the qualities of the good administrator, Weber noted, because politicians have responsibilities different from those of administrators. Ultimately, the administrator is judged by the ability to carry out assigned tasks. The politician is judged by the capacity for independent action; and for this he alone is responsible. On this basis, he, as an individual, as opposed to being part of an institution, is evaluated by his constituents and his fellow politicians. His ability to realize independent action is based on his ability to enlist supporters. While willing to make compromises, these is not his raison d'etre. Never can he explain his actions in terms of personal conviction and decided commitment. He acts; Weber said, with "passion, a feeling of responsibility, and a sense of proportion."[26]

Legislative staffers work for politicians, not for administrative officials. Their worth to "the boss" surely must be related to their ability to assist him in his role. For those staffers who work for committees or other units within the legislature, as opposed to working directly and solely with a legislator, the same rule would probably hold. As a lateral organization, the legislature as an institution can only be understood in terms of the felt needs of the legislators. Consider, for example, the oft-mentioned recommendation that diminishment of the volume of legislation introduced in a session would effect enormous rationalization of the legislative process. A staffer might be brought to this conclusion in the name of the institution, the legislature, and the process, if he looked at that institution and that process as superseding the individual interests of legislators. Ultimately, we believe, what happens of consequence in a legislature will be consonant with the fact that it is a lateral organization maintaining itself in terms of the individual political interests of the legislators. In the case of the recommendation for decreases in numbers of bills introduced: So long as legislators relate the numbers of bills they introduce to the nurturance of their capacity for independent action and "political clout," there will be no decrease.

A temptation to which staffers sometimes may be prone is to attempt relating their raison d'etre to their ideas on what a legislature should mean to the society at large. This, in my view, is a mistake and, if succumbed to, will lessen the effectiveness of the staff person in the legislative process. Legislators are motivated actors, but the motivations are particularized, not deduced from concepts of broad social goals. This should come as no surprise. As Joseph A. Schumpeter observed, political activity, like economic activity, cannot be understood in terms of generalized, societal purposes. For example, he notes,

> The reason why there is such a thing as economic activity is of course that people want to eat, to clothe themselves, and so on. To provide the means to satisfy those wants is the social end or meaning of production. Nevertheless we all agree that this proposition would make a most unrealistic starting point for a theory of economic activity in commercial society and that we shall do much better if we start from propositions about profits.[27]

Similarly, says Schumpeter:

> The social meaning or function of parliamentary activity is no doubt to turn out legislation and, in part, administrative measures. But in order to understand how democratic politics serve this social end, we must start from the competitive struggle for power and office and realize that the social function is fulfilled, as it were, incidentally—in the same sense as production is incidental to the making of profits.[28]

THE METAPHYSICS OF THE LEGISLATIVE PROCESS

I would like to express some thoughts on a subject seldom, if ever, discussed in books on legislatures—the metaphysics of the legislative process. Is it possible to relate legislative process to any cosmology? Is its existence consistent with broader social truths, and in the framework of such broader truths can we treat it in terms of values? I think so, and I think we should be doing so more than we do. This chapter, this book, is not the place to do so, but we should briefly consider what is involved because it seems to me to be something of importance to an individual who chooses a career as a legislative staffer.

By metaphysics of legislative process, I do not mean the political desirability of a democratic, representative form of government. That is, of course, tremendously significant and important. But I am talking about a broader, more speculative dimension having to do with cosmological processes. In deference to the fact that a section on metaphysics in a book on legislative staff may be surprising, I should explain why I chose to include it. Recently, I attended a conference on legislative studies at which a professor sharing my viewpoints on legislatures presented a thoroughgoing phenomenological analysis of legislatures and our knowledge of them. His approach was criticized on a number of grounds, the most salient of which was that he allegedly proposed rejection of *telos* in dealing with the subject. Precisely, the criticism was that the phenomenological approach to legislatures leaves us unable to establish criteria by which to compare and evaluate them. To vernacularize the criticism, it goes like this: The phenomenological approach leaves us with an ability to say, "They are what they are and that's what they are," and no more. "What you see is what you get."

The criticism of a phenomenological approach on these grounds draws us inevitably into metaphysics because it is based on a metaphysical assumption that reality is knowable only in terms of permanence. Legislatures are best understood, we suggest, in terms of process rather than in terms of permanence. Furthermore, the history of philosophy and science justifies the integrity of reality as process and impermanence, as well as permanence. To put it another way: Legislatures manifest a reality of change that cannot be understood in terms of permanent categories such as "legislatures are democratic institutions," or "legislatures are mechanisms for the recruitment of political elites," or "legislatures are conservative," or "legislatures are liberal." One cannot find an abiding quality of legislatures to fill in the following blank: "Legislatures are _____." One can say: "Legislatures are." And that is the truly important statement. They *are*.

My studies of legislatures indicate that they are sometimes conservative, sometimes liberal, sometimes this, sometimes the opposite. The only abiding quality of legislatures appears to be that they are part of the process of the societies in which we find them. They do not have a universal reality by which we can know them in all places and at all times, except that common names are given to them, such as parliaments, assemblies, legislatures, etc.

Because this is an unusual kind of diversion—i.e., this reflection on metaphysics—let me try to delineate what I am trying to do, why I am trying to do it, and why I think it needs to be done:

(1) I am attempting to discuss legislatures as participants in an open-system universe where change is fundamental, as opposed to being in a closed system universe where things stand still.

(2) I am attempting to demonstrate that a changing universe is philosophically and scientifically legitimate.

(3) I am doing this for two reasons: (a) to provide a place for legislative staff to stand in the philosophical cosmos; and (b) to provide a point of view for studies of legislatures.

(4) I think it needs to be done because legislative staffers and persons conducting studies of legislatures are so easily threatened by persons who insist that legislatures have certain universal functions.

Points 3 and 4 interrelate. Legislative staffers who grasp their roles in a reality of flux, knowing that this reality is true and moral, are not defenseless when they are challenged to show the permanent aspects of legislative process. For example, consider a legislative staffer who is asked to justify the existence of his role and his institution in terms other than that the institution enables the society to have a place to bargain between differing viewpoints. If the staffer realizes that such a function is crucial to the maintenance of the society, and, further, grasps the cosmological dimensions of that function, he can regard himself with pride rather than with regret. Similarly, studies of legislatures do not need to find justification in the massaging of universal categories if they are tied to the kite of legislatures as flux.

We will first discuss the philosphical and scientific legitimacy of process (flux) as reality, and then discuss legislatures as instances of that reality. Since the beginning of thought about the universe there have been two different ways of treating an experience: It could be classed along with other experiences, or it could be considered as a unique happening. Various names were given to this difference. Liebnitz used *verites eternelles* versus *verites de fait*. Windelband and Rickert used the terms nomothetic studies and idiographic studies. Today we speak of scientific versus historical relevance. And there are many manifestations of the difference. The difference to which these names refer is that between a reality that goes beyond an immediately preceived experience and a reality that is unique to the immediately perceived experience. For example, science classifies me in various ways (homo sapiens, skeletal, etc.) which have nothing to do with the way in which *I* experience *myself.*

Perhaps the most eloquent and brilliant philosophy of process was written by Alfred North Whitehead.[29] That "all things flow," said Whitehead, is a primary element in man's experience:

> It is the theme of some of the best Hebrew poetry in the Psalms; it appears as one of the first generalizations of Greek philosophy in the form of the sayings of Heraclitus; amid the later barbarism of Anglo-Saxon thought it reappears in the story of the sparrow flitting through the banquetting hall of the Northumbrian king; and in all stages of civilization its recollection lends its pathos to poetry. Without doubt, if we are to go back to that ultimate, integral experience whose elucidation is the final aim of philosophy, the flux of things is one ultimate generalization around which we must weave our philosophical system.[30]

A process approach to reality begins with *assemblage* rather than *system;* it is primarily an attempt to understand what is happening rather than with the formulation of a system of concepts and models with which we purport to capture the essences of things. The issue is well expounded in Plato's *Theatetus:*

> Socrates: But now, since not even white continues to flow white, and whiteness itself is a flux or change which is passing into another color, and is never to be caught standing still, can the name of any color be rightly used at all?
>
> Theodorus: How is that possible, Socrates, either in the case of this or any other quality—if while we are using the word the subject is escaping in the flux?[31]

The wisdom of ancient Greece was refound by modern science in the twentieth century by means of the Heisenberg Indeterminancy Relations, according to which we lose accuracy in determining natural states of things as we gain accuracy in studying them. In order to accurately determine a particle's position we must use a microscope which provides light by sending out unpredictable and uncontrollable quanta of light which collide with the particle and thereby put it into a form of motion that would not have existed had the microscope not been used.

For Whitehead the complete problem of metaphysics is wrapped up in the phrase "Abide with me/Fast falls the eventide."[32] Modern political science approaches to legislatures, in my view, are frequently uninformed by the truth of constant flux, though they are usually inspired to some degree by

America's most seminal thinker on politics as process, Arthur Bentley. In his classic study, *The Process of Government,* Bentley set out "to attempt to fashion a tool."[33] This, he hoped, would be a tool for studying and understanding a political world as a world in the process of constantly becoming, rather than being.

Paul F. Kress has pointed out in a brilliant analysis of the subject that while American political scientists have "accepted and stressed secondary strains in Arthur Bentley's social thought," such as the popular notion of group analysis, "there is almost no discussion in the literature of process per se."[34] American political science, for the most part, has closed what Bentley tried to keep open. It has looked for systems by which to order the process of group conflict rather than, in Whitehead's terms, first coming to grips with assemblages resulting from flux.

SUMMARY

—The role of staff is related to the fact that the legislature is an organization, having organizational needs such as information management and organizational characteristics such as being an instrument of power.

—The legislature is a lateral, not a scalar, organization.

—Legislators are politicians. Politicians differ from administrative officials; they act from commitment and passion, taking full responsibility as authors of their actions for the repercussions of those actions, as opposed to being effective instrumentations of "orders from above."

—Staffers are, and need to be, responsive to the constraints and possibilities existing in this kind of context. The application of "scientific, rational thinking" is, of course, important, but if carried to points where it conflicts with the nature of the legislative lateral organization, it will cause (and be in) trouble.

—Looking at legislatures in terms of metaphysics, we see them as a process where changes are not predictable but nonetheless rationally interpretable in a mode of understanding compatible with a respectable cosmology. We have not proposed an anti-rational and/or an anti-philosophical way of talking about the legislative process.

NOTES

1. W. F. Willoughby, *Principles of Legislative Organization and Administration* (Washington, D.C.: Brookings Institution, 1934), p. 579.
2. Ibid.
3. Ibid., pp. 578-579.

4. Ibid., p. 579.

5. John F. Bibby, "Reforming the Committees While Retaining the Unique Role of the House," in Committee Organization in the House: Panel Discussions before the Select Committee on Committees, 93rd Congress, 1st Session (Washington, D.C.: Government Printing Office, 1973), Vol. 2, part 3, p. 526.

6. Charles Perrow, *Complex Organizations* (Glenview, Ill.: Scott, Foresman, 1972), p. 14.

7. Ibid., p. 32.

8. Ibid., p. 12.

9. Congressional Research Service, *Modern Information Technology in the State Legislatures* (Washington, D.C.: Government Printing Office, 1972), p. 1.

10. Robert R. Arnold, Harold C. Hill, and Alymer V. Nichols, *Modern Data Processing* (New York: John Wiley, 1972), p. 3.

11. Richard Nunez, "Inappropriate Uses of Computers in the Legislative Process," unpublished paper presented at the Second International Conference on Legislative Development, Albany, New York, January 20-23, 1975, p. 10.

12. Wallace Notestein, *The House of Commons 1604-1610* (New Haven: Yale University Press, 1971), pp. 464-474.

13. Eric Redman, *The Dance of Legislation* (New York: Simon & Schuster, 1973), pp. 16-17.

14. Edgar Crane, "Program Evaluation and Performance Audit by Legislative Bodies: A New Thrust for a Traditional Tool of Government Accountability," *Comment,* August 1974, Vol. 1, No. 1, p. 1.

15. Richard Nunez, "The Nature of Legislative Intent and the Use of Legislative Documents as Extrinsic Aids to Statutory Interpretation: A Re-examination," *California Western Law Review,* Vol. 9 (Fall, 1972), p. 134.

16. Vilfredo Pareto, *Manuel d'Economic Politique,* Deuxieme Edition (Paris: Marcel Girard, 1927), pp. 233-234.

17. Chester Barnard, "Planning for World Government," in *Organization and Management* (Cambridge: Harvard University Press, 1948), pp. 134-175.

18. James P. Mooney and Alan C. Reiley, *Onward Industry* (New York: Harper, 1931), p. 31.

19. Barnard, "Planning for World Government," pp. 156-157.

20. James J. Heaphey and Abdo I. Baaklini, "Legislative Institution Building in Brazil, Costa Rica, and Lebanon," *Sage Professional Papers in Administration and Policy Studies* (Beverly Hills: Sage, forthcoming).

21. See Kenneth J. Arrow, *Social Choice and Individual Values* (New York: John Wiley, 1951), pp. 26-28.

22. Karl Mannheim, *Ideology and Utopia* (New York: Harcourt, Brace, 1936), p. 114.

23. Ibid., pp. 114-115.

24. Ernest Barker, *The Politics of Aristotle* (New York: Oxford University Press, 1958), p. 359.

25. Mannheim, *Ideology and Utopia,* p. 105.

26. These comments on Weber were drawn directly from Reinhard Bendix, *Max Weber: An Intellectual Portrait* (Garden City, N.Y.: Anchor, 1962), pp. 440-441 and from Weber's, "Politics as a Vocation," in H. H. Gerth and C. Wright Mills (eds.), *From Max Weber* (New York: Oxford University Press, 1958), p. 115.

27. Joseph A. Schumpeter, *Capitalism, Socialism, and Democracy* (New York: Harper Torchbooks, 1962), p. 282.

28. Ibid.

29. Alfred North Whitehead, *Process and Reality* (New York: Harper Torchbooks, 1960).

30. Ibid., p. 317.

31. Paul F. Kress, *Social Science and the Idea of Process* (Urbana: University of Illinois Press, 1970), p. 3.

32. Whitehead, *Process and Reality*, p. 318.

33. Arthur Bentley, *The Process of Government* (Bloomington, Ind.: Principia Press, 1949).

34. Kress, *Social Science*, p. 182.

LEGISLATIVE STAFFING:
A REVIEW OF
CURRENT TRENDS

A L A N   P.   B A L U T I S

Substantial effort is now being devoted to the reform of legislative institutions. Although empirical evidence is lacking, nearly everyone involved in reform efforts agrees about what the problems are and what should be done to solve them:[1] legislatures maintain too many standing committees, therefore committees should be consolidated; compensation is too low to attract able men, therefore salaries should be increased; legislatures do not meet often enough to do their jobs, therefore they should convene annually and have longer sessions. If there is one type of problem and one type of solution on which agreement by reformers is virtually unanimous, it is professional staffing.[2] According to the Advisory Commission on Intergovernmental Relations: "One of the most critical factors conditioning the capacity of legislative leaders, committees, and individual members to respond to their growing responsibilities is staff."[3] Without staff, the reform argument goes, legislators cannot possibly arrive at competent judgments, independent of governors, bureaucracies, and interest groups. They need greater assistance in gathering, processing, and assessing information. As Duane Lockard states, there is no satisfactory alternative, for "by not providing desperately needed help the legislature is assuredly undermining its own foundation."[4]

Yet the recommendation for increased professional staffs, like other aspects of legislative reform, has been made before political scientists have produced descriptive and analytical accounts of the staff which legislatures already employ. Over ten years ago in a review of the literature on legislative behavior, Norman Meller stated, "Staffing as a factor in the shaping of legislative product and the facilitating of legislative action remains almost wholly unresearched."[5] Even today, little is known about this aspect of the legislative process. Indeed, a review of the current state of actual knowledge concerning the role of professional staff and their effects upon legislative operations is an unrewarding task, for knowledge of this kind is impressively slight.

A major difficulty arises. Having become persuaded of the utility of professional aides, there is a growing tendency among legislators and legislative reformers to regard staffing as a panacea. Moreover, little concern has been given to possible dysfunctional consequences of increased staffing. As Norman Meller has pointed out, indiscriminate staffing "could well lead to the institutionalizing of the legislator, and eventually to each legislator becoming the captive of his own staff."[6] It might prove useful, then, to examine the direction of current reform efforts and to identify areas for future research.

LEGISLATIVE REFORM

A wide variety of aides currently services Congress and our state legislatures.[7] Legislative housekeeping staffs—from attendants in the mail room to Xerox machine operators—may constitute the bulk of employees, but their numbers are swelled by the corps of clerks who process the legislature's work and keep its necessary records, the technical and secretarial staffs of standing and joint legislative committees, the librarians and researchers of reference bureaus, the analysts and administrative staffs of legislative councils, compilers and codifiers of statute revisors, legislative auditors, and the various categories of personal aides provided at governmental expense to legislators. The rapid expansion in their size and diversity during the last quarter-century conceals the fact that housekeeping services tended the convening of the first American legislatures[8] and that even early state constitutions occasionally provided for legislators receiving legal opinions[9] and bill-drafting services.[10]

Several observers have noted that legislative staffs have grown fairly steadily in recent years. Samuel C. Patterson has noted the increase in the size of congressional committee staffs[11] and argued that they have become much more professionalized with tenure in staff positions now secure in most committees, and salaries competitive with those of executive agencies.[12] In addition, increases in the numbers of committees and subcommittees have produced increases in the numbers of professional staff employees. In 1947, House committees employed about 222 persons; staff size reached 770 employees in 1967. Senate committee staffs grew from about 340 persons in 1952 to more than 620 in 1967. Increases in staff activity have been reflected in steady increases in committee expenditures for inquiries and investigation.[13]

Harrison Fox and Susan Hammond found that the number of staff authorized for each congressperson also has increased very rapidly in recent years,[14] and, as a result, the total number of individuals employed on office staffs of congresspeople has expanded accordingly.[15] To a certain extent, the institutionalization of the House has been reflected in the institutionalization of House staff.[16] In the Senate, the personal staffs of senators have quadrupled in size since the passage of the Legislative Reorganization Act in 1946.[17]

In a survey of current trends in the movement for modernization and improvement of our state legislatures, Karl Kurtz identified seven major themes. Two of the seven dealt with increased professional staffing:

> The most substantial efforts toward legislative improvement have been made in the area of improving the Legislature's ability to make independent judgments concerning taxation and spending by state government. This has been achieved primarily through the addition of specialized fiscal staff. Sixth, a major emerging trend is for the Legislatures to provide specialized staff to their standing committees, as well as to make the committees more effective instruments of the Legislature in the interim, so as to improve the quality of information and legislation available for consideration by the legislators.[18]

A survey conducted by the Citizens Conference on State Legislatures revealed that more respondents noted changes in the areas of staffing and services—mainly improvements—than in any other category. Questionnaires from forty-three states (eighty-six percent) reported changes in staffing and services. Reports from thirty-nine states noted increases in professional staffing; twenty-three of those also noted expansion of clerical staffs.[19]

The trend in legislative modernization efforts seems clear. As Kurtz concludes, "The early 1970's appear to be a period for the diffusion of the innovations of the 1960's in staff services to a larger number of States and for the expansion of existing staffs."[20]

Two questions naturally follow. First, why the great effort at legislative reform and increased professional staffing at this point in history? Second, what difference have these changes made? What consequences flow from the reform effort? The first question is answered briefly in the next section, but the latter question requires lengthier consideration and is the subject of the last section of this chapter.

WHY REFORM AT THIS TIME?

It has been the contention of many political scientists studying legislatures, and often of reformers within the legislature itself, that increases in staff expertise and a general upgrading of information resources are necessary if legislatures are to retain or regain their lawmaking capacities and to escape complete dominance by the executive. As one New York State Senator, long an advocate of reform, noted:

It's pretty common to find legislators who don't think they need experts to advise them because they are "generalists." Generalism is often just a euphemism for ignorance. Legislators come to Albany with a mind not only open but vacant. In this fallow field the Governor sows his executive seeds.[21]

One of the most visible capabilities of professional staff, then, involves the intelligence function of the legislature. The whole legislative process "is built around the process of acquiring information and intelligence with respect to particular conditions and situations, and the application of that information to the fashioning of laws."[22] An experienced Democratic legislator in New York made the argument:

When the legislature depends on the executive agencies or private interest groups for research instead of relying on its own sources of information, it makes its choices from the alternatives offered by the interest groups or the executive. Now we have an independent check because we have professional staff. They provide us with alternatives.

It is a common assumption that "bad" or "wrong" decisions in politics as in business stem from insufficient or improperly processed information,[23] and increased legislative staffs have been justified on the basis of providing more complete and accurate information.[24]

As thousands of bills pile up on their desks annually, legislators are expected to exercise intelligent choice in sifting beneficial legislative proposals from those that are harmful or unsound.[25] For the most part, members of the legislature are laymen representing diverse professions, businesses, and trades.[26] The legislature is essentially a political arena. Its informational requirements "cannot be analyzed solely in terms of the factual inputs needed to define an issue, generate alternative solutions, select the 'best' solution to meet some simple objective criteria such as cost or profit, and then control implementation in terms of 'economy and efficiency.' "[27] "Facts" and competent analysis—these alone are not the essence of legislating. "Get the facts and let the legislator decide" may be a neat and popular slogan, but it is not necessarily a valid assumption about the way in which laws are made.

The argument might well be made that our legislatures are already swamped by information,[28] that their input channels and information-handling machinery are simply not equipped to handle the mass of available data in a practical manner for decision-making. The problems of legislative access to information might be better defined as a problem of information management.[29] As one upstate New York Senator put it in describing the role the staff plays in investigating, researching, scheduling, editing, compiling, and distributing much of the information on which legislative decisions are based:

> The legislature is already swamped by information and the legislators themselves are simply not equipped to handle the mass of available data in a practical manner for decision making. That's where the staff comes in. They analyze the information and present it so that it's meaningful to us as legislators.

As Donald Matthews noted, modern legislation is complex and technical, and it comes before the legislature in a crushing quantity.[30] Legislatures have created staff research agencies, then, to provide them with two essential ingredients of good policy decisions: (1) accurate, thorough, relevant information, carefully analyzed from the legislative perspective; and (2) the necessary time for the legislators to apply this information and analysis accurately in evaluating available policy alternatives. In a real sense, the staff acts as gatekeepers,[31] as an intervening bureaucracy in a two-step flow of demands, requests, information, and so on between the members of the legislature and the network of advocates seeking legislative action. They filter the competing demands for legislative attention and help decide who and what is to be granted access. They specialize in interpreting technical aspects in terms comprehensible to the legislator. Thus, by supplying the first ingredient, the research staff helps to make the second possible.

The matter of the increasing quantity and complexity of matters before the legislatures also merits attention. Legislation was seldom a simple problem, but today it is more difficult than at any other time in our national history. Annually, thousands of bills are introduced in every legislature. In New York, for example, in 1972 more than 15,000 individual proposed pieces of legislation were put into the hopper. If the legislature, as a whole, were to consider these individually and spend ten minutes on each bill, it would have to meet ten hours a day, five days a week for fifty weeks of the year.[32] As the number of bills has grown each year, so too has the complexity of the decisions facing legislators increased.[33]

Moreover, legislators often deplore, as did one U.S. Senator, that "we have provided endless equipment for the executive and administrative agencies to take care of themselves; but we have not provided ourselves with the machinery to do those things that we ought to do."[34] The result has been, as another legislator noted, that "the legislature doesn't appreciate the importance of many decisions requiring technical expertise and, as a result, they are made not in the chamber of the legislature, but elsewhere; not by the elected representatives, but by unknown administrative officials."[35]

With but few exceptions, there is general agreement among most political scientists that legislatures have declined in power vis-à-vis the executive, and that the decline in power is most visible in the decline of legislatures as initiators of legislation and innovators of public policy. Increasingly, it seems, the formulation of policy alternatives falls to the executive, aided and influenced by the expert advice of civil servants, while the legislature reviews, approves, modifies, or vetoes.

Professional staffers provide the legislature with an innovative capability. One of the reasons members of the legislative staff like their work is that they have the opportunity to innovate, to initiate public policy, or to see it initiated.[36] Eugene Eidenberg has attempted to show quantitatively the relationship between staff bureaucratization and committee innovation. Based upon data from committee staff interviews, he ranked House committees according to the degree of bureaucratization, using indices of specialization, hierarchy, coordination, impartiality, and merit employment. He also ranked committees in terms of the extent to which members initiated bills independent of the executive branch. He found that staff bureaucratization and committee innovation were highly correlated ($r = .55$), with staff specialization contributing most to innovation.[37] Eidenberg suggests that "perhaps the bureaucratic staff allows members to initiate more, by doing the routine noninnovative things which otherwise the member must do for himself."[38] It may be added that staff members, especially those with long tenure in key staff positions, are about as likely to initiate legislation as are legislators themselves.[39]

The staffing of legislatures has introduced a third force of experts into the policy process to serve as a corrective to the bias of the special interests and to the substantive recommendations of the executive. Larger staffs are seen as a major factor in reversing the trend in the direction of the ascendance or even the virtually complete dominance of the executive over the legislative branch. With a larger staff, reformers assert, the legislature could legislate in detailed instead of broad terms and could initiate legislation instead of ceding the formulation of policy alternatives to the executive.[40] Professional staff members can provide legislatures with that independent innovative capacity.

Frequently, conflict has spurred legislative modernization. For example, an important impetus for legislative modernization in New York was conflict with the executive branch. In 1964, for the first time in many years, the Democrats gained control of the legislature. As one staffer described it,

"When the Democrats took over the legislature, they sought to use it as a focus of opposition to the incumbent governor and they thought it would be useful to further staff Assembly Ways and Means. Fiscal staffing was thought necessary in order to enhance legislative power." In California, the establishment of a special legislative budget committee resulted from sharp antagonisms between the legislature and the governor.[41] The election of an aggressive governor in Illinois in 1969 is said to have contributed to changing the legislature in that state.[42] The change in the party system in Wisconsin in the 1960s, and especially the confrontation between a Democratic governor and a Republican legislature from 1961 through 1964, prompted the drive for a stronger legislature.[43]

The Supreme Court's decisions in Baker v. Carr and Reynolds v. Simms can also be viewed as a factor in increased efforts toward legislative improvement and modernization. The Citizens Conference on State Legislatures argues:

> The prospect that state legislatures could, once more, genuinely reflect and represent their people and respond to their needs—that they could, once more, count for something in the public life of the nation—made it all the more imperative that they be strengthened and improved to the point where they could really function as the democratic decision-making bodies they were designed to be.[44]

Moreover, recently it has become apparent to people of every political persuasion that our political system does not work unless all of its parts are alive and well. Legislatures have long been the main, although not the only, "drag" upon the capacity of government to respond to public problems. As John Burns forcefully noted in *The Sometime Governments:*

> We are rediscovering the states and their legislatures not out of filial respect for our forefathers, or a fine regard for our political heritage, but for the most pragmatic of reasons: our federal system simply will not work well without them, and it is the only system we have.[45]

Finally, the movement toward reform of our legislative institutions has been aided by the work of several national organizations composed of legislator members—notably the National Legislative Conference and the National Conference of State Legislative Leaders. A number of non-legislator organizations, including the Citizens Conference on State Legislatures, the Eagleton Institute of Politics at Rutgers University, Common Cause, and the League of Women Voters also have served as major vehicles for reform. As a result of the efforts by these organizations—together with those of other private and public organizations, and those of many state legislators and congressmembers—the pace of legislative reform has accelerated in recent years.

SO WHAT?:
THE CONSEQUENCES OF LEGISLATIVE STAFFING

According to Malcolm Jewell and Samuel Patterson: "The enduring motif in both popular and academic discourse about American legislatures has been that of reform."[46] Although we may not know exactly how the legislative reform movement began, one thing we are sure of is that it has resulted in a mass of newspaper and magazine articles, a welter of speeches, and numerous reports and studies. Thus no one can say that the movement for legislative modernization suffers from lack of information. The what, the what's wrong, and, to a certain extent, the what ought to be done, have been adequately covered, to say the least.[47]

But the specific effects of particular staff patterns, the consequences of legislative reform efforts, have been largely ignored.[48] Senator Earl Brydges, former Majority Leader of the New York State Senate, expressed this point well when he said: "To help us in decisionmaking, we need not just more staff, not just full-time staff, not just better-trained staff, so glibly urged by the traditional reformers." Even more important, he continued, "We need to know what kinds of staff we need."[49]

Several recent studies, however, have provided the outline for a more complete exploration of the actual roles, functions, and impact of professional legislative staffs. A study by James Cochrane[50] begins with the premise that congressional committee staff members "are not neutral servants" and "are as actively involved in the legislative process as are the members of Congress."[51] Because professional experts do not necessarily agree in their views of problems and solutions, the way is paved for the formation of a committee staff that leans toward one particular partisan view. Thus, congressional committee staffs range from the kind envisioned in the Legislative Reorganization Act, "the highly professional, very nonpartisan staff which renders excellent service to all committee members," to the highly partisan staff.

It should not be assumed, then, that legislative staff members are but "neutral servants," who unerringly supply the legislature with indisputably objective evidence. The staff members are inexorably involved in the political struggle within the legislative system, and their role behavior may have fundamental policy implications.[52]

The activities of legislative staff are illustrated in a number of case studies of congressional committees. Not infrequently does the advice and recommendation of the committee staff determine whether an item or provision is included in a bill reported by a committee.[53] The ability of professional staff to influence or affect the legislative process is tremendous. Some have gone so far as to contend that "at the top of the heap . . . one can, practically speaking, say that the power is divided almost equally between legislators and staff members."[54] Robert Sherrill has stated:

> There are plenty of exceptions, of course, and there are degrees of involvement, but as a rule, it is the administrative assistants, the legislative assistants, the staff counsels, and the staff economists—not the members—who think up the legislation, make the deals, listen to the lobbyists, keep the backhome political pipes flushed out, determine what mail the member sees and what he misses, and determine who gets to see him and who has to settle for a flunky.[55]

Recently, the question of the consequences of legislative staffing changes—functional and dysfunctional, intended and unanticipated—has been considered in two studies. Alan J. Wyner seeks to describe in some detail the changes that have taken place in the California state legislature in recent years and to focus on the consequences, if any, for legislative procedures, personnel, and, to some extent, policy.[56] In assessing the impact on procedures, Wyner finds that, although the cost of legislative operations rose from $3.4 million in fiscal year 1951 to $7.0 million in 1961 to $24.5 million in 1970, legislative costs as a percentage of total state expenditures have increased only slightly. Wyner also finds that the availability of staff, coupled with annual sessions, has contributed to the legislature's workload—more bills are introduced, and more are passed. It seems that increased staffing may not necessarily lighten the burden of work for legislators. As Bertram Gross pointed out a number of years ago:

> The man who tries to do a better job often turns out to be one who sees that the better job is actually a bigger job. Moreover, imaginative staff aides often uncover new problems, new opportunities, and new challenges. They tend to create—or at least attract—heavier burdens.[57]

Wyner also attempts to assess several predicted consequences of staff increases. More staff allegedly means: (1) more information for legislators; (2) more independence from the governor, bureaucracy, and lobbyists; and (3) more help with many time-consuming "service" chores. He finds that whether "one speaks only about the number of formal, written statements and research reports now generated or about the more casual verbal interjection from staff," there is little doubt that "more 'bits' of information are inserted into the California legislative process as a result of staff increases."[58]

While the evidence is somewhat impressionistic, Wyner also asserts that "today's California legislature has more independence than in prior times."[59] He claims that the role of most lobbyists and almost all bureaucrats now requires different kinds of interactions because of increased staff. Lobbyists and bureaucrats now must interact more with staff personnel than legislators and must present a more detailed and widespread justification for their proposals. This development poses the danger, raised by Arthur Macmahon, that the growth of a legislative bureaucracy will insulate the legislator from, or dilute the relationship with, either constituents or executive officials.[60] Macmahon believes that it is the duty of the legislator, immediately in touch with constituents, to bring "practical public sense" to bear in the oversight of administration. The legislator interjects the criticism of a "robust, imaginative, lay mind into highly technical operations."[61] Macmahon fears that these values might be lost if the politician-legislator dealt with administrative officials vicariously through an intermediate legislative bureaucracy.

Finally, Wyner finds that while the staff has allowed legislators to escape some constituents' errand-type demands, they have not freed them completely from "case work." The reform efforts have also resulted in more legislative-gubernatorial conflict, as measured by gubernatorial reductions in the appropriations bill passed by the legislature and vetos of legislation.

Staff impact on policy was noticeable in two areas: (1) a change for the better in the "technical" characteristics of legislation was evident and (2) the legislature's resumption of an initiatory stand in several policy areas, especially mental health, air pollution, and education.

Alan Rosenthal of the Eagleton Institute of Politics at Rutgers University has been a major figure in the area of state legislative reform for several years now. In his study,[62] Rosenthal seeks to evaluate the effects of caucus and fiscal staffs on legislative adjustment, decision-making, integration, and performance in Wisconsin. He finds that legislative analysts in Wisconsin provide both tangible and symbolic benefits to members. By furnishing members with information and publicity and enhancing their sense of security and self-esteem, staffers facilitate the adjustment of many individuals to the trials of legislative life.[63]

Although the evidence is indirect, Rosenthal claims that staffing the fiscal bureau and party caucuses led to an increase in the centralization of decision-making influence in the Wisconsin Legislature. One arrangement strengthened an already strong finance committee; the other aided individual legislators, but also increased the control of leaders over party caucuses. The latter also promoted greater intraparty unity and interparty conflict. Both staffs, at least indirectly, contributed to a decline in the power of substantive committees in the legislature.[64] While the evidence is sketchy and somewhat impressionistic, the fact that a particular staffing arrangement may result in some alteration in the balance of power in the legislature merits attention.[65]

While this alteration may not necessarily be harmful, legislators and legislative reformers should be aware of the ramifications of various staff changes. The probabilities of who gets what, when, and how should be considered before a legislature decides on one type of staff rather than another. Legislative staffers serving individual members, specialists serving standing committees, and political aides serving legislative leaders may have different effects. The first group may enhance the capability of individual legislators, the second may add to the strength of the committees, and the third may increase the power of the leadership. Such consequences should be anticipated so that those advocating legislative reform will get the type of staff that will meet their needs.

Rosenthal found, as Wyner did, that the staff increased, rather than lightened, the workload of legislators—by uncovering problems, perceiving opportunities, and passing on information and research to their patrons.[66] But the staff was responsible for considerable improvement in legislative performance. The fiscal staff reinforced the legislature's customary budgetary role and contributed to legislative economizing. It also served as a deterrent, cautioning the governor and executive departments and agencies against excessive budget demands. Caucus staffing also fostered improvement in two interrelated respects:

> First, it has helped the legislative parties, and especially the minority, exert continuous pressure on the executive branch, and thereby has enhanced legislative control. Second, it has enlarged the number of alternatives that can be considered by the legislature, and thereby has contributed to legislative modification of proposals advanced by the governor and the executive departments and agencies.[67]

Rosenthal concludes:

> In Wisconsin, staffing did not make a weak legislature strong; rather it made a strong legislature stronger. This, of course, is what the leaders had in mind when they decided to experiment with several demonstration projects. . . . They hoped merely to reinforce existing institutional patterns, and this is just what happened.[68]

Further research is clearly necessary to determine the effects of specific staffing patterns in various state legislatures and in Congress. Especially relevant would be research aimed at discerning the unexpected and dysfunctional results of increased staffing.

A number of authors have questioned whether or not large and efficient staffs may be a mixed blessing.[69] Perhaps the most cogent criticism of the opponents to increased staffing is that staffing in itself cannot solve many problems. Whether a legislator will initiate an investigation, follow through on hearings and committee action, and actually vote for legislation may depend on a range of factors completely apart from the availability of staff. Staff may offer only an illusory hope that legislators can escape the burdens of uncertainty, difficult choice, and continuing frustration.

In a recent study, for example, John Kingdon found that, in terms of the importance of voting decisions which congresspeople themselves reported, the staff was not at all important.[70] Congressmembers spontaneously mentioned staff as being involved in their decisions only five percent of the time, the lowest figure for any actor in the system. Kingdon concludes:

> In terms of our standard importance coding, the staff is of major or determinative importance only 9 percent of the time, and of no importance at all a full 66 percent, the highest percentage of all the actors. In short, if staff members are important in voting decisions, their influence is either extremely subtle, or is restricted to those issues in which the congressman has a particular interest and asks his staff to do more extensive work.[71]

Correlating the Citizens Conference indicators of state legislative reform with various policy output indicators, Leonard G. Ritt suggests that, on the whole, reformed legislatures are not more likely to have different policy outcomes than are unreformed legislatures. The overall conclusion is that reform has little impact on expenditure or tax levels and may result only in a reshuffling of men and institutions with minimal impact on the allocation of public resources.[72]

CONCLUSIONS

Recommendations for reform for legislative institutions are likely to be troublesome for both the legislator and the academician, for they reveal a gap in our knowledge. No one really knows whether proposed reforms will do what their sponsors say they will. No one has said much about the unintended consequences of these changes. No one really knows whether major changes in the legislative process, in structure or procedures, will make the legislature a better place in which to work, a more nearly equal partner to the executive, a more resourceful institution for the generation of imaginative political ideas. No one should expect legislators to take quixotic risks for the sake of tenuous political theory. We need to know what happens when specific changes are introduced. In order to anticipate intelligently how proposals for change may work in the future, it is necessary to evaluate how changes have worked in the past. It seems clear that no prescriptions will carry much weight unless they meet functional tests.

In one area of legislative reform, that of professional staffing, a great deal of careful research needs to be done. We have a number of prescriptive studies; we lack descriptive and analytical studies. The consequences of legislative reform efforts have been largely ignored. This chapter has attempted to ascertain what can be said about the legislative reform movement as we enter the last third of the twentieth century. It has also sought to describe what work is currently going on and to speculate as to what lies ahead and what remains to be done.

The only adequate test of the validity of the many diverse and often conflicting perceptions of legislative staffing is how they have worked in practice. Since a number of state legislatures now have been operating with a sizable professional staff for some time, it would be desirable to examine the nature and workings of these staffs. State legislatures provide an ideal location to examine the effects of professional staffs—anticipated and unexpected, functional and dysfunctional. For example, most state legislators serve in their jobs on a part-time basis. The legislative session may last only thirty, sixty, or ninety days, as it does in many states; few go beyond six months. In a number of states, regular sessions are held only once every two years. Even during the session, legislators do not devote all their time to legislative tasks; they also operate their businesses or professions back home and actually may be in the capitol only three days a week. In a setting with part-time legislators and full-time staff, the role of the staff may take on greater significance, and the dangers of staff autonomy may be greater. Moreover, research in several state legislatures would allow for more meaningful comparisons of various factors identified as important in affecting staff influence: party, partisanship, size of the legislature, seniority, nature of the district, legislators' role orientations, ideology (liberal-conservative), and so on.[73] As a result of changes currently being made in the staffing patterns of state legislatures, there is considerable opportunity for analysis of the effects of professional staffing. Such studies could contribute significantly to our understanding of the legislative process.

NOTES

1. Donald Herzberg and Jess Unruh, *Essays on the State Legislative Process* (New York: Holt, Rinehart & Winston, 1970), esp. pp. 103-111.

2. In a recent compilation of recommendations, more pages were devoted to staff and services than to any other subject. Citizens Conference on State Legislatures, *Compilation of Recommendations Pertaining to Legislative Improvement in the Fifty States* (Kansas City, Mo.: The Conference, April 1967). See also John C. Wahlke, "Organization and Procedure," in Alexander Heard, ed., *State Legislatures in American Politics* (Englewood Cliffs, N.J.: Prentice-Hall, 1966), p. 131. Surveys conducted in Maryland, Connecticut, New Jersey, Mississippi, Florida, Wisconsin, and Rhode Island also indicate widespread legislator agreement on the need for professional staff. See the Strengthening the Legislature series prepared by the Center for State Legislative Research and Service, Eagleton Institute of Politics, New Brunswick, New Jersey.

3. Advisory Commission on Intergovernmental Relations, *Fiscal Balance in the American Federal System* (Washington, D.C.: The Commission, October 1967), p. 243.

4. Duane Lockard, "The State Legislator," in Heard, *State Legislatures,* p. 114.

5. Norman Meller, " 'Legislative Behavior Research' Revisited: A Review of Five Years' Publications," *Western Political Quarterly,* Vol. 18 (September 1965), p. 177.

6. Norman Meller, "Legislative Staff Services: Toxin, Specific, or Placebo for the Legislature's Ills, *Western Political Quarterly,* Vol. 20 (June 1967), p. 388.

7. For one listing, see the Council of State Governments, *Permanent Legislative Service Agencies* (Lexington: The Council, 1970).

8. See Albert J. Abrams, *The Staff of Liberty,* Report to the Legislative Staffers of the United States (Salt Lake City, Utah: National Legislative Conference, August 1970).

9. 1792 Constitution of Kentucky, Article II, Sec. 16.

10. 1867 Constitution of Alabama, Article VI, Sec. 16.

11. Samuel C. Patterson, "The Professional Staffs of Congressional Committees," *Administrative Science Quarterly,* Vol. 15 (March 1970), pp. 22-38.

12. Ibid., p. 23.

13. Ibid., p. 24.

14. Harrison W. Fox, Jr. and Susan Webb Hammond, "Congressional Staff and Congressional Change," paper presented at the annual meeting of the American Political Science Association, September 4-8, 1973, p. 7.

15. Since 1946, personal staffs have more than tripled. Ibid., p. iii.

16. Nelson W. Polsby, "The Institutionalization of the U.S. House of Representatives," *American Political Science Review,* Vol. 62 (March 1968) pp. 144-168.

17. Fox and Hammond, "Congressional Staff," p. 21.

18. Karl T. Kurtz, "The State Legislatures," in *The Book of the States* (Lexington: Council of State Governments, 1974).

19. Citizens Conference on State Legislatures, "Legislatures Move To Improve Their Effectiveness," Research Memorandum No. 15 (Kansas City: The Conference, April 1972).

20. Kurtz, "The State Legislatures."

21. See Alan P. Balutis, "Professional Staffing in the New York State Legislature: An Exploratory Study," (Ph.D. dissertation, State University of New York at Albany, 1973). Unless otherwise indicated, quotations in the text are taken from this study.

22. H. Alexander Smith, "Information and Intelligence for Congress," *Annals of the American Academy of Political and Social Science,* Vol. 289 (September 1953), p. 114.

23. John S. Saloma III, *Congress and the New Politics* (Boston: Little, Brown, 1969), p. 209.

24. For a discussion of this point, see William J. Siffin, *The Legislative Council in the American States* (Bloomington: Indiana University Press, 1959), pp. 218-223.

25. David Brinkley opened a November 1965 NBC-TV News Special Report, entitled "Congress Needs Help," standing next to mountainous piles of paper that passed through a typical congressperson's office in a single session.

26. For an examination of the social and political background characteristics of American legislators, see Malcolm E. Jewell and Samuel C. Patterson, *The Legislative Process in the United States* (New York: Random House, 1966), pp. 101-123.

27. Charles R. Dechert, "Availability of Information for Congressional Operations," in Alfred de Grazia, ed., *Congress: The First Branch of Government* (Garden City, N.Y.: Anchor Books, 1967), p. 156.

28. Warren Weaver, Jr., has argued, "The problem is not that Congress gets too little information, but that too little of the great mass it gets is relevant and readily, rapidly

available. . . . Buried in this information glut are useful facts and provocative arguments, but the members and committees of Congress, with limited manpower and no mechanical assistance at all, have rarely been able to separate the worthwhile bits from the great mass of repetition and special pleading and then store those bits where they can be readily found." *Both Your Houses: The Truth About Congress* (New York: Praeger, 1972), p. 165.

29. See Dechert, "Availability of Information," and Ed Crane, "Legislative Service Agencies," in *The Book of the States* (Lexington: Council of State Governments, 1971), pp. 76-78. Crane argues that "the ability of the legislative branch to realize its full potential in the coming decades rests substantially on development of effective means of 'managing' itself" (p. 76).

30. Donald R. Matthews, *U.S. Senators and Their World* (New York: Vintage, 1960), p. 97.

31. It was the late Kurt Lewin who applied the term "gatekeeper" to a phenomenon which is of considerable importance to students of mass communication. See Kurt Lewin, "Channels of Group Life," *Human Relations*, Vol. 1 (1947), p. 145. For a further discussion of the conceptual underpinnings of "gatekeeper" studies, other studies utilizing this concept, and its relevance to the study of legislative staffs, see Balutis, "Professional Staffing," pp. 201-209.

32. Peter A. A. Berle, *Does the Citizen Stand a Chance?* (Woodbury, N.Y.: Barron's Educational Series, 1974), p. 25.

33. This seems to be one of the reasons for the movement toward regularly scheduled annual sessions and extensions of session length among state legislatures. See the Citizens Conference on State Legislatures, *Legislatures Move To Improve Their Effectiveness*, p. 6.

34. As quoted in Arthur Macmahon, "Congressional Oversight of Administration: The Power of the Purse," *Political Science Quarterly*, Vol. 58 (June 1943), p. 186.

35. As quoted in Alan P. Balutis, "Science, Technology, and the State Legislatures," proposal submitted to the Committee on Science and Technology of the National Legislative Conference, Palm Beach Shores, Florida, February 16, 1973, p. 2.

36. For a discussion of this staff capability at the congressional level, see Patterson, "The Professional Staffs of Congressional Committees," pp. 27-28.

37. Eugene Eidenberg, "The Congressional Bureaucracy" (Ph.D. dissertation, Northwestern University, 1966), pp. 70-117.

38. Ibid., p. 112.

39. Ibid., p. 124.

40. Kenneth Kofmehl, *Professional Staffs of Congress* (West Lafayette, Ind.: Purdue Research Foundation, 1962), p. 5.

41. See D. Jay Doubleday, *Legislative Review of the Budget in California* (Berkeley, Calif.: Institute of Governmental Studies, University of California, 1967), p. 36.

42. Samuel K. Gove, "Policy Implications of Legislative Reorganization in Illinois," in James A. Robinson, ed., *State Legislative Innovation* (New York: Praeger, 1973), p. 129.

43. Alan Rosenthal, "Professional Staff and Legislative Influence in Wisconsin," in Robinson, *State Legislative Innovation*, p. 186.

44. Citizens Conference on State Legislatures, *The Sometime Governments* (New York: Bantam, 1971), p. 3.

45. Ibid., p. 15.

46. Jewell and Patterson, *The Legislative Process*, p. 517.

47. Herzberg and Unruh, *Essays on the State Legislative Process*, pp. 104-107.

48. An exception is the recent provocative work in the Praeger Special Studies Program: Robinson, *State Legislative Innovation.*

49. Earl W. Brydges, "New Frontiers in Legislative Staffing," *State Government,* Vol. 39 (Autumn, 1966), p. 227.

50. James D. Cochrane, "Partisan Aspects of Congressional Committee Staffing," *Western Political Quarterly,* Vol. 17 (June 1964), pp. 338-348.

51. Ibid., p. 338. For a stimulating article on whether "professionalism"—in the sense of "neutral competence"—is the hallmark of several congressional staff aides, see David E. Price, "Professionals and 'Entrepreneurs': Staff Orientations and Policy Making on Three Senate Committees," *Journal of Politics,* Vol. 33 (May 1971), pp. 316-336.

52. See Max Kampelman, "The Legislative Bureaucracy: Its Response to Political Change, 1953," *Journal of Politics,* Vol. 16 (August 1954), pp. 539-550.

53. It is one of the major themes of a dissertation by Seymour Mann that Gerald Reilly, staff aide to the Senate Labor and Public Welfare Committee, was the evil genius who, through his skill as a legislative draftsman, shaped the Taft-Hartley Act in a much more anti-labor direction than it otherwise would have taken. See Seymour Mann, "Congressional Behavior and National Labor Policy: Structural Determinants of the Taft-Hartley Act" (Ph.D. dissertation, University of Chicago, 1951), pp. 127-128, 198, 262-263, 266-272, 326-327, 398-407, 427-428.

54. Robert Sherrill, "Who Runs Congress?" *New York Times Magazine,* November 22, 1970, p. 53. This view is supported by Kenneth Schlossberg in "The Ablest Men in Congress," *Washingtonian,* Vol. 3 (August 1968), pp. 61-63 and 72-75 and by P. Wyden, "Ghosts on Capitol Hill," *Newsweek,* January 28, 1957, p. 33.

55. Sherrill, "Who Runs Congress?" p. 53.

56. Alan J. Wyner, "Legislative Reform and Politics in California: What Happened, Why, and So What?" in Robinson, *State Legislative Innovation,* pp. 46-100.

57. Bertram Gross, *The Legislative Struggle* (New York: McGraw-Hill, 1953), p. 422.

58. Wyner, "Legislative Reforms and Politics," p. 87.

59. Ibid., p. 88.

60. Macmahon, "Congressional Oversight," pp. 161-190.

61. Ibid., p. 187.

62. Alan Rosenthal, "Professional Staff and Legislative Influence in Wisconsin," in Robinson, *State Legislative Innovation,* pp. 183-225.

63. Ibid., p. 195.

64. Ibid., pp. 200-206.

65. For a further discussion of this subject, see Alan Rosenthal, "The Consequences of Legislative Staffing," in Donald G. Herzberg and Alan Rosenthal, eds., *Strengthening the States: Essays on Legislative Reform* (Garden City, N.Y.: Anchor, 1972), pp. 75-88.

66. Rosenthal, "Professional Staff and Legislative Influence," p. 213.

67. Ibid., p. 216.

68. Ibid., p. 220.

69. A number of criticisms and the replies of advocates of enlarged staffs are discussed in Saloma, *Congress and the New Politics,* pp. 159-168. See also Balutis, "Professional Staffing," pp. 47-50.

70. John W. Kingdon, *Congressmen's Voting Decisions* (New York: Harper & Row, 1973), pp. 192-197.

71. Ibid., pp. 192-193.

72. Leonard G. Ritt, "State Legislative Reform: Does It Matter?" *American Politics Quarterly,* Vol. 1 (October 1973), pp. 499-510.

73. See Balutis, "Professional Staffing," pp. 209-230.

LEGISLATIVE INFORMATION NEEDS AND STAFF RESOURCES IN THE AMERICAN STATES

H. OWEN PORTER

Members of a citizens' lobby in a large industrial state were recently monitoring the legislative debate over an air pollution control bill when they learned that an amendment was about to be offered which would alter the prescribed heat level of industrial furnaces and affect the balance between leftover hydrocarbons and nitric oxides. The observers were dumbfounded. "What does this do?" "How does it affect our position?" They did not and could not know until complicated technical questions were explained. More information was needed.

This type of situation would not cause great alarm if it exemplified the quandaries of average citizens alone, because their part in governmental decision-making can usually be confined to merely selecting those who will represent them. They can and usually do vote for individuals who are better educated than themselves and who for a variety of reasons have chosen to make the public business their personal concern. But the variety and complexity of issues may frustrate the elected representative as well if he or she lacks the information and understanding which rational decisions require.[1] Unfortunately, representatives are bedeviled by these same difficulties much of the time. Legislators at both national and state levels must make numerous decisions often in a short space of time, but the information which they need is often not readily available. Recent increases in staff services in the states represent efforts to deal with these difficulties.[2] But legislators' information needs are more complex than reformers may have realized and the value of staffing depends upon how these services are integrated within the information-processing system which already prevails. In this chapter, I will describe certain aspects of this problem of securing adequate information as it appears in state legislatures, drawing particular insight from recent studies in Michigan and Virginia.

AUTHOR'S NOTE: The Virginia portion of this study was funded by the Institute of Government, University of Virginia.

DIMENSIONS OF THE PROBLEM

Legislators confront a number of difficulties in performing their tasks but in both the Congress and the states they are most troubled by insufficient time and information. Almost twenty years after the Congressional Reorganization Act rationalized the committee structure, provided substantial staff for committees and individual members and expanded the Congressional Reference Service, most representatives still identified lack of information and the complexity of decision-making as their most serious concern.[3] While several observers have noted a substantial improvement in the information-gathering and -processing abilities of Congress, many still call for further reforms to provide more information more quickly.[4]

The testimony by state legislators is similar. In both Michigan and Virginia, representatives feel as harassed as their congressional counterparts. As revealed in Table 1, a third of the recent appraisals by members of the Michigan House and over half those by Virginia delegates refered to these related problems. Yet the Michigan legislature, with unrestricted annual sessions, an established reference service, committee staff and personal aides, was ranked among the top ten in the nation in a recent comparative study.[5] Even though the Virginia House was less "professionalized" than Michigan, a reference service, interim study commissions, and personal staff are all available. The complaints of Virginia delegates regarding the volume of work and constraints of time would probably be mitigated in part if sessions were longer. The greater emphasis upon the difficulties of becoming informed in Virginia might also be reduced if committee staff and more time were available.[6] But it is also likely that, even when alleviated, these problems will continue to be the most serious which legislators confront.

We might expect that the difficulties of acquiring information would be most serious for freshmen legislators. It takes time to learn how to utilize the research services which are available and to hire and train individual aides. Also, the freshman has no past recollection of bills or issues to provide him with guidance with regard to current debate. The testimony of new legislators in both states confirms this assumption, although a substantial majority of senior legislators also complained. "You can't keep well informed especially on questions that aren't controversial," commented one Virginia representative with six years of experience. A senior legislator in Michigan agreed. "There are about 4,000 bills submitted," he said. "If you wait for the calendar there are 1,000. I have neither the time nor the inclination to become more than superficially informed on all of the bills I vote on." Some senior members did point out that the problem had become less serious for them as a result of experience. Many measures are recognized as amendments to recent or well-known legislation, and the representative can recall a previous position or assess the legislation anew, but opinions in both states demonstrate that seniority alone does not provide solutions.

TABLE 1
DIFFICULTIES OF LEGISLATIVE WORK (in percentages)

Question: What do you find is the most difficult part of your job?

Type of Difficulty	Proportion of Total Responses[a]	
	Virginia	Michigan
Getting adequate information; becoming knowledgeable on proposals, understanding the effects of legislation	25	20
Keeping up with the volume of work; finding enough time to do all of my work	33	13
Communicating with constituents, trying to satisfy constituents	9	16
Achieving success for my own legislation; convincing my colleagues on an issue	4	12
Making choices; voting on controversial legislation	3	10
Attending all committee meetings, tediousness of work on the floor; wasting time in debate	7	9
Making the job compatible with normal life; unable to have a private life; keeping up with another job	5	4
Financing state government	3	3
Campaigning	2	2
Other	9	11
TOTAL	100	100
FREQUENCY	150[b]	89

a. The Virginia data were collected by personal interviews with 87 of the 100 members of the House of Delegates during the spring of 1974. The Michigan data was collected by similar interviews with 75 of the 110 members of the House in 1970. Although the 75 Michigan legislators were not intentionally drawn as a random sample, they were closely comparable in terms of partisanship and tenure to the entire House, and there is no evidence to indicate that their responses should not be considered representative. For an earlier presentation of these data and a detailed description of the Michigan study, see "Legislative Experts and Outsiders: The Two-Step Flow of Communication" *Journal of Politics,* Vol. 36 (1974), pp. 703-730.

b. The total exceeds the number of legislators interviewed because of multiple responses.

Underlying Causes of the Problem

The difficulties of acquiring information arise from several factors which are peculiar to legislative institutions. In the first place, the volume of legislative business by any standards is enormous and still increasing. The U.S. Congress in 1969 and 1970 considered over 24,631 bills, enacting 941. In California during the 1970-1971 sessions over 7,000 bills were submitted and almost 3,500 passed. Since 1950, the volume of legislation in the ten largest and ten smallest states has increased on the average by fifty percent and, as Table 2 indicates, in some it has more than doubled. The diversity of this legislation requires encyclopedic knowledge and virtually assures that no single legislator will be well informed on all or even most questions before him or her.

TABLE 2
STATE LEGISLATIVE WORKLOAD BILLS ENACTED: 1950-51, 1970-71

Ten Largest[a] States	1950-1951	1970-1971	Percentage Change	Ten Smallest States	1950-1951	1970-1971	Percentage Change
California	1791	3449	+ 92.57	Rhode Island	691	715	+ 3.47
New York	1666	2262	+ 35.77	N. Hampshire	337	559	+ 65.88
Pennsylvania	569[b]	588	+ 3.34	Idaho	287	629	+119.16
Texas	505	1067	+111.29	Montana	229	444	+ 93.89
Illinois	1040	2411	+131.83	S. Dakota	473	607	+ 28.33
Ohio	242	187	− 22.73	N. Dakota	348	611	+ 75.57
Michigan	279	486	+ 74.19	Delaware	458[b]	761	+ 66.16
New Jersey	664	739	+ 11.30	Nevada	558	681	+ 22.04
Florida	1512	1978	+ 30.82	Vermont	373	272	− 27.08
Massachusetts	1724	2016	+ 16.94	Wyoming	161	270	+ 67.70
	average change + 48.53				average change + 51.51		

Combined total for ten largest and ten smallest states: + 50.02%

SOURCE: *The Book of the States,* Lexington, Ky.: Council of State Governments, Vols. IX, X, XIX.

a. States were chosen on the basis of their population size in 1970. Alaska and Hawaii, among the ten smallest in 1970, were not states in 1950 and were not included.

b. There were no figures given for Pennsylvania and Delaware in 1950. These are for 1949.

In the second place, the questions which are put before legislators are often quite specific and detailed and do not lend themselves to evaluation on the basis of ideological or partisan perspectives alone. Having articulated a conservative or liberal position on major issues of the day does not help very much when the issue is technical and complex. Third, because a system of standing committees is widely used in this country to distribute the legislative workload, legislators must specialize. Those who do confine their attention to their committees' jurisdictions place themselves in even greater jeopardy with respect to all those other areas of policy which they are forced to ignore. The legislature as a whole gains expertise, but the individual representative becomes more narrow and less well-informed. Fourth, even though many state assemblies have in the last ten years switched from biennial to annual sessions and have lengthened the period of their deliberations, most are still cramped for time.[7] Regardless of the length of a session, the end-of-session logjams, a chronic condition of American assemblies, squeezes many decisions on to a crowded calendar. The all too common practice of turning back chamber clocks to permit voting after a legally mandated adjournment does not characterize thoughtful decision-making. All these factors conspire to prevent elected officials from informing themselves and carefully evaluating their options before making a choice.

The Legislator's Perspective

It would not be necessary for a public official to inform himself, of course, if the consequences of his decisions are thought to be trivial. A legislator from inner-city Detroit does not need to examine very closely the provisions of a bill to alter the state bounty paid for predatory animals to hunters. His relative ignorance is itself rational. The legislation will have no impact on his constituents or on most of the state at large. Thus, assuming that rational behavior for him means helping or at least not hurting the voters in his district, he can enjoy the luxury of indifference. But such inattention is a luxury because in many cases it is not obvious that constituents will be unaffected by or disinterested in the choice the legislator makes. (A legislator from the working-class suburbs of Detroit would probably be wise to look carefully at changes in the deer hunting laws.)

The consequences of a decision may also be seen as trivial if legislators do not really care very much what their constituents want or need. If, for instance, the representative does not wish to remain in office, then securing approval from a majority in her district by "correct" votes in the assembly need not be important. While the high voluntary turnover rate in the American states lends some initial plausibility to this latter view, there is contrary evidence that most of the state assemblymembers do measure their conduct against constituency needs, if not desires.[8] Whether they describe their roles as delegates or trustees, most do not appear to be indifferent and because they are not, they work in an environment of uncertainty where information is constantly needed to make decisions.

The problem of securing adequate information is not merely an inconvenience and source of frustration. It afflicts legislators in these ways to be sure, but far more disturbing is the very real prospect of a legislature's incompetence with regard to its principal tasks. Inadequate information can prevent responsible representation by individual legislators, and contributes to the recurrence of sessional charades where the ill-informed legislators only go through the motions of making policy while outsiders really provide the important direction.[9] Staff assistance to committees, research and budget divisions, and aides to individuals can counteract these tendencies, but only at certain points in the decision process and only with regard to certain kinds of information. There are, after all, different kinds of information. Facts and figures, explanations of the intent or meaning of a measure, appraisals of impact or need, determinations of feasibility, and statements of group or party opinion are all types of information needed by most legislators during the course of decisions, but they are not all needed at the same time, and they cannot be packaged and produced by the same staff.

The structure and perspectives of legislative staff services vary greatly. Following the suggestion of Norman Meller, we can conceive of them as varying along at least two dimensions. One describes the degree of "personal involvement" of staff members in their work and ranges from intense involvement to anonymous objectivity.[10] The other refers to the clientele of the agency or service and varies from services which are assigned and responsible to the whole assembly to those which serve individual legislators. Staff members assigned to a Legislative Council which does not issue specific recommendations following its studies would represent a high degree of objectivity while providing little in the way of personal assistance. The staff of a party caucus would certainly be less objective but provide only slightly more assistance for individuals. An administrative assistant to a state representative would, of course, exhibit relatively great personal involvement. Most current recommendations for improved staffing tend toward objectivity and institutional responsibility.[11] Some of these service agencies can provide some kinds of information but not others, and some information probably lies beyond the competence of all. The limitations upon staff abilities are, in fact, imposed by the information-processing system which characterizes the institution itself.

INFORMATION-PROCESSING SYSTEM

A legislative information-processing system is marked by formal and informal channels and filters which include standing committees, bill-drafting and research divisions, influential individuals, and party organizations. The multiplicity of these points reflects the dispersion of lawmaking across stages and among various subunits. The policy-making process is thus fragmented and diffused unless and until the whole membership is called to a vote. Individual members and outsiders take the initiative as the authors of bills, committees dominate the early stages of review and recommendation, party leaders control the agenda, and all members participate in the final choices.[12]

The kinds of information which are needed by most legislators during the early and mid-points of this process and the kinds which are needed later are, in most instances, not the same. An author, during the early stage, needs information to perfect the content of a bill. What is the law now or the practice in other states? How should this be written to conform to legal codes? These are researchable questions which legal staff or personal aides can help to answer. Committee analysis and reformulation also deals with the content of legislation, and committee staff can lighten the workload and improve the final product.

In addition, other kinds of information are relevant during this stage. Determinations of potential impact and statements of preference and position by various interest groups and public officials are appropriate. But this is essentially political information which professional staff are less competent to provide. Much of it is a consequence of lobbying, and only long experience working for a committee will make staff members sensitive to the public and private interests involved. Finally, during the floor stage, when many legislators are appraised of a question for the first time, the need for essentially political information dominates, and staff services are least useful.

Reliance on Colleagues

The evidence from Virginia and Michigan supports these observations, especially with regard to the latter stages. When legislators in these states must reach decisions they do not rely primarily upon their staff—either institutional service agencies or personal assistants. As demonstrated in Table 3, outsiders such as lobbyists or bureaucrats and members of the governor's office are more attractive. But most important of all are the legislator's own colleagues within the House. When representatives in Michigan described their efforts to secure information in order to make decisions, over forty-five percent of their responses referred to this collegial interaction. Virginia delegates also mentioned this strategy more frequently than any other. "When I am not well informed about an issue," observed one Michigan representative, "I turn to other members whose judgment I respect, and who could explain it and the importance of it to me if we had time. I buy their conclusions, not their data."

This dependence on colleagues is no doubt due in part merely to their availability. They are readily at hand when information is needed, whereas informed outsiders may be unavailable. In addition, their candor and reliability has been tested before.[13] When a legislator needs information or advice on a question outside his or her own field of concentration, there is often a colleague who can provide it. This type of collegial exchange continues right up to the voting stage. When representatives have not previously decided how to vote but are called upon to do so, they often seek cues from associates. Over fifty-five percent of the Michigan representatives' descriptions

TABLE 3
SOURCES OF INFORMATION AND ADVICE (in percentages)

Question: What do you do when you must reach a decision and yet do not have enough time to become well informed in legislation outside of the area of your specialization?

Source	Proportion of Total Responses[a]	
	Virginia	Michigan
Turn to, go to, seek advice from other more knowledgeable legislators	38	46
Depend on discussion or debate in committees, on the floor, or in caucus	21	10
Turn to lobbyists	6	8
Turn to administrative agencies, governor's office	3	6
Turn to legislative staff, legislative aides	6	3
Turn to people who are informed (general)	6	3
Turn to constituents, vote the way constituents want me to	2	5
Move to postpone the vote, abstain, or vote "no"	2	7
Rely on my own feelings	5	2
Do extra reading, study on my own	2	1
Doesn't ever happen to me, I am always informed	2	2
Other	6	7
TOTAL	100	100
FREQUENCY	181[b]	212

a. Portions of the data first appeared in H. Owen Porter, "Legislative Experts and Outsiders," p. 709.

b. The number exceeds the number of respondents because many members mentioned more than one source.

of efforts to resolve such last-minute indecisions referred to this behavior. The strategy in Virginia is comparable, and references to this interaction in Congress have been frequent as well.[14]

The obvious importance of collegial information exchange also suggests the reason for it. Fellow legislators, after all, have a near monopoly on a particular kind of information—namely, the political—including judgments as to the practicality and feasibility of particular measures as well as the potential impact on local constituencies or the state at large. Such information is not likely to be readily available elsewhere.

Many of the representatives in Virginia and Michigan explained their cue-taking at the moment of voting with reference to the "similar constituency," "party membership," or "common ideology" of their colleague, and the same desire for such information leads them to depend on their colleagues prior to the voting stage as well. "Getting information is easier now than it was several years ago," commented one senior member. "We have staff people now. But they are not experienced politically. Legislators need to know the real meaning of a bill. Staff people may be brilliant but they don't see the whole picture. Other legislators are more practical and can judge the impact of it." This legislator no doubt spoke for many others who also need information which is politically relevant. As representatives, they need to know how a particular measure or amendment will affect their constituents or what the general consequences will be. Such activity was also described in California, Ohio, New Jersey, and Tennessee.[15]

Need for Political Information

The desire for political information is readily apparent when we look at the types of requests which are made of legislators by their colleagues. In Michigan, forty percent of the requests legislators receive are for evaluations of the likely consequences of impending bills. As revealed in Table 4, these are general requests or references to constituents and particular groups. As one representative described it, "Basically, my colleagues want to find out the ramifications of a bill and what are the political overtones—for instance, how it affects a township in their district." The most frequent request obviously calls for a description of the content of a bill or an interpretation of the meaning, but some portion of even these must be made with political consequences in mind. Virginia delegates testified to a similar emphasis. When

TABLE 4
TYPE OF INFORMATION SOUGHT IN MICHIGAN

Question: What kind of information or guidance do other legislators who are not specialists in your field seek from you?

Type of Information	Frequency	Percentage
Description of the content of proposed legislation, "What does it say?"	41	33
Effects on district or constituency or particular groups	26	21
Effects and consequences, costs (general)	23	19
Description of the present situation or problem to which the bill is aimed	6	5
Information needed to respond to specific requests by constituents	5	4
Information on supporters or opponents, "Who is for it, against it?"; "What are the pros and cons?"	5	4
Practice, policy in other states	3	2
Other	15	12
TOTAL	124	100

the eighty-seven members interviewed rated how frequently they were asked to interpret the impact of a bill on a colleagues constituency, more than fifty-five percent said that such requests came frequently or very often.[16]

Of course, in many cases the potential impact of a proposal is immediately apparent. Representatives can judge for themselves. This is especially true when the bill or amendment has been widely discussed. But, for a great number of decisions outside a representative's specialty, this is not the case. Since his own time and energy is limited, a legislator must find some economical way to decide if the item in question is likely to affect his constituents or particular groups and in what way. If a legislator feels concern for the interests of an organized group, he/she may secure the needed direction from lobbyists themselves. She/he merely needs a statement of preference. The more general appraisals of the merits of consequences of legislative may also be secured from interest groups if they are seen as legitimate spokespeople within a certain field.[17] But when questioned, the most active lobbyists in the fields of education, labor, health, and transportation in Michigan indicated that while legislators do request appraisals of their constituents' interests, such inquiries are relatively rare.[18] This is primarily because such outsiders have difficulty losing a stigma a special pleaders.[19]

When a legislator focuses his attention on the state at large, his problem is altered by the size of his reference group and by the more readily available guidance for questions which affect a broad public.[20] The party or the executive branch, having taken a position with regard to this broader constituency, may provide him with easy answers. The reliance upon lobbyists, bureaucrats and executive personnel, which was revealed in Table 3, no doubt derives in part from these latter needs for statements of preference and opinion. But neither the governor nor the party leadership often take stands. Moreover, the facts and reports which are readily available from agencies do not provide information in an easily interpreted form. "I occasionally go to departmental people," one Michigan legislator said, "but they sometimes give me voluminous material to digest. I don't have the time."

A legislator's difficulty is greatest when she/he believes that her/his unorganized constituents might be affected, but the impact upon them is unclear. The local businessman, the farmer, local government officials, and citizens are not likely to be represented by a well-staffed lobby in the Capitol. A legislator can sometimes "just know" because he is a resident of his district. But when the potential impact of an amendment or bill is not readily apparent, then his knowledge of constituency predispositions does not help very much and in such cases the constituents themselves are not much help. "On the vast majority of the bills," said one Michigan legislator, "neither my party nor my constituents have taken a stand or if they have, they have not communicated it to me." Another agreed, pointing out that "my constituents are not aware of over seventy-five percent of the bills which come before the legislature, so on many they can't advise me at all."

If a representative were assured that silence guaranteed subsequent indifference, then she could decide how to vote with impunity, acting on uninformed first impressions and in a sense "guessing." But too often constituents develop opinions after a vote has been taken and legislation has begun to take effect: then legislators' decisions may be appraised. Confronted with such silence among constituents, the representative must look for information and advice elsewhere.

Reliance on Staff

Are existing legislative services able to provide this political information? The answer from Michigan and Virginia is no. We have already seen in Table 3 that, when decisions have to be made, legislators do not often turn to personal staff, committee aides, or the members of a reference service. Even when representatives have more lead time to initiate study, they do not ask the institutional research personnel who are available. The six staff members of the Michigan Legislative Reference Service in 1970 said that most of the requests they receive from legislators are for copies of existing legislation or bills in progress, and these go mostly to constituents. Although the researchers encourage requests for "spot" or in-depth research, they agree that less than twenty percent of their assignments fall into these categories. One senior member of the staff could only remember four requests for in-depth research from members of either house in the previous three years. Spot research, which refers to specific limited questions, can easily be handled by the staff, but they are rarely asked. The Virginia Division of Statutory Research and Drafting gave similar accounts. Yet these services are placed within the respective capitol buildings within easy reach of the representatives. The problem is that they do not provide the politically relevant information which the legislators so often need. As another member of the Michigan reference service put it, "We can't give them what they often want to know—whether something is good or bad, right or wrong for them. What we can give are facts and figures—but that's not all that's needed."

The same situation exists in other states. "[There] is a suspicion of the trained mind among many legislators," Gladys Kammerer observed after appraising legislative services in Kentucky. "Such suspicion may induce the lawmaker to starve research or at least to ignore insofar as possible the findings of the research staff."[21] Similar observations have been applied to as varied states as California and Connecticut.[22] The legislative environment requires that, to be useful, information must be cognizant of political realities. The problem is not simply an inadequate supply of information but the relevance and usefulness of that which is available.[23] When legislators themselves conduct research as members of interim committees or separate commissions, they can attract the attention of their colleagues because they relate findings of fact to constituency interests.[24] Most legislative staff cannot or will not do this.

These staff limitations are much less serious during earlier stages of the policy-making process, when the content of legislation is determined by sponsors themselves or by committee specialists. Here research capabilities are important and personal aides and committee staff more helpful. Indeed, a committee which is served by experienced consultants can occasionally become a mere "holding company" for its staff.[25] Thus, when members of the Virginia House were asked to evaluate the general usefulness of various potential sources of information, they rated their personal aides highly. In Table 5, their ratings of sources of information are presented. Personal aides are obviously appreciated, as are administrative personnel and lobbyists. But the most impressive ratings go to fellow legislators. The preferred mechanism for information exchange is still collegial.

The Institutional Reference Service is also given recognition. No doubt this approval refers to the bill-writing and early technical character of the divi-

TABLE 5
SOURCES OF INFORMATION:
EVALUATIONS BY MEMBERS OF THE VIRGINIA HOUSE, 1974
(in percentages)

Question: How useful is each of these sources when you need information? (It would be useful if you could note each on a scale running from 0 for not at all useful to 8 for very useful)

Source	Proportion of Responses		
	Not Very Useful (0-2)	Moderately Useful (3-5)	Very Useful (6-8)
Colleagues who are particularly knowledgeable in some field	0	23	77
Personnel in administrative agencies	6	32	62
Personal legislative staff	19	21	60
Individual constituents	7	39	54
Interest group spokesmen in home district	12	41	47
Division of legislative services	16	45	39
Committee staff	30	32	38
Party leaders	31	34	35
Interest group spokesmen in Richmond	24	50	26
Governor's staff	34	43	23

sion's work. Standing committees in Virginia are served by consultants on an ad hoc basis, and this deficiency was often criticized by legislators in additional comments. Still, in Table 5 we see that some legislators rated these aides highly as well. An increase in the number and tenure of these staff members would be appreciated.

Personal assistance for state legislators has been one of the most popular recent reforms, and Virginia's experience is quite new. Certainly the evaluations presented here argue for such assistance. But again one must be careful to note that the information-gathering abilities of personal aides are generally maximized through research. In Table 6, we see that, when the Virginia delegates were asked to describe in detail the most important services their assistants performed, they most often mentioned background research preparatory to bill-drafting.

TABLE 6
EVALUATION OF SERVICES PERFORMED BY PERSONAL STAFF: VIRGINIA HOUSE OF DELEGATES, 1974[a]
(in percentages)

Type of Service Performed	Percentage of Delegates Who Rated Service Among Most Important or Valuable (n = 82)[b]
Research related to specific measures	42
General research and information gathering	32
Helping with correspondence and newsletter	32
Serving constituents; communicating with public	30
Handling office, schedules, and appointments	17
Attending meetings; monitoring committees	10
Running errands	6
Keeping up with calendar or specific measures	5
Contacting state agencies	3

a. This information first appeared in "Personal Legislative Staff: The Virginia Experience," *Newsletter,* Vol. 50, No. 11 (July 1974), Charlottesville, Va.: Institute of Government, p. 44.

b. Five of the 87 respondents did not have assistants during the 1974 session. Percentages exceed 100 because many respondents mentioned more than one service.

The contribution of personal aides to the delegates' knowledge of questions outside of their own individual fields is much less, and contributions to their supply of essentially political information must be minimal. It is possible that this limitation of personal aides in Virginia reflects the inexperience and youth of most personnel. Salaries are not adequate there to retain employees from year to year, and many of these positions are filled by college and law students. It is reasonable to assume that the advice and appraisals of constituent interests which legislators need cannot safely be acquired from such assistants.

PROSPECTS FOR IMPROVEMENT

The difficulties of acquiring information cannot be remedied by the installation or improvement of legislative service agencies alone, and it is quite possible that for the individual legislator "the problem" is beyond complete solution. Legislative services can bring improvements, however, if service agencies are integrated into the existing components of legislative systems and if innovations are guided by recognition of significant variations in such systems among the states. In particular, the need for political information, especially for individual interpretations of constituency interests, cannot be met without careful evaluation of the ongoing processes of communication. Those services which are responsible to the whole legislature and which are characterized by objectivity will thus be of little *direct* value to individuals.[26] The staff to legislative councils, aides to standing committees, reference services, and legislative budgetary personnel provide substantial assistance to the whole assembly but relatively little in the way of direct personal aid.[27] However, they can indirectly alleviate some of the problems individual representatives experience by supporting the development of legislative experts who, as we have seen, provide the information, interpretations, and opinions which the larger body of nonspecialists prefers.

It has been demonstrated elsewhere that legislative experts occupy key positions in a two-step flow of communication between interested groups and individuals on the outside and the rest of their colleagues on the inside.[28] The addition of competent staff to standing committees probably transforms this into a multistage communication process wherein the consultants themselves become intervening or additional access points, filtering data and proposals before they receive serious consideration by committee members and adding their information to the existing supply. In this way, experienced committee staff can facilitate the development of expertise among the legislators themselves.

When staff support goes to members of legislative council subcommittees who also serve on regular standing committees, this training process should function most efficiently. Legislators who in the interim supervise a study of existing mental health programs and who subsequently serve on the relevant standing committee can best provide guidance for their colleagues in this area.[29] The principal focal point for indirect improvements in individuals' access to information obviously becomes the standing committee. In addition to requiring a carryover between interim council and committee personnel, additional support for the standing committees themselves can also help.

Standing Committees

Increased staffing will be of little avail, however, if the legislative membership of committees is unstable. At present, standing committees in most states are unstable in part because of the relatively high turnover of legislators.[30] A recent study of turnover in a sample of states revealed that the average proportion of members reappointed to committees from 1958 to 1972 nowhere exceeded fifty percent.[31] If such turnover results from electoral defeats, we might accept it as a necessary price of a vigorous competitive process, but most withdrawals are voluntary and reflect the relatively low prestige and inadequate salaries of officeholders.[32] Increases in committee staff without a reduction in legislative turnover could merely encourage a displacement of influence from elected representatives to hired professionals. In such a case, the non-committee-member's need for information which is satisfied best by informed colleagues will not be filled.

Other factors influence stability in addition to general turnover. Those committees which deal with the most recurrent and pressing questions—such as appropriations and finance—retain their membership longest and generally meet the needs of other legislators.[33] In Michigan, legislators felt deprived with regard to questions in other areas, where the turnover in membership of some committees was higher. "It is more difficult to get information in some areas," one representative acknowledged. "For instance, we are sadly lacking in anyone who is tops in public health. The area of transportation is also one of our weaker areas."

This disparity in the adequacy of information among policy fields could be alleviated in part by party leaders who actively encourage development and maintenance of expertise in these areas primarily by sustaining committee membership. The leadership will not find this an easy task, especially in areas such as health, which attract few individuals with prior educational or occupational experience. But they can make improvements. Having identified legislators who appear motivated to work hard at their tasks and who aspire to a legislative career, party leaders can encourage them to specialize in areas which are relatively impoverished. Committee work alone can produce the type of politically aware experts upon whom the rest of the legislators depend. Only then will supporting staff realize their full potential in producing better-informed legislators.

Caucus Staff

Staff provided to the party caucus can also assist individual legislators, although, as is the case with other services responsible to a large group, their utility for individuals is limited. Ogle includes caucus staff among his recommendations for assisting members of the Connecticut Assembly. He argues that such a service could "interpret the partisan and political ramifications of technical information and report to leaders, individual members and the party caucuses."[34] Obviously these assistants would serve some of the function

of interpreters and intermediaries for individual legislators at least on questions where the party has an interest. In such cases, ordinary members can
rely on the staff for assessments of the effects of various policy options on
their party.[35] In Wisconsin, such staff have helped the minority party in
particular and the entire legislature in general to offer alternatives to proposals emanating from the governor's office.[36] Apparently such caucus
assistance in turn encourages development of stronger legislative parties.[37]

Yet there are several limitations to the benefits to be derived from caucus
staff. In the first place, the staff can probably serve the interests of individual
legislators only in highly competitive states where the parties represent
opposing policy interests. Connecticut and Wisconsin, from which the pre-
ceding testimony derives, have such competitive two-party systems. In these
states, the caucus staff can assist relatively cohesive, issue-conscious parties in
an environment which encourages the use of partisan views and voting
cues.[38] Especially where the parties represent different constituencies and
a relatively high degree of similarity exists among the member's districts, the
parties can achieve maximum utility as a source of direction for individual
members.[39] Districts have been "sorted out" between the parties.[40] But
competitiveness does not describe more than one-half of the states, and the
number of those in which the parties do represent distinctive constituencies is
considerably smaller. In the remaining states, where one party clearly dominates, caucus staffs are not going to be of much use to the individual
legislator. Wide disparities in outlook and constituent needs will prevent them
from providing useful partisan counseling.

In the second place, party interest, and thus party position, occurs on only
a minority of questions even in states with two cohesive organizations. In
Michigan, for instance, where the competitive parties do speak for different
constituencies, legislators as well as staff emphasized that there was little
party interest (and thus direction) on most issues. Wayne Francis has described the low level of party conflict in most other states as well.[41] A
substantial increase in the assistance available to the party might increase
partisan awareness and thus conflict. However, the independent effects of
such reform would probably not be very great, and the party in essential
noncompetitive states will thus remain an inadequate vehicle for the generation of information and advice on a host of questions which legislators will
confront. This would certainly be the case in Virginia.

Personal Staff

Staff assigned to an individual legislator will necessarily be the most
responsive to his or her personal needs and the most aware of his or her
political environment. Such administrative and even secretarial assistance can

also divert much work from the legislator and release him for more important tasks—including the efforts to keep well-informed. Assistants who have been with a legislator for a long time can also gather information for him and to a certain extent interpret it for him in light of his past positions. Attending committee meetings, listening to floor debate, contacting agencies and interest groups, and performing spot research are ways of securing such information. Most congressional assistants who serve longer than their counterparts in the states would recognize some of these tasks.[42] Yet the degree of direct staff influence over the Congressperson's voting seems to be small. Some Congressmembers do have their staffs prepare summaries of legislation, major anticipated amendments, and the major issues which their legislator should consider. Yet these legislators appear to be a small minority of the total House. In most cases, if the staff, through its information-gathering activities, is involved in the legislator's decision, it is only peripherally.[43] Individual aides in the states will not likely help the legislators very much in gathering the political information they most need.

CONCLUSION

In the anecdote which introduced this chapter, I suggested that the citizens who could not understand the ramifications of a technical change in a pollution control bill were facing a difficulty which most legislators confront many times. That comparison was too simple. In fact, the citizens had laid before them a "puzzle" which could be solved by merely determining whether or not the changes in permissible heat levels would result in a higher and perhaps undesirable level of emissions.[44] Science could provide a definitive answer to their first question, leaving them to decide what they would consider desirable. After they had informed themselves and taken a position, they could attempt to persuade legislators to support them.

But the representatives who have to make the final choices face a different situation. They too need a solution to the technical puzzle. But, having received an answer, they still must surmount the difficulty of finding out what would be best for their constituents and themselves. Their difficulty does not lend itself to one solution, but can only be reduced, surmounted, or ignored. Additional information, including answers to questions of fact, will help them to satisfy themselves regarding the best choice, but factual information alone is insufficient because the "correct" decision is a political one.

The information-processing systems found in state legislatures channel the flow of both technical and essentially political information. While the significance attached to differences between parties and across policy fields varies, all the systems attempt to fulfill a representative function, as well as a problem-solving one. The representative aspect especially provides the basis for the preferred collegial information exchange which we have observed. It is no doubt possible to develop criteria for judging the quality of legislative decisions which allow no place for this representative function. One might then determine that "right" decisions were best made by experts without reference to constituent desires or opinions. Such standards alone would have no place in a scheme of representative government, however, and fortunately none is recommended by current reformers. Yet many of the reforms in staffing which are recommended do not pay very close attention to this representative aspect of legislative decision-making and to the particular kinds of information which this function often requires. Future discussions and recommendations should attend to these needs but consider as well the constraints upon staffing which they imply.

NOTES

1. For a complete discussion of the concept of rational decision-making used, here see Donald Matthews and James A. Stimson, "Decision-Making by U.S. Representatives: A Preliminary View," in *Political Decision-Making,* edited by Sidney Ulmer (New York: Van Nostrand Reinhold, 1970), pp. 16-17.

2. Ed Crane, "Legislative Service Agencies," *Book of the States* XIX (Lexington, Ky.: Council of State Governments, 1972), p. 78. There is some debate over whether or not Wisconsin or New York established the real forerunner of legislative reference services in the United States. See E. A. Fisher, "Legislative Reference in the United States," *American Political Science Review,* Vol. 3 (May 1909), pp. 223-226.

3. For a complete description of the content of this act, see George B. Galloway, "The operation of the Legislative Reorganization Act of 1946," *American Political Science Review,* Vol. 45 (March 1951), pp. 41-68. For a discussion of the legislation's impact on the Legislative Reference Service, see W. Brooke Graves, "Legislative Reference Service for the Congress of the United States," *American Political Science Review,* Vol. 41 (April 1961), pp. 289-293. For the results of this survey, see Roger Davidson, David Kovenock, and Michael O'Leary, *Congress in Crisis: Politics and Congressional Reform* (Belmont, Calif.: Wadsworth, 1966), pp. 76-78.

4. Kenneth Janda, "Information Systems for Congress," in *Congress: The First Branch of Government* (Washington, D.C.: American Enterprise Institute for Public Policy Research, 1966).

5. John Burns, *The Sometime Governments* (New York: Bantam Books, 1971), pp. 104-109.

6. The Virginia General Assembly inaugurated annual meetings under the 1971 Constitution with alternating sixty- and thirty-day sessions. Personal assistants were provided beginning in 1972, and in 1973 the Legislative Audit and Review Commission was established with professional staff.

7. In 1970-1971, thirty-three state legislatures provided for annual sessions. In twenty-nine states, sessions were limited in time by constitutional restrictions. *Book of the States 1972-1973,* XIX (Lexington, Ky.: Council of State Governments, 1972), p. 52.

8. John C. Wahlke, Heinz Eulau, William Buchanan, and LeRoy C. Ferguson, *The Legislative System: Explorations in Legislative Behavior* (New York: John Wiley, 1962); see especially chapters 12 and 13. Studies of the motivations and resulting behavior of legislators have not gone far enough to fully account for representative-constituent relations, however. Relatively little has been done at the state level. One exception is James A. Barber, *The Lawmakers: Recruitment and Adaptation to Legislative Life* (New Haven: Yale University Press, 1965).

9. See R. J. Huckshorn, "Decision-Making Stimuli in the State Legislative Process," *Western Political Quarterly,* Vol. 18 (March 1965), p. 173; John A. Perkins, "State Legislative Reorganization," *American Political Science Review,* Vol. 40 (June 1946), pp. 516-518; "American State Legislatures in Mid-Twentieth Century," *State Government,* Vol. 34 (Autumn 1961), pp. 245-250; Donald G. Herzberg and Jesse Unruh, *Essays on the State Legislative Process* (New York: Holt, Rinehart & Winston, 1970), p. 29; Ruth A. Ross and Barbara S. Stone, *California's Political Process* (New York: Random House, 1973), p. 81; Jesse M. Unruh, "Science in Law-Making," *National Civic Review,* Vol. 54 (October 1965), pp. 466-472; David B. Truman, ed., *The Congress and America's Future* (Englewood Cliffs, N.J.: Prentice-Hall, 1965), p. 1; William J. Keefe and Morris S. Ogul, *The American Legislative Process: Congress and the States* (Englewood Cliffs, N.J.: Prentice-Hall, 1965), p. 483; and K. C. Wheare, *Legislatures* (New York: Oxford University Press, 1963), p. 221.

10. Norman Meller, "Legislative Staff Services: Toxin, Specific, or Placebo for the Legislative Ills," *Western Political Quarterly,* XX (June 1967), pp. 383-384.

11. Ibid.

12. Richard F. Fenno, Jr., "The Internal Distribution of Influence: The House," in *The Congress and America's Future,* edited by David B. Truman (Englewood Cliffs, N.J.: Prentice-Hall, 1965), pp. 59-60.

13. William Buchanan et al., "The Legislator as Specialist," *Western Political Quarterly,* XIII (September 1960), p. 647. R. J. Huckshorn, "Decision-Making Stimuli," pp. 174-175.

14. Relatively little attention has been directed toward information exchange in state legislatures. Exceptions include Huckshorn, "Decision-Making Stimuli," and H. Owen Porter, "Legislative Experts and Outsiders: The Two-Step Flow of Communication," *Journal of Politics,* Vol. 36 (August 1974), pp. 703-730. The literature on Congress has paid more attention to this phenomenon although the treatment of the subject even there is not very systematic. See especially Matthews and Stimson, "Decision-Making by U.S. Representatives"; David Kovenock, "Influence in the House of Representatives: Some Preliminary Statistical 'Snapshots,' " (presented to the Sixty-Third Annual Meeting of the American Political Science Association, Chicago, September 1967); Donald R. Matthews, *U.S. Senators and Their World* (New York: Random House, 1960), pp. 251-253; Charles L. Clapp, *The Congressman: His Work as He Sees It* (Washington, D.C.: Brookings Institution, 1963), pp. 123-126.

15. John C. Wahlke, Heinz Eulau, William Buchanan, and LeRoy C. Ferguson, *The Legislative System* (New York: John Wiley, 1962), pp. 208-209.

16. The eighty-seven members of the Virginia House of Delegates were asked the following question: "There are probably many different kinds of information that other legislators might seek regarding matters outside of their fields of concentration. Here is a list of some of the kinds of information legislators tell us that they give to their colleagues. Would you look over this list and using a scale of 0 to 8 indicate how often, if at all, you provide such information." Approximately fifty-five percent of the respondents rated the frequency of "constituent requests" with a five or higher. Twelve delegates scored this type of information with an eight.

17. John A. Straayer, *American State and Local Government* (Columbus, Ohio: Charles E. Merrill, 1973), pp. 195-196.

18. In 1970, as part of the study cited in note 24, interviews were conducted with the twenty most active lobbyists and administrators in the four fields. There was good reason to believe that these were among the most influential to interact with the legislature. For a more complete description, see Porter, "Legislative Experts and Outsiders."

19. R. J. Huckshorn, "Decision-Making Stimuli," pp. 173-174; J. A. Perkins, "State Legislative Reorganization," pp. 516-518.

20. The reference group, if there is any, and the perspective which the legislator takes vary. Eulau and his colleagues found that some representatives attend especially to their own districts' interests while others focus upon the state. All probably vary their perspective from group, to district, to state, to relative indifference—depending upon how the issue is presented to them. See Heinz Eulau, John C. Wahlke, William Buchanan, and LeRoy C. Ferguson, "The Role of the Representative: Some Empirical Observations on the Theory of Edmund Burke," *American Political Science Review,* Vol. 53 (September 1959), pp. 742-746.

21. Gladys M. Kammerer, "The Development of a Legislative Research Arm," *Journal of Politics,* Vol. 12 (November 1950), p. 652.

22. Norman Meller, "The Policy Position of Legislative Service Agencies," *Western Political Quarterly,* Vol. 5 (March 1952), p. 113. David B. Ogle, *Strengthening the Connecticut Legislature* (New Brunswick, N.J.: Rutgers University Press, 1970), pp. 174-175. Herzberg and Unruh, *Essays on the State Legislative Process,* p. 38.

23. Alan Rosenthal, *Strengthening the Maryland Legislature* (New Brunswick, N.J.: Rutgers University Press, 1968), p. 87; Lewis Anthony Dexter, " 'Check and Balance' Today: What Does It Mean for Congress and Congressmen?" in *Congress: The First Branch of Government,* Alfred de Grazia, ed., (Washington, D.C.: American Enterprise Institute for Public Policy Research, 1966) p. 93; Fred Schwengel, "Problems of Inadequate Information and Staff Resources in Congress," in *Congress: The First Branch of Government,* p. 97.

24. Frederick H. Guild, "Legislative Councils: Objectives and Accomplishments," *State Government,* Vol. 22 (September 1949), pp. 218-226.

25. Fenno, "The Internal Distribution of Influence: The House," p. 55.

26. Meller, "Legislative Staff Services: Toxin, Specific, or Placebo."

27. Harold Davey, "The Legislative Council Movement 1933-1953," *American Political Science Review,* Vol. 47 (September 1953), p. 792.

28. Porter, "Legislative Experts and Outsiders: The Two-Step Flow of Communication."

29. Alan Rosenthal, "Between Sessions—The Effectiveness of Legislative Study and Interim Work," *State Government,* Vol. 44 (Spring 1971), p. 97.

30. Paul Beckett and Celeste Sunderland, "Washington's State Law-Makers," *Western Political Quarterly,* Vol. 10 (March 1957), pp. 180-202. Preliminary analysis of data on committee turnover in twenty states by the author supports this generalization. See also Keefe and Ogul, *The American Legislative Process,* pp. 196-197.

31. H. Owen Porter and David A. Leuthold, "Acquiring Legislative Expertise: Appointments to Standing Committees in the States," (presented at the annual meeting of the American Political Science Association, Chicago, Illinois, August 29-September 2, 1974), p. 11.

32. Keefe and Ogul, *The American Legislative Process,* pp. 135-136.

33. Porter and Leuthold, "Acquiring Legislative Expertise," p. 26.

34. Ogle, *Strengthening the Connecticut Legislature,* p. 178.

35. M. Rosenthal, "An Analysis of Institutional Effects: Staffing Legislative Parties in Wisconsin," *Journal of Politics,* Vol. 32 (August 1970), p. 548.

36. Ibid., pp. 556-559.

37. Ibid., p. 540.

38. Austin Ranney, "Parties in State Politics," in *Politics in the American States,* edited by Herbert Jacob and Kenneth N. Vines (Boston: Little, Brown, 1971), pp. 86-87; John Fenton, *Mid-West Politics* (New York: Holt, Rinehart & Winston, 1966), pp. 44-74.

39. Hugh L. LeBlanc, "Voting in State Senates: Party and Constituency Influences," *Midwest Journal of Political Science,* Vol. 13 (February 1969), pp. 35-37.

40. Ibid.

41. Wayne L. Francis, *Legislative Issues in the Fifty States.* (Chicago: Rand McNally, 1967), pp. 44-45.

42. Kenneth Kofmehl, *Professional Staffs of Congress* (West Lafayette, Ind.: Purdue University, 1962), pp. 167-180. Clem Miller, *Member of the House,* edited by John W. Baker (New York: Charles Scribner's, 1962), p. 27.

43. John W. Kingdon, *Congressmen's Voting Decisions* (New York: Harper & Row, 1973), pp. 192-197.

44. The distinction made here between political difficulties, problems, and puzzles is borrowed from T. D. Weldon, *The Vocabulary of Politics* (Baltimore: Penguin, 1953), pp. 75-83.

CHARACTERISTICS OF CONGRESSIONAL STAFFERS

SUSAN WEBB HAMMOND

Events of the early 1970s have focused the attention of both political scientists and the general public on the U.S. Congress, and, more broadly, on the role and functions of legislative bodies in the political system. To the general public, it may not appear that Congress has changed in recent years—committees remain important, incumbents are generally reelected, and constituents are unable to identify their congresspeople in polls. But a number of changes in the congressional process, now apparent on close study, may be expected to have significant consequences for the policy process, and, indeed, for the role of Congress in our political system. Among these changes are the increase in, and the changing roles of, congressional staff, particularly the professionals serving on personal staffs.

It has long been accepted that committee staff play a significant role in the development of legislation and in the exercise of legislative oversight. It is clear from the data analyzed in a larger study,[1] from which this chapter is derived, that professionals on personal staffs of House members similarly make a significant and extensive impact on both these areas.

Personal staff operate as independent professionals in an increasingly complex environment. They brief congresspeople on pending legislation. They coordinate and advise on co-sponsorship. They research issues, gather background data on specific legislative matters, and draft legislation. Staff draft testimony, statements, and reports. They offer their opinions and act as a "sounding board" for the congressman or congresswoman. They may, on occasion, argue vigorously for a certain policy position. Personal aides have substantial responsibilities for the congressperson's committee work; the intensity of involvement varies with the committee assignment, with the issue, and with seniority and control of committee staff. Staff responsibility for coordinating legislative strategy is increasing. And, in what appears to be a growing number of offices, professional staff participate in the identification and development of issues to be introduced into the legislative process.

Focus

The focus of this chapter is on personal staffs in the U.S. House of Representatives, and is based on data, including a number of semi-focused interviews, from the Ninety-Second Congress (1971-1972).[2]

State legislatures, or, indeed, the parliaments of other countries, do not have legislative staffs similar to those of the U.S. Congress. Indeed, the U.S. Congress may be unique and more organizationally developed (in degree of organizational specialization, for example) than other legislative bodies in staffing arrangements. Examination of staff recruitment and the background of staff in the House of Representatives assists analysis of staff roles and functions and should also serve to shed light on aspects of staffing in other legislative bodies. It appears that the recent changes in the size and professionalism of staffs in the U.S. House have contributed to an increased congressional capability for analysis and informed decision-making. Ultimately, the significant question is what effect staffing changes have on the legislative and policy processes.

History of Staff Growth[3]

In the House, "clerk-hire" paid by public funds was first authorized in 1893, eight years after the Senators had voted monies for Senate personal staff aides. As in the Senate, authorization was initially for clerks to congresspeople who were not committee heads and applied only during the congressional session. In 1896, clerks were authorized year-round; by 1902, all representatives, including committee heads, received a clerk-hire allowance. In 1919, the names of personal staff members were put on the official payroll of the House, with salaries paid to the staff aide by the Clerk of the House through the Disbursing Office, rather than by the representative. Clerk-hire salary allotments and numbers authorized gradually increased.[4] Between 1956 and 1972, staff number was tied to district size, and members with districts of more than 500,000 were entitled to an additional staff member. In 1971, the House delegated to its Committee on House Administration the authority for making changes in staffing allowances; the committee notifies the House of changes, but a formal House vote is not required.

The number of staff authorized for each representative has increased very rapidly in recent years (see Figure 1), and as Table 1 indicates, the total number of individuals employed on office staffs of congresspeople has expanded accordingly. As of 1974, congressmen or congresswomen may appoint sixteen staff aides to work at the Capitol or in a district office. Salaries may be set by the congresspeople; a yearly allotment of $173,052 is authorized, one-twelfth of which must be used each month. One aide may be paid a maximum salary of $33,710.[5] An additional amount up to $20,952 is available if the representative wishes to hire a research assistant as one of the employees. Professional staff specialize more now than they did fifteen years ago. The majority of House members now have legislative assistants, and a small number of offices have several legislative aides. The number of press secretaries is increasing, and at lower staff levels there are increasing numbers of researchers, legislative secretaries, or federal program assistants. Decision-making regarding staffing has become more automatic.[6] In short, the institutionalization of the House is reflected in the institutionalization of House staff.[7]

Senate personal staffs also have increased rapidly in recent years, quadrupling since 1946. As in the House, there is a specific allotment for staff salaries (based in this case on a state's population), as well as a maximum salary for a top aide. But there is no limit on the number of staff aides who can be employed. In some ways, Senate staffs differ from House staffs. For example, because Senate staffs are generally larger (ranging from ten to more than fifty), they are frequently more highly organized with the work more routinized. Personal aides in the Senate also tend to be more specialized than in the House. In addition, in the Senate there is often far less delineation between personal and committee staff than is found in the House. This is

TABLE 1
MEMBERS' CLERK-HIRE,
HOUSE OF REPRESENTATIVES, SELECTED YEARS[a]

Year	Number Employed
1947	1440
1957	2441
1962	3071
1967	4055
1968	4156
1969	4301
1970	4545
1971	4934
1972	5280
1973	5516

a. SOURCE: Hearings, Subcommittee on Legislative Appropriations, U.S. House of Representatives, FY 1949-FY 1974. *N.B.* figures quoted are based on clerk-hire payroll for a selected month during the year. Months vary.

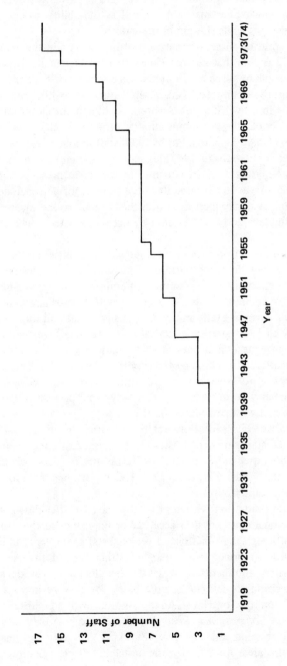

a. 1956-1972: Members with districts of more than 500,000 were entitled to one additional clerk.

SOURCE: *Congressional Record; Statutes at Large;* Disbursing Office, House of Representatives.

FIGURE 1: Increase in Number of Staff Authorized per Representative since 1919[a]

presumably a result of the multiple committee, and particularly subcommittee, assignments which Senators hold, as well as the ability to control some committee staff slots while still junior in seniority.

Nevertheless, in spite of these differences, staffing changes in the Senate have occurred much as they have in the House—that is, incrementally with similar changes often taking place at about the same time. In 1885, Senators who were not chairing committees were given authority to hire personal clerks during the session; by 1893, the Senators could appoint clerks on an annual basis. For a period, the maximum number of personal clerks was set by law and applicable to all Senators, but in 1939, staff numbers were set on the basis of a state's population. In 1947, legislative limits on staff numbers were removed, and Senators were free to hire as few or as many personal aides as they wished. As in the House, the total number of personal aides employed by Senators gradually increased, with the largest increase, measured both by actual numbers and by percentage, occurring since 1947 (see Figure 2).

Although this study is not primarily concerned with committee staffs, it is useful to note that much the same pattern of incremental increases and a gradual shift from temporary (per session) to permanent and professional expertise is evident for committees also. Committee staff changes have tended to precede those for personal staff, and hence set significant and important precedents. As early as 1840, part-time clerical committee staff were authorized, and in 1856, revenue committees in each House could hire full-time clerical aides. Thereafter, the number of committees hiring staff increased rapidly. The move toward larger staffs and senior aides with recognized professional expertise has occurred at a particularly rapid pace since World War II—as is also the case with personal staffs.[8]

The 1946 Legislative Reorganization Act had a significant impact on all types of congressional staff support. By specifically authorizing professional staff for standing committees, the principle of staff professionalism, whether as committee or personal aide, was recognized. This in turn created a milieu where professionalism could flourish.

What is the present situation with regard to personal staff aides in the Congress? First, personal aides are now accepted as important to the operations of Congress; although the functions of personal staffs may vary, no one seriously quarrels with the principle of personal staffing. Second, the issue of staff numbers and salary allotments is far less devisive than in previous years. The 1971 House decision to delegate responsibility for changes in staffing allowances to the Committee on House Administration, with announcement of the changes in the *Congressional Record,* and a House vote only after a legislative effort to rescind the changes, results in relatively automatic decision-making in this area. And, finally, the principles of specialization and

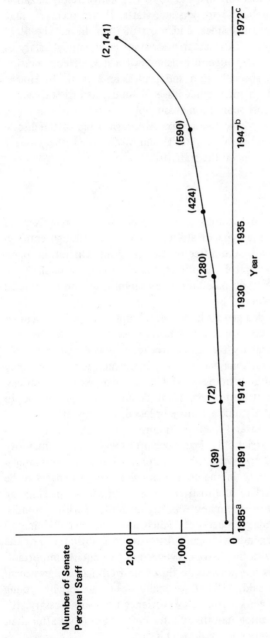

Number of Senate Personal Staff

a. No specific number was authorized.

b. Numbers of staff between 1885 and 1947 are based on authroized positions. Number of staff between 1948 and 1972 are based on proportionate increases in clerk-hire funds.

c. Based on *Report of the Secretary of the Senate.*

SOURCE: Fox and Hammond, "Congressional Staffs." The data is from the section on the Senate, compiled by Dr. Fox.

FIGURE 2: Increase in Senate Personal Staff

professionalism are at least implicitly recognized. The 1946 Legislative Reorganization Act laid the basis for this; the 1970 Legislative Reorganization
Act is more specifically applicable to personal staffs. House members may
now establish titles for personal aides, and most of them have. The 1973
authorization for appointment of a research assistant at an annual salary of
up to $20,000+ is a further step toward assistants with specialized expertise.
In spite of the increase in specialization and professionalism in the House,
professionals make up only a small percentage of total personal staff aides.
Some offices (usually of most senior congresspeople) operate with only one
staff professional; others may have five or six. Although some of the discussion which follows covers all staff, secretarial and professional, the primary
concern is with the professionals on the staff.[9]

Staff Recruitment

Congressional recruiting procedures and representatives' perceptions of
their staffing needs affect the type of staffer hired. And although employment offices run by the Joint Committee on Congressional Operations operate on both sides of the Capitol, recruitment and hiring, particularly of
professional staff, continue to be based primarily on informal, nonroutinized
contacts and "who knows whom."

New congresspeople are deluged by hundreds of applications. For them, as
for incumbent representatives, applicants who come recommended by contacts offer at least a preliminary screening procedure which can save time.
Other representatives send on someone who is job hunting; constituents may
leave resumés; wide acquaintance in the district—all serve as personnel sources.
A congressman said, "Recruitment is haphazard. People really choose you. In
a way, the congressman and his staff are more or less driven together."

House members weigh several factors in hiring staff. A major one is
whether to hire from the district only. Many begin this way, and the majority
of first-term representatives do have staffs—both professional and secretarial—
with district ties. At this stage in the congressional career, it appears to be
both easier and more natural to hire district people; contacts in the state are
widespread, and there may not be many Washington contacts. Hiring nondis-
trict people requires screening procedures, which involve either Washington
trips or close Washington friends who can substitute. In addition, during the
first term, cultivating ties with the district is viewed as particularly important,
and hiring district people is one way to do this. One freshman congressman,
in discussing this balance, said, "[What we really need] are bright, young
people who are willing to work hard. Hill experience isn't so necessary. It's
important the first two to three months of a freshman's term, but after that,
staff without experience can really get along O.K."

Hiring district people has dysfunctional consequences, however, which may make professionalization more difficult. One congressman noted, "The problem of firing is complicated by taking people from the district." And a staff member to a senior congressman commented on the "split" life of staff members from the district—a problem of great concern to congressional families, also[10] : "At first we tried to have everyone from the district. It didn't work for secretaries, though. They'd cut their hours to go out [to the district] to see their boyfriends, or they'd even live here and go back to see their husbands every weekend. Now we just look for competent people."

Nevertheless, most offices prefer staff with district ties, and most of the top-level professional staff do come from the district. Administrative assistants (AAs), who often handle political chores in the district in addition to Washington duties, generally have district ties. More senior congresspeople are somewhat less likely to have AAs from the district, but many still do anyway. Legislative assistants (LAs) are less likely to be from the district; press secretaries—or the professional staffer handling press—more often are; TV and radio tapes, and contacts with local press are an important aspect of the communications function of the Washington office. Also, a press aide who is not from the district may be, initially at least, at a disadvantage in dealing with journalists representing local media.

Of the offices surveyed, a minority insist that all employees, including secretarial personnel, be from the district; a very large majority (eighty percent) prefer that most personnel have district ties; a small minority (twenty percent) do not look for staff with district ties at all. This latter group uses the Joint Committee on Congressional Operations' Office of Placement most extensively.[11] In offices where there is an effort to have staff from the district, sixty-two percent of the professional staff *are* from the district. Many offices look for people from the state if no one with district ties is available. Tables 2-6 delineate the relationship between staffing and localism more precisely.[12]

TABLE 2
LOCALISM OF STAFF AIDES, BY JOB

	From District	N
AA	73%	22
LA	59%	17[a]
Other professionals	43%	14[a]
Aide handling press duties	81%	21
	60%	Total percentage professional staff from district

a. Number of aides on which pertinent data are available.

TABLE 3
LOCALISM OF STAFF AIDES, BY SENIORITY OF CONGRESSMEN

Seniority Quartile	% of all professionals with state ties	% AAs with district ties
Most senior	71 (n = 7)	60 (n = 5)
Next most senior	66 (n = 15)	83 (n = 6)
Third most senior	59 (n = 20)[a]	71 (n = 7)
Most junior	71 (n = 31)	75 (n = 4)

a. May be skewed by one office with atypically large number of professionals, none from district.

TABLE 4
LOCALISM OF AIDES, BY PARTY

Republican offices		Democratic offices	
14/22	64%	17/28	61%

TABLE 5
LOCALISM OF AIDES, BY POLICY ATTITUDE OF BOSS

Conservative Coalition Support Scores, 1971[a]	n	Percentage Aides Local
0-19 (n = 9)	27	52
20-19 (n = 8)	14	71
80-100 (n = 8)	17	76

a. As reported in *Congressional Quarterly,* weekly editions, and *Congressional Quarterly Almanac* (Washington, D.C.)

TABLE 6
LOCALISM OF AIDES, BY REGION OF DISTRICT

	Percentage Aides "Locals"	Percentage AAs "Locals"
East (n = 3)[a]	80	33
South (n = 6)	80	100
Midwest (n = 10)	69	80
West (n = 6)	50	66

a. N refers to number of offices. Professionals in the offices are: eastern offices—5; midwestern offices—29; southern offices—10; western offices—10.

As is the case in many matters pertaining to staffing, the party variable is not a significant determinant of whether or not the aides are locals. Seniority also appears to make little difference; the pattern is mixed, with the most senior and most freshman congresspeople employing the same proportion of local aides. When only AAs are considered, senior representatives appear to consider an AA with local ties less important than their more junior colleagues.

Policy attitudes, as measured by *Congressional Quarterly*'s conservative coalition scores, appear to affect staff localism. House members with the lowest conservative coalition support hired the fewest local aides, and the strongest supporters of the conservative coalition hired the most local aides. However, other variables may converge with policy attitude to cause this result. For example, Southern congresspeople, many of whom are strong conservative coalition supporters, also hire the most local aides.

An unexpected finding appears from the data in Table 6: Western congresspeople hire fewer local aides than their colleagues from other regions, although most Western congresspeople *prefer* that their top staff be from the district. This may be an indication of the difficulty in persuading prospective staff from districts a long distance away to move to Washington.

Another consideration in staffing is balancing the need for Hill experience with knowledge of the district (assuming that both cannot be found in one employee). Both can enhance a staffer's value. For first-term representatives, the specific balance appears to be a particularly important decision.

Most congresspeople find that a mix of the two is useful. Certain jobs lend themselves to staff with Washington experience: a number of people have made the federal casework slot a quasi-professional career.

All the offices of freshmen representatives in the survey had hired some staff who were not from the district but who did have Hill experience, and all felt this had proven useful. Truly competent secretarial help is in short supply on the Hill, as elsewhere, and most congresspeople do not insist that their secretaries be from their district. Most offices do, however, try to have as a receptionist someone with district ties. If a secretary or clerk has district ties, he or she is often also the receptionist.

Most offices try to hire personnel of the same party and inclination as the representative, although a very small group specifically stated that this was never investigated and did not matter as long as the employee did the job well. In recruiting, the political background of applicants is usually known, especially if the office relies on the "informal contact" recruitment system. Very often staff people feel they cannot work for someone whose ideas they do not support, and want to feel that "the boss" and they are thinking along similar lines. Occasionally, an applicant will be asked how the congressperson views an issue and how this could be made clear—in a letter or a press release—to constituents. In a way, this is as much a skill test as a political test, as obviously one aspect of staff success is ability to interpret the congressperson's position correctly. Generally, party similarity is the litmus test for compatibility.[13]

Very occasionally, representatives hire in order to have the presence of specific attitudes or geographic or party groups in the constituency. One administrative assistant had been hired because he was acceptable to all elements of the party after a particularly hard-fought and bitter primary; a number of applicants for the job had worked for primary opponents of the elected congressman. Although the AA had been involved in the primary fracas, he had convinced the congressman that he fully supported him, and would be loyal. In another instance, a black administrative assistant had been hired twenty years earlier as a staff assistant by a white congressman in order to represent the black element in the district. The staffer had stayed on the Hill, for most of the time with that district and through several other congressmen representing it. Representation of district groups is usually not a significant consideration in recruitment, however.

Staff Background

Education. In looking at staff background, it is useful to distinguish among different positions. As Congress has become more specialized, the more recently added professional jobs, such as legislative assistant and press aide, are filled by staff with specific expertise.

Most House offices (eighty-four percent of the sample) are headed by an administrative assistant. All AAs are regarded as the staff director; in the office hierarchy, no matter how loosely organized, they are at the top. The AA continues to be the generalist job, whether measured by job content or by education and training.

In contrast, legislative assistants tend to have more specialized training. Of all Ninety-Second Congress' AAs listed in the biographical section of the *Congressional Staff Directory, 1972,*[14] 9.8 percent had never attended college; 13.6 percent had some college; 41.1 percent held bachelor's degrees; 14.7 percent had master's degrees; 18.5 percent had law degrees; and 2.3 percent had Ph.D. degrees. In contrast, a higher proportion of LAs have more formal educational training, and far fewer have no college at all (see Table 7).

As might be expected, the LA, a position which has come into its own more recently and which came about as a result of increased specialization, makes use of more specialized training. Looking at the field of specialization, LAs are trained more specifically for a legislative function. Of the staff in the

TABLE 7
EDUCATION OF AAs AND LAs[a]
(in percentages)

	No college	Some college	BA	Masters	LLB	PhD
AA (n = 265)	10	14	41	15	18	2
LA (n = 189)	4.2	2.6	46	19	25	2.1

a. Derived from data in the *Congressional Staff Directory, 1972.* Data in the Directory also show that Senate AAs have more law degrees and are slightly better educated (as measured by formal degrees) than House AAs. They also tend to be somewhat younger.

offices surveyed, twenty-three percent of the AAs versus thirty-nine percent of the LAs were trained in political science; the same number (but a slightly higher percentage) of LAs (twenty-eight percent) as compared with AAs (twenty-three percent) were lawyers. Altogether, slightly less than half the AAs (forty-six percent) but a large majority of the LAs (sixty-seven percent) had training specific to their legislative duties (see Table 8).

Older AAs are less likely to have formal educational training than are younger AAs. All the AAs of thirty or less had college degrees; fifty percent also held master's or law degrees. All the AAs in the sample who had not finished college were over forty-five (twenty-seven percent of those over forty; sixteen percent of the AAs). Thirty-six percent of the AAs over forty held a college degree; thirty-six percent held master's or law degrees. Older staff may not have attended or finished college due to the depression or World War II; this appears to be the pattern for both the sample and for others whose biographies are listed in the *Congressional Staff Directory.*

Of the LAs in the sample, ninety-two percent (eleven of twelve) of those under thirty held B.A. degrees; thirty-three percent held law degrees; one LA was still attending college, but was a senior in his final semester. Of the LAs

TABLE 8
STAFF EXPERTISE, BY FIELD OF EDUCATION

		AA (n = 22) % of AAs	LA (n = 18) % of LAs
Political Science		23	39
	n	(5)	(7)
Law		23	28
	n	(5)	(5)
Journalism		18	11
	n	(4)	(2)
Other		36	22
	n	(8)	(4)

over forty, one held an M.A. in political science; one held a B.A. degree but had no further formal educational training; and one had some college. All of the remaining LAs, aged thirty to forty, had some graduate work, and two of the three held a graduate degree (M.A. or law). For other professional aides, the B.A. is ordinarily the only professional degree necessary. Of the staff members surveyed, only one "other professional" did not hold a college degree, although most did not hold degrees beyond the bachelor's.

Press assistants have specific expertise in media work, with journalism training and prior experience in radio, TV, or newspaper work. Of the four press assistants in the offices surveyed, two were journalism majors and one majored in English. All had worked in journalism prior to their present positions. In one other office, a lower-level staffer who assisted the AA in press work also majored in journalism in college and had worked in radio-TV.

A number of staff professionals have a journalism background, as both my data and a glance through staff biographies indicate. These professionals may perform some press duties, but are not designated as "press assistants" and hence are not treated as a separate group.

The data above do not show the proportion of aides engaged in further formal training. A number of staff assistants in the House are currently attending law or graduate school, and another group has had some graduate work or some law school.

Age. Administrative assistants tend to be older than legislative assistants. Legislative assistants are, in turn, older than other staff professionals, although as with other professionals, a large majority are thirty or less. Table 9 indicates the age distribution of professionals in the House offices.

One explanation for age differences in staff positions is that congresspeople most usually recruit close campaign workers as AAs. They may be somewhat older than other staff professionals when appointed. And, once in Washington, the AAs stay on with their bosses (although representatives with many years' seniority may need to recruit a replacement). Longer tenure and the more generalist nature of their jobs converge so that AAs are older and have somewhat less formal education than other personal staff professionals.

TABLE 9
AGE OF STAFF ASSISTANTS TO CONGRESSMEN (in percentages)

	(n = 50)		
	30 or less	31-40	more than 40
AA	18	23	59
LA	69	12	19
Other professional assistants[a]	90	10	

a. Excludes executive assistants.

Previous Political Activity. A majority of the staff members (fifty-five percent) in the survey had been active in politics prior to coming to the Hill. For some, this meant working in recent presidential campaigns. A large minority (forty percent) were directly involved in some aspect of the congressperson's most recent congressional campaign. (A majority of the AAs were involved.) A growing number of younger staff people have been recruited after college study of political science—with perhaps some direct involvement in political activity as part of their study. Another minority (not necessarily exclusively those involved in campaigning) have been active in local party matters or college political clubs.

Because AAs generally have the closest district ties and the closest personal ties to the congressperson, it is interesting to look at their involvement in their district's politics. Fifty-nine percent of the AAs had worked in district or state politics prior to Hill employment; indeed, in many cases, it was because of this involvement that the AA had come to Washington as a staff employee. All but a very few AAs are involved in district politics as part of their jobs, whether or not this was the case prior to coming to the Hill. And many AAs spend several months in the district at the time of congressional elections.

Previous Experience in Other Governmental Positions. Like their bosses, professional staff assistants do not often have executive branch experience. In twenty-nine percent of the offices surveyed, no staff member had had any experience in any branch of the federal government. Twelve percent had served in positions in state government, one having served on the staff of a state legislature. Twenty-five percent had held jobs in the executive branch of the federal government (thirty-three percent of these positions had been in legislative liaison). Eight percent had worked on staffs in other offices. It would appear that staff jobs are filled primarily by men and women with a legislative and local orientation, reflecting to a great degree their bosses' experience.

Staff Profiles. Before turning to a discussion of staff tenure, it may be useful to summarize briefly the attributes of staff in the different professional positions. Staff background varies considerably in the different jobs, as is evident from the data above, and representatives view those positions as requiring different kinds of training, experience, and expertise. Many expect differing lengths of tenure also.

Typically, the administrative assistant has worked with the congressperson in a first campaign, and joined the staff upon the member's election. Of the AAs in the sample, seventy-three percent came to the Hill with the representative at the time of his or her first term.[15] Although there is, of course, some turnover in staff among representatives who have been in Congress for some time, nevertheless a large proportion of the AAs have remained with their bosses. Table 10 breaks down AA tenure by seniority groups.

When House members replace administrative assistants, they may promote a staff aide who has already served on the staff over a period of years, or a personal friend or professional acquaintance is brought in. Of AAs who were replacements (six), thirty-three percent had previously been legislative assistants in the office. Fifty percent had come to know the congressperson in the course of his or her congressional duty—either in work with the executive branch or through local politics. The remainder were appointed in a typical recruitment search.

Table 11 summarizes the age and training of administrative assistants.

TABLE 10
TENURE OF ADMINISTRATIVE ASSISTANTS

Quartile	No. AAs	No. AAs from 1st term	% stayed
Most senior	5	2	40
Next most senior	6	4	66
Third most senior	7	5	71
Most freshman	4	4	100

TABLE 11
PROFILE OF HOUSE ADMINISTRATIVE ASSISTANT

Age	Education	Field of Training
Median: 41	No degree: 9%	No degree: 9%
Range: 27-65	B.A.: 46%	Journalism: 18%
Less than 30: 9%	M.A.: 27%	Political Science: 23%
30-39: 32%	Law: 23%	Law: 23%
40 or more: 59%		Other: 27%

Legislative Assistants

Fifteen years ago, few members of the House had legislative assistants, although staff aides performed some of the duties now assigned to LAs. Today, a majority of House offices do employ LAs (sixty-four percent of the offices surveyed). And there also appears to be a trend to divide the legislative workload among two, or even more, legislative assistants, as Senators do. This reflects the specialization of House staff, the increasing workload, and what appears to be an increased emphasis on the legislative function by more House members. Legislative assistants are, as previously noted, generally younger and more specialized than administrative assistants. They are recruited on the basis of skill, training, and background. In some instances, they are recruited from within the staff. They generally have had job experience or educational training which gives them some subject matter competence and at least some general expertise in the legislative process. They tend to be issue-oriented, often concerned about national priorities, and are, quite naturally, also oriented toward finding legislative solutions to problems.

A large majority of legislative assistants (seventy-three percent) hold degrees in law or political science. Although they are younger than AAs, their training is more directly related to law and/or the congressional function. Of those surveyed, thirty-nine percent were trained in political science (twenty-five percent of these hold graduate political science degrees); twenty-eight percent hold law degrees; eleven percent (two) were trained as journalists; twenty-two percent (three) were trained in other fields. Training increasingly appears to have a political science or legal orientation, either from formal education or previous work experience. When the prior jobs of legislative assistants trained in fields other than law or political science are considered, ninety percent of all legislative assistants bring knowledge of congressional processes and functions to their LA jobs.

Press assistants are young professionals with journalism training and media experience. A few offices (four, or sixteen percent of the sample) hire research assistants who perform a variety of research—collecting data for a speech or working on issues which may eventually result in legislation. All the research assistants hold college degrees; several are engaged in graduate training or expected to attend graduate school in the future. During the Ninety-Second Congress, research assistants were lower-level professionals, often appointed to a first job at relatively low salaries. This can be expected to change somewhat with the Ninety-Third Congress' specific provision for appointment of research assistants at a salary considerably higher than that of a number of legislative assistants. It may well be that, in the future, the typical research assistant of the Ninety-Second Congress will continue to work side by side with a more experienced and more senior counterpart.

Office Managers and Executive Secretaries

In some congressional offices, an office manager now shares supervisory responsibility with the administrative assistant. The office manager hires and supervises secretarial personnel, overseeing daily workloads and taking responsibility for much of the mail and the work flow. In twenty-three percent of the offices with AAs, there were also staff aides performing this function. Their titles were "Office Manager" or "Executive Secretary"; occasionally, the representatives's personal secretary acts in this capacity. Office managers are usually women, with a number of years experience on the Hill in a variety of positions. Often they have worked for several different House members. Typical office managers begin as secretaries, usually handle casework, and have wide contacts among staff in both the executive and legislative branches. They bring continuity, judgment, and often good political sense to the office staff. Because they have handled a variety of assignments, they are particularly helpful in supervising younger secretarial staff. A staff organized this way is similar to a committee staff with a clerk-professional staff distinction (where professional staffs are headed by a professional supervisor and clerical staff aides are headed by a clerical supervisor; much of the coordination occurs at the supervisory level).

Staff Tenure and Turnover

The pattern of turnover in the professional jobs varies. In the administrative assistant positions, the most prestigious and probably the most diversified, there is not a great deal of turnover. In several instances in the offices surveyed, when turnover came, the new appointee had already had several years' experience on the congressional staff of the congressperson. There is also less movement from one congressional office to another at the AA level.[16] At even the most senior level (congressmen in the most senior quartile), fifty percent of the Republicans and thirty-three percent of the Democrats had employed the same AA since their first election.

Sixty-six percent of the congresspeople employing AAs had hired their present AA upon first entering the House. The average tenure of employment is nine years; the median is eight. Two AAs have served twenty years in the same office; five more have served ten to fourteen. In offices where there has been AA turnover, the average length of tenure is five years; the median is four and one-half. In a system where contacts and precedents are important, experienced staff assistance can increase the effectiveness and output of the House member. An experienced AA can draw on previous patterns and information with regard to office procedures, grant assistance, and patterns of legislation. The importance of Hill experience in hiring staff has been discussed. Several congressmen noted that they preferred some professional staff turnover as they valued creativity and fresh ideas. One added, "But an exception is probably the AA."

Legislative aides have shorter tenures. The average is 2.3 years, with 6 years the longest any of the sample had stayed with the same congressman. LAs are promoted to AA (two in the sample), move to another office (three had worked for other congressmen), or move to committee staff jobs or the Senate. Many LAs, however, look forward to moving to jobs outside the Congress after several years, and a number of representatives seem to encourage this. ("It's probably good not to have people stay on the staff too long," one congressman said.) Lawyers may move to private law firms or to legal positions in the executive branch. Non-lawyers often join research organizations or do other government-related work. The fact that there is a higher proportion of law degrees may mean greater ease of movement to non-Hill jobs for LAs.

As with legislative aides, turnover is also greater for press personnel, as well as lower-level backup staff. In part, this is due to youth. For several staff members, this was one of their first jobs; predecessors had left to pursue careers in law outside Congress, to return to graduate school or, in the case of women, had dropped out of the job market with marriage. More staff members in these jobs had had experience in other congressional offices or in other areas of endeavor (teaching, executive secretary work). Their recruitment was not tied so directly to the election of a congressperson—that is (except in the case of first-term representatives), they had not worked on the campaign or stayed to move to Congress with the elected representative.

The pattern for staff who are office managers or handle individual casework is different. Many caseworkers have had long experience in congressional casework and have developed expertise in the field. Although occasionally caseworkers move to a legislative assistant or other staff slot, more likely they have moved up from secretarial duties and will continue in jobs with secretarial content. Most caseworkers are women. Many can move with ease from one office to another on the Hill. Office managers show a similar pattern: Usually starting on the Hill in a secretarial job, they develop an administrative expertise which enables them to move between offices with ease. They are more likely to be involved in policy matters than are caseworkers, but they may occasionally change party when changing positions.

Length of stay is, of course, affected by a number of variables. A significant one is the amount of responsibility the staff assistant has; this is measured both by the actual job content (does she draft the newsletter, the press releases, or does she rework the House member's drafts; does he work on independent legislative projects, developing his own information sources and having his own suggestions accepted?) and place in the office hierarchy. Salary and age are also important. Young staff are often expected to leave after a while—for graduate school, or perhaps for higher-level jobs on another staff.

Women outnumber men on staffs on Capitol Hill. The percentage of women has remained fairly constant (sixty-five to seventy percent) in recent years so that, as staffs have increased, the number of women and men employed have increased at a constant ratio (see Table 12). As Table 13 indicates, the proportion of women on staffs does not appear to vary significantly by party.

The significant factor, however, in assessing the role and function of the professional staff is the positions women on the Hill occupy. The percentage of women drops sharply when professional positions only are considered.

TABLE 12
HOUSE PERSONAL STAFF, BY SEX, 1961-1971
(n = 25) offices; in percentages)

	Women	Men
1961	63.5	36.5
1967	71	29
1971	71	29

SOURCE: Records, Clerk of the House.

TABLE 13
STAFF AIDES, BY SEX AND PARTY, 1961-1971
(n = 25 offices; in percentages)

	Republican Women	House Members Men	Democratic Women	House Members Men
1961	62	38	65	35
1967	73	27	69	31
1971	72	28	70	30

SOURCE: Records, Clerk of the House.

And even then, although given a professional title and professional responsibilities, a woman may be expected to handle typing and routine office chores which would not be expected of a man holding the same position. Trevor Armbrister, Congressman Riegle's assistant in writing *O Congress*, inadvertently alludes to this dual role when, in his foreword, he graciously thanks the congressman's legislative and federal projects assistants for devoting "evenings and weekends to typing the final manuscript."[17] Both are mentioned later in the text in connection with their professional duties.

Of the administrative assistants in the sample, five are women (twenty-three percent of the total). Once women attain AA rank, a majority have pay and duties similar to those of their male colleagues. However, the route to the AA position generally differs: The secretarial route was used by four of the five women AAs.

The situation is somewhat different at lower professional levels. Of the eighteen legislative assistants, four were women. They had duties generally comparable to those of male LAs. They were paid less, but they were also younger and had fewer graduate degrees. They did, however, have more pertinent prior work experience than male LAs. All the professional office managers and executive secretaries in the offices surveyed had started as staff secretaries.[18]

Freshman Offices: Recruitment and Expertise

Freshmen representatives feel strongly the lack of guidance on the role and function of their professional staff. Congresspeople do not agree on whether or not office organization and needs change as seniority increases. But many note that the skills and expertise they require of staff members have changed during their tenure in office. It is difficult to separate the causal factors involved in this: increasing seniority, changes in the overall congressional workload, changes in committee assignments which force changes in staffing, realization that the function of the staff is different from the perception of the House member prior to actually taking a seat in the House—all appear to contribute to change.

The three freshmen in the sample staffed their first-term offices in quite different ways. A common thread which ran through their experience was the use of contacts; as previously noted, these are significant in all hiring on the Hill. Other members of the state delegation, both House members and Senators, were particularly important in advising and also in assisting in the actual hiring of staff.

All the first-termers tried to weigh the need for staff from the district, for Hill expertise versus district ties, and for technical knowledge. All followed the pattern set by their state or city delegations in the division made between district and Washington offices, and seemed to be satisfied that the system was working properly.

Initial staffing for freshman congresspeople is similar in many respects to the replacement hiring of incumbents. The same factors are weighed, and new House members benefit from the advice of those more senior. "Contacts" and who knows whom are also significant. But in many cases, staffing a fresh-man's office is haphazard. It is clear that more help—organized and institu-tionalized (as one representative put it)—is needed by newly elected members. Contacts will undoubtedly continue to be important, and different congresspeople-elect will give priority to different needs based on their own perceptions and constituency needs; but freshmen-elect need some general body of information about staff duties, available applicants, and information sources, and it is not presently available.

LEGISLATIVE STAFF: A CAREER?

As congressional staffs have become larger and more specialized, several trends are evident. First, a career of being a Hill aide has developed. The most salient example may be in the field of federal casework. Congressional secretaries move between offices, and across the Capitol fairly frequently. (One AA listed turnover in secretarial personnel during the past year; nearly all had left for better-paying jobs in other offices.)

At the professional staff level, too, a Hill career is possible. One Senate AA interviewed had moved from a job as AA to a House member, to LA to a

Senator, and then to AA to the Senator. A staff man (with legal training and experience) had moved from a committee staff to a Senator's personal staff, and back to the staff of a different House committee. Presumably because of the closer local ties of representatives, there is a somewhat lower frequency of movement among their top staff, but there is some. There is also movement between the legislative and executive branches, especially in those positions where the same expertise is useful. Lawyers move between committee and executive branch staff jobs, as do some foreign affairs experts. Legislative liaison and LA or AA functions are easily exchangeable. (Following a change in administrations, a reverse flow may occur between executive and legislative.) Hence, Hill experience is valuable and a Hill career may mean that the staffer spends different stages of a career in jobs in another governmental branch.

One administrative assistant reflected on changes in congressional staffing: "A congressional staff aide is really a whole new career field. There's a healthy tendency to get people who are more qualified. People are much more interested in the content of the work—it's more than just a job. Actually, they are much more idealistic, too." Two staff aides felt that both specialization and professionalism had increased, but one commented, "Yes, House aides are more professional, but in function, not necessarily in training." Another aide felt that the generalist nature of the House staff jobs, although more specialized than previously, detracted from the professionalization, and noted, "We're not all lawyers—the Senate is more professionalized." He also mused on his future—what type of training was his LA position giving him for a non-Hill job?

Several congressmen commented on the increasing expertise required of staff, and one freshman stressed the importance to him of having a lawyer as a legislative assistant. Congress is becoming more sophisticated, and, measured by both formal education and by job content, staff is following a similar trend.

Extensive job histories of professional staff, both those who then held staff positions as well as the previous incumbents, were gathered in 1969.[19] Some data, although less complete, are available for the expanded Ninety-Second Congress study. It is not possible to determine conclusively whether a pattern exists in congressional personal staff careers. However, the outline of a typology seems visible; it is presented here as both tentative and speculative, for purposes of discussion and as a basis for further research.

It would seem a reasonable hypothesis that staff oriented toward certain types of career patterns may have different types of impact on the policy formation process, and analysis of career patterns will be useful in various ways. For example, do aides who tend to emphasize Hill rather than professional contacts have narrower communications nets than aides who put a profession first and the place of practicing that profession (the Hill) second? Or, alternatively, do aides emphasizing very broad professional contacts miss significant political inputs from the Hill which may be crucial to passage of legislation? Do aides with a career Hill orientation get "locked into" certain approaches, with a consequent, possibly dysfunctional impact on policy formation? Or are aides who see their Hill work as a steppingstone to something else more interested in looking for the next position than in the negotiation and attention to detail which may accompany passage of obscure legislation? Are they too flexible? Identification of career patterns can yield further insights for the congressional process.

Table 14 sets forth a preliminary typology. The categories are closely linked to role orientation—that is, to how the staffer views the job as well as the types of skills used in the job.

TABLE 14
CAREER ORIENTATIONS OF PERSONAL PROFESSIONAL STAFF

Hill Professional
Hill Specialist
Professional Specialist
Impermanent Careerists

Those who are "Hill professionals" use typical congressional skills such as compromise and negotiation to facilitate the functioning of the office (and the member in his or her job). The supplementary aspect of staff jobs is emphasized. Professional Hill people tend to emphasize Congress first and a profession second. The staffer uses skills more specific to Congress, and as time goes on, less specific to the practice of his profession. Hill professionals tend also to be Hill careerists; they see their new careers as serving on Hill staffs (personal or committee), and expect to stay on the Hill if their present boss is defeated or retires.

The Hill specialist also typically uses congressional-type skills, often in an administrative capacity. However, in contrast to the Hill professional, the Hill specialist's skills are easily transferable to an area outside Congress, if he or she wishes. Like Hill professionals, their primary orientation is not generally to a specific profession, but because of their particular expertise and the job they fill, they move to jobs off the Hill more easily (and more often).

In contrast to these two categories, the professional specialist is more oriented toward a profession. He uses his professional training on the Hill. Her skills are transferable and her own career is not necessarily submerged in that of her boss. These staff aides tend to have somewhat temporary Hill careers; they move from the Hill after awhile, in order to pursue a profession of their own less tied to a personal staff role.

A number of younger staff are what might be called "impermanent careerists." The aide has professional training, but is not entirely clear where or how, over time, that training should be used. The staffer does not consider the job in Congress as permanent, but does not have any specific plan for where to move next. A number of these staff aides are college-trained women, in lower-level professional positions, who may not continue to work full-time, or who may shift to volunteer work. These staffers appear to combine a professional role with strong personal ties to the particular House member for whom they work.

STAFFING: REPRESENTATIVES' REQUIREMENTS

What do congresspeople look for in hiring staff assistants? The tangible and measurable qualifications of expertise: law or journalism (increasingly, with experience in TV news), secretarial skill, research, and writing experience. Many seem to look, also, for staff with communications and interpersonal relations skills: a political scientist with experience in community organization; a journalist with public relations experience; a lawyer who has handled legislative liaison work; a media and engineering expert with experience running a division in a federal government agency program. Several representatives and aides mentioned the critical need for having staff who write well—for mail, newspaper columns, testimony and statements, and so on. One congressman said, "I constantly underestimated the need for writers [before I was sworn in]. There is enough communicating with the district to keep one person busy.... My LA and the interns are rapidly becoming writers." Another congressman noted "the critical shortage of people who can draft letters, statements, testimony, well."

House members also look for qualities which are not easily measured: someone who "enjoys government and doesn't mind the long hours." Another congressman said, "I look for staff who are highly motivated, with a desire to serve. Flexible people. A deep sense of idealistic responsibility." This congressman has "made an effort" to hire young people, and is proud of the number of alumni of his office in government service. He views staff employment as a time to instill a sense of public service, and as training in the functioning of government.

A senior Republican looks for employees who will be conscientious ("Not la de da," he said) and have compassion. He tries to assess how well applicants will work together, as "it's really got to be a coordinated team. I also must have people who will say 'wait'—the staff *must* bring both the pros and cons of an issue to me."

It seems to add up to loyalty, long hours, conscientious application to the work, willingness to learn and ability to apply native intelligence to one's work. One staffer said, "The most important thing is to think along the boss' lines," and this was echoed by others. Most, but not all, would agree with a senior congressman who said, "The staff philosophy must reflect the members' philosophy."

There is no agreement on whether a congressperson is best served by bright, young staff who do not stay very long, or by older, more experienced staff, who are knowledgeable in the ways of the Hill. It appears to depend primarily on the representative's own inclination and organizational ability. Frequent turnover puts greater demands on congresspeople and staff aides, and may prove dysfunctional during the learning process. But longevity may be dysfunctional also, as staff settle into routines which are rarely jolted. In fact, as noted above, there is fairly frequent turnover of lower-level professionals, and among secretarial staff as well. But there is continuity in staffing achieved with the longer tenure of the administrative assistant. Most congressmembers would probably agree that this is a pretty good mix.

The data reported in this chapter indicate that some staffing patterns are related to certain attributes such as seniority and policy attitude. Thus, staff of different groups of congresspeople may have different types of impact on legislative operations. The ramifications of these differentiated patterns extend broadly to the actors in and operations of the governmental subsystems, to theories of responsiveness and representativeness, and to our understanding of the congressional policy formation process. It should also be noted that, although differing patterns of staffing exist, certain patterns are common to virtually all offices. Hence, recruitment of professional aides is generally informal, somewhat haphazard, and dependent on contacts. This tends to provide House members with staff who in some important ways mirror their bosses (local ties and background, for example), and perhaps reinforce predilections for certain types of policy and processes of policy formation.

Data on staff can also tell us something about the legislator.[20] This study indicates increasing expertise, specialized training, and professionalization, as well as some growing differentiation of staff positions. This may be a result of the heavier and more complex congressional workload, but also may reflect changes in the training, experience, and perhaps the role perceptions, of representatives themselves. In my view, the data raise a number of significant questions, research on which can contribute to our understanding of congressional actors and the legislative policy process.

Staffing has become more institutionalized, of course. The increase in allowances has contributed both to bureaucratization of the office organization and to the attractiveness of top slots as a career post. But the comments of both congresspeople and staff indicate overwhelmingly that personalization of staffing continues on the Hill. Prized qualities include personal loyalty and "ability to think along the same lines." House members do want more expertise and technical skill, but the staff people reflect by and large their bosses' own roles—expert generalists in a personalized job situation.

NOTES

1. Susan Webb Hammond, "Personal Staffs of Members of the U.S. House of Representatives," unpublished Ph.D. dissertation, Johns Hopkins University, 1973.

2. See note 1. Published sources for the data include the *Congressional Record* and Hearings of the Subcommittee on Legislative Branch Appropriations of the Appropriations Committee, U.S. House of Representatives. Congressional records of clerk-hire salary payments (Office of the Disbursing Clerk, U.S. House of Representatives), and clerk-hire allotments were also used. Seventy-two semi-focused interviews were conducted with virtually all professionals and most congresspeople in a random sample of twenty-five House offices; the sample was stratified by party, seniority, and region. See Harrison W. Fox, Jr., "Personal Professional Staffs of U.W. Senators," unpublished Ph.D. dissertation, American University, 1972, for analysis of Senate staff activities. Harrison W. Fox and Susan Webb Hammond, "Congressional Staffs and Congressional Change," paper presented at the American Political Science Convention Annual Meeting, New Orleans, Louisiana, 1973, compares House and Senate staffs in some areas.

3. Portions of this section are drawn from Fox and Hammond, "Congressional Staffs," pp. 6-9 and 19-21.

4. The typical one or two aides in 1893 rose to a maximum of five by 1946.

5. Personal staff aides may receive the five and a half percent pay raise for government workers effective October 1, 1974, at the discretion of each House member.

6. For example, the House vote in July 1971 to delegate to the House Committee on Administration the decision on allowable staff numbers and funds (as well as changes in certain other office allowances).

7. See Nelson W. Polsby, "The Institutionalization of the U.S. House of Representatives," *American Political Science Review,* Vol. 62 (March 1968), pp. 144-168, for discussion of some of the factors important to increasing institutionalization.

8. Material on committee staffing is based largely on *Congressional Quarterly's Guide to the Congress of the United States,* Congressional Quarterly Service, Washington, D.C.: 1972, especially pp. 160-161.

9. Professionals are here defined primarily by function—those aides who perform professional, press, administrative, or similar duties. Secretarial and clerical staff, in contrast, perform routine duties under close supervision and do not exercise independent judgment and/or initiative in substantive areas. The distinction is not always clear-cut; in some instances relatively routine duties may include professional aspects, as, for example, when caseworkers identify possible areas for legislative or administrative remedy from constituent complaints. Such caseworkers are classified as "lower-level professionals" for purposes of this study. Making a distinction between professional and secretarial staff by means of a salary level, which is sometimes done, would result in either omitting some aides who do in fact perform professional duties, or setting a salary floor which would include some secretarial employees.

10. Donald Riegle with Trevor Armbrister, *O Congress* (Garden City, N.Y.: Doubleday, 1972). Abigail McCarthy, *Private Faces/Public Places* (Garden City, N.Y.: Doubleday, 1972).

11. Discussion applies to Washington staff. Field office staff are necessarily from the district.

12. Localism here is defined as district and/or state ties (residence, previous job experience, education).

13. Many congressmembers distinguish between professional staff and secretarial staff in looking for compatible attitudes. In general, when the entire office staff (including secretaries) works closely together as a team, all the staff share similar policy attitudes. But because secretarial work is a skill which, strictly speaking, does not involve policy, secretaries transfer most readily. One Republican, generally regarded as conservative, had recently hired a secretary from a "liberal" Democrat. Other offices would regard this kind of transfer as difficult to make.

14. Charles L. Brownson (ed.), *Congressional Staff Directory* (Washington, D.C.: Congressional Staff Directory, 1972).

15. Includes one representative with discontinuous service. Present AA came at time of election to most recent continuous service.

16. The Senate would seem to present a different pattern, with more movement of high-level aides from one office to another. It is perhaps because Senators have longer terms and do not always need to maintain local ties to the same extent. There is also more movement between AA and subcommittee and committee staff, perhaps because Senators control committee staff much earlier in their careers than do representatives.

17. Reigle, *O Congress,* p. ix.

18. For further data comparing men and women staff assistants, see Hammond, "Personal Staffs," especially Chapters IV and V.

19. See Susan Webb Hammond, "The Office Staff of the Congressman: Organizational and Recruitment Patterns," unpublished M.A. thesis, Johns Hopkins University, 1970.

20. Donald R. Matthews discusses this and posits a typology of office operation in discussing Senators' offices. See Donald R. Matthews, *U.S. Senators and Their World* (New York: Random House, 1960), pp. 82-87. Also, see the discussion by Eric Redman of how changing perceptions of senatorial function affect staff hiring in *The Dance of Legislation* (New York: Simon & Schuster, 1973).

ROLE CONSENSUS AND CONFLICT IN LEGISLATIVE STAFFING: THE FLORIDA EXPERIENCE

MICHAEL A. WORMAN

INTRODUCTION

In early 1969, the Securities and Exchange Commission named Martin Sweig as one of two co-defendants in a civil suit involving a stock manipulation. Sweig was serving at that time as administrative assistant to House Speaker John McCormack. As the case developed, there unfolded a fascinating story of the techniques utilized by Sweig in the performance of his duties as McCormack's aide.[1]

The role of administrative assistants in the legislative process is a crucial one, for, as the Sweig affair showed, they may often wield great influence. Several questions are therefore worthy of exploration, questions pertaining to their basic functions, their degree of independence in the legislative process, and the establishment of guidelines for their actions. Were the actions of Martin Sweig within these guidelines or were they atypical?

One of the purposes of this study is to determine the norms for the behavior of administrative assistants. The method of analysis known as role theory seems particularly suitable for this task. One of the most authoritative works in this area defines role theory as follows:

> The study of the behavior of the individual in terms of how that behavior is shaped by the demands and values of others, by their sanctions for conforming and non-conforming behavior, and by the individual's own understanding and conceptions of what his behavior should be.[2]

[86]

The above definition implies description. More important than this, however, is that it stresses determinants of behavior in terms of expectations of others. This is particularly applicable to this study because the administrative assistant to the legislator must have a thorough knowledge of the desires and expectations of his boss. Therefore, if we are going to describe the behavior of the aides, we must also attempt to determine the boundaries or determinants of that behavior. The terminology and the analytical framework of role analysis helped to organize the data gathered in this study.

This is not to imply that role theory is by any means a hard and fast set of terms and concepts. The attempt will be made in this chapter to determine the role of the administrative assistant and to explore the degree of role consensus and conflict regarding his or her position.[3]

METHODOLOGY

Sampling Procedure

The universe for this investigation was the body of legislators and their aides serving in the Florida Legislature in the 1970 session. At the time of the survey this included 32 senators and an equal number of assistants, and 31 representatives and their assistants, for a total of 126 individuals.[4]

In Florida, there are two different pay grades for this position—administrative assistant I and II. The duties as stated in the personnel manual are identical.[5] The sole difference between the two is the amount of experience required in staff or administrative work prior to employment.

The data and findings of this chapter are drawn from a doctoral dissertation on Florida legislative staffing. For the study, a questionnaire was submitted to aides and legislators serving in the 1970 session of the legislature. Two basic categories of questions are pertinent to the matter of role conflict and consensus.

Role Expectation Questions

In this series of questions, an attempt was made to ascertain both the legislators' and aides' conceptions of the attributes of the ideal aide. Questions were asked which elicited their conception of the ideal educational background an aide can possess as well as the ideal college major. The respondents' views as to the ideal occupational background were also requested.

The two most important questions in this section were those dealing with the ideal personal traits an aide can possess and also the ideal activities an aide can perform. In both of these areas, care had to be taken to compose a list of personal traits and activities which was inclusive of those having a bearing on the role of the aide and yet not so detailed as to make the obtained data unmanageable.

The list of personal traits and activities utilized in this study was composed primarily from my personal experience as an administrative assistant to a representative for the period of one year, and from another year's experience as a legislative assistant in the office of the House Majority Leader.

The final question of this section dealt with the communication of role expectations between the legislator and the aide.

TABLE 1
LEGISLATION RESEARCHING EXPECTATIONS OF
LEGISLATORS AND AIDES

	Rating of Importance							
	V.I.		I.		D.K. & N.R.		U. & V.U.	
	n	%	n	%	n	%	n	%
Legislators	25	55.6	18	40.0	2	4.4	----	---
Aides	25	53.2	22	46.9	----	----	----	----

Role Description Questions

In this section, both legislators and aides were asked to estimate the percentage of time the aide spent in performing certain activities. The response to this question would describe what aides actually do during the course of a day.

The interaction between the legislators and the aides was examined through two questions. The first asked the frequency of the legislators' soliciting of advice from the aides on certain matters. The second asked them to rate their personal relationships with each other.

The final and most important question in this section was that dealing with activities the aide is permitted to perform independently and how strongly the legislator would approve or disapprove of certain stipulated activities. The list of activities was composed in the same manner as the list of ideal activities previously mentioned.

Validity of Questionnaire

No pretest of the instrument was conducted because of the difficulty in persuading legislators and, to a lesser degree, their assistants, to respond to a questionnaire one time, much less a potential three times.

Instead, after the questionnaire was composed, it was submitted to five aides and five legislators (four representatives and one senator). It was also submitted to the Director of the Florida Legislative Service Bureau, a unit which at the time processed legislators' research requests. Finally, it was also submitted to a member of the Department of Government at Florida State University. These twelve individuals constituted the panel of expert judges for this questionnaire. The legislators and their aides were chosen because of their obviously intimate involvement in the legislative process. The Director of the Service Bureau was chosen because of his day-to-day contact with the legislators. The Florida State University professor was chosen because of his experience with Florida legislators in various capacities since the late 1940s.

Administration of Questionnaire

Questionnaires were mailed to the subjects at the end of the legislative session. Cover letters from myself and the Director of the Legislative Service Bureau accompanied the instrument. The total responses to the questionnaire numbered ninety-two, or seventy-three percent of the universe. Aide responses outnumbered legislator responses, but only slightly. In the House of Representatives, twenty-two legislators and twenty-three aides responded, and in the Senate, twenty-three senators responded as compared to twenty-four aides. The high rate of response was probably a result of the Director's letter and my own employment as an aide. The ninety-two individuals who responded to the questionnaire serve as a solid base for analysis of role conflict and consensus in the position of administrative assistant.

Role Expectations for the Position of Aide

Every individual employed by another individual performs his or her task within a double set of expectations. First, he performs according to the expectations of the individual paying his wage. This is obviously the most important set of expectations, for ultimately it is this individual who has the power of hiring and firing.

Second, the individual who is employed has her own set of expectations concerning her position. Her enactment of her role will be colored by her expectations also.

Theoretically, these two sets of expectations will be in some sort of agreement or role consensus, at least in a condition of continuing employment. It is possible, however, for these expectations to be dissimilar, thus creating the condition termed role conflict.

In this chapter, we shall examine role consensus and conflict with regard to ideal aide activities and the perceived degrees of freedom within which the aides operate.

IDEAL AIDE ACTIVITIES

The most important type of role expectations for the position of aide are those which set the standards for role performance. To determine these expectations, legislators and aides were requested to rate by importance eight general categories of activities in terms of the role of the ideal aide. These activities were felt to adequately represent the universe of possible aide activities.

Researching and Drafting Legislation

Preparing a bill for introduction is basically a two-step process. First, the bill must be researched. The background of similar bills in other states might be uncovered, the effect of the bill must be estimated, etc. In addition to researching the bill, there remains the essentially technical task of putting the desired thought into legal language.

In Florida, there exist legislative staff services which will perform both these tasks at the legislator's request. This accounts for the wording "researching legislation or having it researched," and "drafting legislation or having it drafted" in this question. Often, however, the legislator or the assistant will perform both these tasks.

TABLE 2
LEGISLATION DRAFTING EXPECTATIONS OF
LEGISLATION AND AIDES

| | Rating of Importance | | | | | | | |
| | V.I. | | I. | | D.K. & N.R. | | U. & V.U. | |
	n	%	n	%	n	%	n	%
Legislators	16	35.6	22	48.9	3	6.7	4	8.9
Aides	20	42.6	23	53.2	1	2.1	1	2.1

As will be observed shortly, researching legislation or having it researched had the second highest rating of all the items in terms of importance. A full 95.6 percent of the legislators rated this type of activity as either very important or important in terms of the role of the ideal aide. One hundred percent of the aides rated research as either very important or important.

Drafting legislation was 20 percentage points behind researching legislation in the very important category for legislators and 10.6 points behind for the aides. On the whole, legislators ranked this activity as being less important than did the aides. Four legislators, or 8.9 percent, felt that this type of activity was either unimportant or very unimportant, while no aides expressed this sentiment. Drafting legislation was the third highest ranked activity for both groups.

Public Relations

One of the main types of activity an aide performs is that of public relations. Often an aide will write speeches, press releases, newsletters, etc. Both legislators and aides ranked public relations fourth on their list of ideal activities as can be seen in Table 3.

While both groups placed public relations fourth, aides rated this activity higher than did the legislators. In addition to the difference in importance, 8.9 percent of the legislators stated that this activity was either unimportant or very unimportant. The slightly lower rating of public relations may have been due to the sensitive nature of such work. To issue a press release, write a newsletter, or perform some other activity of this type, the aide should possess a thorough knowledge of the legislator's thinking on several subjects. This ability takes time to develop. Since most of the aides had served a relatively short time, legislators might be understandably reluctant to emphasize this function.

TABLE 3
PUBLIC RELATIONS EXPECTATIONS OF LEGISLATORS AND AIDES

	Rating of Importance							
	V.I.		I.		D.K. & N.R.		U. & V.U.	
	n	%	n	%	n	%	n	%
Legislators	13	28.9	23	51.1	5	11.1	4	8.9
Aides	20	42.6	23	48.9	3	6.4	1	2.1

Constituent Relations

Rated as most important as an ideal activity by both legislators and aides was the conduct of constituent relations. A legislator's job has often been characterized as that of an errand boy for constituents. During the course of a single day he or she may be asked to arrange a tour through the capital for a group of school children, have a flag flown over the building, secure a state job for an unemployed neighbor, obtain action from a state agency, or a number of other favors. As one senator wrote on his questionnaire, "When I check 'constituent relations' I mean helping constituents with personal problems—when they call their senator for help and the request is reasonable, they deserve prompt help!"

In addition to processing requests, constituent relations also means corresponding with constituents regarding pending legislation. Depending on the issue and the legislator's constituency, he may receive literally hundreds of letters on any given issue. It is characteristic of most legislative offices that incoming mail is answered as promptly as possible. It stands to reason that a legislator simply does not have the time to read hundreds of letters opposing or favoring a bill. Consequently, it is usually the responsibility of the aide to compose a form letter in response to these letters. In addition to this, of course, there are matters requiring the legislator's individualized attention, and they get it.

Over half (57.8%) the legislators rated constituent relations as very important, with the remainder rating it as important. An even higher percentage of the aides (59.6%) rated it as very important, with 36.2 percent rating it as important. Surprisingly, two aides (4.3%) rated constituent relations as very unimportant.

Secretarial Expectations

Rated eighth on the legislators' list and seventh on the aides' was secretarial activities.

Despite the fact that all aides occasionally do some typing and filing, secretarial activities had the highest negative response from the legislators of all activities listed (46.6%). The combined very important or important scores of both groups were practically identical.

TABLE 4
SECRETARIAL EXPECTATIONS OF AIDES AND LEGISLATORS

| | Rating of Importance | | | | | | | |
| | V.I. | | I. | | D.K. & N.R. | | U. & V.U. | |
	n	%	n	%	n	%	n	%
Legislators	3	6.7	13	28.9	8	17.8	2	46.6
Aides	5	10.6	12	25.6	9	19.1	21	44.7

Personal Expectations

Occasionally in every aide's career there arises the necessity for performing some sort of personal chore for the legislator. Personal tasks include such things as driving him to the airport, buying the sandwiches for lunch, renting his apartment for the session, etc.

Personal chores rated fairly low on both groups' lists of ideal activities. It ranked sixth on the legislators' list and seventh on the aides'. But while only a small number of respondents cited it as very important, both groups rated it as at least important. In addition, it had a small negative response among the aides, although almost one-quarter of the legislators (24.4%) felt it was unimportant.

Personal chores probably should not be deprecated. In theory, at least, every minute saved the legislator can be devoted to legislative matters.

Performing personal chores can amount to a good deal more than a few minutes. Just ask the aide who has spent hours searching for the best deal on an apartment for the session!

TABLE 5
PERSONAL CHORES EXPECTATIONS OF LEGISLATORS AND AIDES

	Rating of Importance							
	V.I.		I.		D.K. & N.R.		U. & V.U.	
	n	%	n	%	n	%	n	%
Legislators	3	6.7	23	51.1	8	17.8	13	28.7
Aides	8	17.0	22	46.9	11	23.4	6	12.8

Official Representation Expectations

Official representation means that the aide attends some function, such as committee meetings, for her employer. This type of activity rated low with both groups, as is shown by Table 6.

Legislators were definitely cooler to the idea of their aides attending an official function on their behalf than were the aides. One reason for this may be legislators' run-ins with aides who played this role a trifle too frequently. This factor was mentioned in Kofmehl's *Professional Staffs of Congress.* [6] According to Kofmehl, many staff people come to believe they actually *are* the legislators and act accordingly, much to the distaste of some legislators.

TABLE 6
OFFICIAL REPRESENTATION EXPECTATIONS OF LEGISLATORS AND AIDES

	Rating of Importance							
	V.I.		I.		D.K. & N.R.		U. & V.U.	
	n	%	n	%	n	%	n	%
Legislators	8	17.8	26	57.8	4	8.9	7	15.5
Aides	19	40.4	48	48.9	2	4.3	3	6.4

Campaigning Expectations

Last on the list of activities was campaigning. This type of activity is unique in that it is the only activity on the list which is forbidden by Florida Statutes.

The illegality of such activity was reflected in the responses. It ranked eighth on the legislators' list of ideal activities with only two of them saying campaigning was very important. The aides ranked it higher, however, making it sixth in their responses. This question also had the highest number of legislators and aides selecting the "no opinion" response or not responding at all to the question.

TABLE 7
CAMPAIGNING EXPECTATIONS OF LEGISLATORS AND AIDES

| | Rating of Importance | | | | | | | |
| | V.I. | | I. | | D.K. & N.R. | | U. & V.U. | |
	n	%	n	%	n	%	n	%
Legislators	2	4.4	8	17.8	16	35.6	19	42.2
Aides	13	27.7	8	17.0	15	31.9	11	23.5

Limits on Aide Activity

The logical question raised by the case of Martin Sweig is, "Just what are the boundaries of aide activity? (What is the aide not permitted to do?)" In this section, an attempt will be made to examine this point.

To determine possible boundaries of aide behavior, legislators were asked the following question: "To what extent would you approve or disapprove of your aide taking the following actions without your approval?" The legislator was then presented with a list of nine actions which included accepting a small gift from a lobbyist and representing the legislator's opinion to the press, to a constituent, to a committee, and to a lobbyist. Other actions included disposing of mail the aide feels would not interest the legislator, hiring or firing a secretary or clerk, researching or drafting a bill, and refusing somebody an appointment. Aides were asked to estimate their employer's approval or disapproval of the same aide activities. The results of this question are presented in Tables 8 and 9.

What is it safe for an aide to do without her legislator's explicit approval? Table 8 tells us that the safest thing she could do is research or draft a bill. A full 33.3 percent of the legislators stated that they would strongly approve of their aides doing this, and 84.4 percent either approved or strongly approved. Again, from personal experience, many aides frequently research and draft bills of interest to them hoping that their employers will introduce them.

It is interesting to note that a much higher percentage of aides thought their legislators would strongly approve of this type of activity. Only one aide thought his boss would disapprove such an act.

The second safest independent action by an aide was disposing of what he perceived to be useless incoming mail. While only 15.6 percent of the legislators strongly approved of such action, over 60 percent approved of it. Again, the aides perceived this slightly differently, with over half feeling that the legislators for whom they worked would strongly approve of such activity. The difference is probably accounted for by the fact that most aides do this without asking, so the legislator never knows how much mail he does not receive.

TABLE 8
LEGISLATOR APPROVAL OF CERTAIN AIDE ACTIVITIES

Type of Activity	Degree of Approval									
	S.A.		A.		D.K. & N.R.		D.		S.D.	
	n	%	n	%	n	%	n	%	n	%
Representing Legislator's Opinion:										
To constituent	4	8.9	20	44.4	2	4.4	10	22.0	13	28.9
To the press	4	8.9	33	73.3	—	—	3	6.7	5	11.1
To a committee	5	11.1	23	51.1	4	8.9	4	8.9	9	20.0
To a lobbyist	3	7.0	19	42.2	5	11.1	11	24.4	7	15.6
Mail disposal	7	15.6	24	53.3	3	6.7	8	17.8	3	6.7
Hiring and firing staff	2	4.4	17	37.8	2	4.4	14	31.1	10	22.0
Bill researching	15	33.3	25	53.3	1	2.1	3	6.7	3	6.7
Refusing an appointment	1	2.2	15	33.3	2	4.4	16	35.6	11	24.4
Receiving gift	—	—	4	8.9	5	11.1	22	48.9	13	28.9

TABLE 9
AIDE ESTIMATION OF LEGISLATOR APPROVAL OF CERTAIN AIDE ACTIVITIES

Type of Activity	S.A.		A.		Degree of Approval D.K. & N.R.		D.		S.D.	
	n	%	n	%	n	%	n	%	n	%
Representing Legislator's Opinion:										
To a constituent	2	4.3	21	44.7	4	8.5	12	25.5	8	17.0
To the press	12	25.6	29	61.7	3	6.4	3	6.4	—	—
To a committee	10	21.2	27	57.4	4	8.5	2	4.3	4	8.5
To a lobbyist	8	17.0	24	51.1	6	12.8	6	12.8	3	6.4
Mail disposal	25	53.2	19	40.4	1	2.1	2	4.3	—	—
Hiring and firing staff	2	4.3	13	27.7	17	36.2	3	6.4	12	25.5
Bill researching	26	55.3	18	38.3	2	4.3	1	2.1	—	—
Refusing an appointment	7	14.9	24	51.1	5	10.7	7	14.9	4	8.5
Receiving gift	—	—	5	10.7	16	34.0	11	23.4	15	31.9

Other safe independent activities for aides included representing the opinion of the legislator to the press or to a committee. While representing his opinion to a committee received the higher strongly approve rating of the two, representing his opinion to the press received the higher overall approval. This is rather surprising when one considers that a misworded press release reaches thousands of individuals.

Representing a legislator's opinion to a lobbyist was borderline as far as approval goes. Only 47.2 percent of the legislators either strongly approved or approved of this.

What is unsafe for an aide without her employer's specific approval? The cardinal sin appeared to be that of accepting a small gift from a lobbyist. Only 8.9 percent of the legislators approved of this, while 77.8 percent either disapproved or strongly disapproved. Aides recognized this as hazardous also, but not to the extent of the legislators. Over one-third (34%) of the aides expressed no opinion on this subject. Another type of risky activity for the aide was that of representing the legislator's opinion to a constituent. No legislator strongly approved of this and only 44.2 percent approved. One-half of the aides (50.9%) either disapproved or strongly disapproved.

The aide who refused to grant an appointment was also running a risk as far as legislators were concerned. Only 35.5 percent of the legislators approved of this while 60 percent disapproved.

Finally, the hiring and firing of staff was generally frowned upon by the legislators. While only 42.2 percent approved of this type of action, 53.1 percent disapproved.

The pattern in all of this appears to be one of diminishing approval rates the closer the independent activity gets to constituents. Certainly, there is no threat to a legislator's grasp on his or her district if an aide drafts or researches a bill. Even the sorting of mail is a fairly mundane task. But the representing of a legislator's opinion to a constituent is another matter altogether. Refusing an appointment is another matter also. Any sort of trouble in one of these activities, any misunderstanding between aide and legislator, could cost votes, as could a charge of impropriety resulting from the receipt of a gift.

Communication of Expectations

What of a misunderstanding? Do legislators actually relate their expectations to their aides? While legislators and aides were in agreement on the highest and lowest of the above items, there was disagreement on those activities between. One possible explanation for this would be a lack of communication.

Both legislators and aides were asked whether or not the legislators' conception of the duties and responsibilities of an aide were communicated to the aide by the legislators. The results of this question are compiled in Table 10.

One can see from Table 10 that there exists a substantial difference of opinion between legislators and aides as to communication. If one counts the no responses as probable cases of no communication, the difference is even greater. This could account for some differences in role expectations of the two groups. The question remains, however, as to whether role conflict occurs when there is no communication between aide and legislator.

TABLE 10
COMMUNICATION OF ROLE EXPECTATIONS BY
LEGISLATORS TO THE AIDES

| | Communication of Expectations | | | | | |
| | Yes | | No | | N.R. | |
	n	%	n	%	n	%
Legislators	36	80.0	9	20.0	——	——
Aides	28	59.6	16	34.0	3	6.4

Role Conflict and Consensus

To check for role conflict and consensus between aides and legislators, we will turn to legislator-aide combinations who both responded to the questionnaire. There were thirty-eight of these pairs, or seventy-six individuals. What we will be examining in this section is whether communication of expectations produces greater role consensus and lack of communication produces or is associated with role conflict.

Communication of expectations was said to occur when *both* the aide and the legislator said it had. A lack of communication was assumed when this agreement was absent.

Role consensus was said to exist when there was either positive or negative agreement between aides and legislators. In other words, both aide and legislator had to approve or disapprove of a certain activity for consensus to occur. They could disagree on the degree of approval or disapproval, but if one approved and the other disapproved of a certain activity, role conflict was said to occur. When both responded that they had no opinion, consensus was said to occur.

In addition, figures were compiled for those legislators and aides who were either in perfect agreement or perfect disagreement concerning any specific activity. Perfect agreement was said to occur when both aide and legislator checked the same response to the question. Perfect disagreement was said to occur when aide and legislator responded in exactly the opposite manner. Perfect agreement and perfect disagreement could be considered manifestations of ideal consensus or conflict.

TABLE 11
ROLE CONFLICT AND CONSENSUS AS REGARDS INDEPENDENT BILL RESEARCHING[a]

| | Communication of Expectations | | | |
| | Yes | | No | |
	n	%	n	%
Consensus	19	51.4	14	37.8
Conflict	1	2.7	3	8.1
Perfect consensus	8	38.1	11	52.4
Perfect conflict			2	9.5

a. The percentage for perfect consensus and perfect conflict is separate from that for consensus and conflict. N = 38 for consensus and conflict except in those instances where not everyone responded to the question.

The activity on which there existed the greatest amount of role consensus was bill researching. A full 89.2 percent of the aides and legislators were in agreement as regards this type of activity. Consensus appeared to be positively related to communication of expectations with 51.4 percent of the agreement occurring when communication had also.

The second highest activity with regard to role consensus was that of mail disposal with an agreement score of 86.4 percent. Consensus again appeared to be related to communication of expectation as 48.6 percent of the consensus occurred under those conditions. It's interesting to note, however, that perfect consensus occurred under opposite conditions with 55.6 percent of the cases occurring when there was no communication.

TABLE 12
ROLE CONFLICT AND CONSENSUS AS REGARDS MAIL HANDLING

| | Communication of Expectations | | | |
| | Yes | | No | |
	n	%	n	%
Consensus	18	48.6	14	37.8
Conflict	7	18.9	3	5.4
Perfect consensus	6	33.3	10	55.6
Perfect conflict			2	11.1

TABLE 13
ROLE CONFLICT AND CONSENSUS AS REGARDS CONSTITUENT RELATIONS

| | Communication of Expectations | | | |
| | Yes | | No | |
	n	%	n	%
Consensus	17	45.9	12	32.4
Conflict	3	8.1	5	13.2
Perfect consensus	17	65.4	8	30.8
Perfect conflict			1	3.8

Third highest in consensus was constituent relations with 78.9 percent. The case is stronger here with both consensus and perfect consensus corresponding to whether or not there had been communication of expectations.

A high rate of consensus existed on the matter of representation of an opinion to a committee. Seventy-three percent reached consensus on this, with both consensus and perfect consensus showing a positive relation to communication of expectations.

After constituent relations, press relations ranked fifth in degree of consensus. It's important to note the ten percent drop-off, however. This is due perhaps to the lack of distinction in the question. Aides see reporters practically every day in the course of their work and may discuss the stands of their legislators. The question tended to formalize the action by sounding more official. No aide with whom I was familiar would have formally issued a position paper without the legislator's prior approval. In this area, again, consensus and communication of expectations occur together.

TABLE 14
ROLE CONFLICT AND CONSENSUS AS REGARDS REPRESENTATION OF LEGISLATORS' OPINIONS TO COMMITTEES

| | Communication of Expectations | | | |
| | Yes | | No | |
	n	%	n	%
Consensus	18	48.6	14	37.8
Conflict	7	18.9	3	5.4
Perfect consensus	6	33.3	10	55.6
Perfect conflict			2	11.1

Very close to press relations in consensus was the acceptance of a small gift from a lobbysit. Sixty-two percent consensus was manifested on this issue, with greater consensus occurring when expectations had been communicated. Perfect consensus, however, was related to communication negatively. The relative lack of consensus could be attributable to disagreement over what constitutes a "small gift." Some might consider a case of beer from the breweries' lobbist as a small gift; others might not. While some legislators were fanatically opposed to this, I would say, based on my personal experience, that most were not.

It was interesting to note that both questions involving lobbyists rated approximately the same. A 60 percent consensus was achieved on this item, and 62.1 percent on the previous, indicating, perhaps, some wariness on this topic. It has been my experience that legislators are cautious about committing themselves to a lobbyist. An aide who would do this would be taking his chances. This is the first question in which consensus occurred most often when communication had not.

TABLE 15
ROLE CONFLICT AND CONSENSUS AS REGARDS REPRESENTATION OF LEGISLATORS' OPINIONS TO THE PRESS

| | Communication of Expectations | | | |
| | Yes | | No | |
	n	%	n	%
Consensus	15	42.9	11	31.4
Conflict	3	8.6	6	17.1
Perfect consensus	13	59.1	8	36.4
Perfect conflict				

TABLE 16
ROLE CONFLICT AND CONSENSUS AS REGARDS ACCEPTING A SMALL GIFT FROM A LOBBYIST

| | Communication of Expectations | | | |
| | Yes | | No | |
	n	%	n	%
Consensus	17	35.1	10	27
Conflict	7	18.9	7	18.9
Perfect consensus	7	46.7	8	53.3
Perfect conflict				

TABLE 17
ROLE CONFLICT AND CONSENSUS AS REGARDS REPRESENTATION OF LEGISLATORS' OPINION TO LOBBYISTS

| | Communication of Expectations | | | |
| | Yes | | No | |
	n	%	n	%
Consensus	10	28.6	8	22.9
Conflict	9	25.7	8	22.9
Perfect consensus	7	46.7	6	40
Perfect conflict			2	13.3

The question of hiring or firing a secretary may have not been the best of questions for Florida aides. Most legislators simply do not have the staff allocation to make this a likely chore for an aide. Still, the senators could have both an aide and a secretary. This is one of the two lowest questions, achieving a consensus of 51.5 percent. One of the reasons for this may be the fact that legislators tend to hire constituents as their staff. To hire or fire without approval would be presumptuous.

The greatest amount of conflict occurred on the question of limiting access to the legislator. One constituent turned away could mean the loss of many votes. Again, communication of expectations appeared to have a limited effect on consensus.

TABLE 18
ROLE CONFLICT AND CONSENSUS AS REGARDS HIRING OR FIRING A SECRETARY OR CLERK

| | Communication of Expectations | | | |
| | Yes | | No | |
	n	%	n	%
Consensus	10	28.6	8	22.9
Conflict	9	25.7	8	22.9
Perfect consensus	7	46.7	6	40
Perfect conflict			2	13.3

ANALYSIS

The material discussed in this chapter has bearing on two basic questions regarding legislative assistants. The first question involves the potential for the abuse of power by the aides. The potential is definitely present, and would appear to be directly related to the nature of the position.

There is not a great deal of contact between the aide and the legislator. If a lawmaker is not in the session, he's in committee or conference. The aide may have a general idea of her tasks for the day, but she has a great deal of leeway in performing those tasks. Therefore, the chance obviously exists for the aide to exceed the wishes of the legislator. In short, the problem appears to be one of lack of communication—which is inherent in the position.

The implications of this for legislators and aides are obvious. If a legislative system wishes to avoid an aide's overstepping permissible boundaries, there are two roads to follow.

One, it may establish strong institutional guidelines for aide behavior. The problem would be one of obtaining agreement among legislators as to the extent of permissible or desirable behavior. Activity between the aide and the legislator's constituency is practically impossible to control since it has little institutional visibility.

The areas which would be more prone to control are those which involve institutional interaction, such as official representation at committee meetings, relationships with lobbyists and, perhaps, campaigning. Of these three, the first two are most controllable. It would be easy to make regulations regarding an aide's filling in at a committee meeting or accepting gifts from lobbyists.

Controls on campaigning are unrealistic. An aide's job, power, and prestige are directly dependent upon the legislator's holding office. To expect aides not to take part in campaign activities is unrealistic. And even if they are not directly involved in campaigning, their performance of legislative functions permit the legislators more time to campaign themselves.

If a legislator decides on these sorts of controls, they must be effectively communicated to the aides. An orientation session for new aides would be a good vehicle for accomplishing this. Legislators should be encouraged to do this also.

The second method of control would be for the legislator to make a greater effort to guide aide behavior. This is likely to be less effective than the first because of the nature of the position as stated above and also because of the personal nature of the position. Aides are generally recruited on the basis of a previously existing personal relationship with the legislator. Such relationships are generally nonconducive to a long list of thou-shalt-nots. If an aide serves as an alter ego to the legislator, he will ultimately reflect the values of that legislator.

Another criticism of aides regards their impact on the output of the legislature itself. Several authors have stated that the volume of work of the already overwhelmed legislator may actually be increased by having an administrative assistant—in that they will have more time to devote to "pet" legislation. As Bailey and Samuel put it:

> And once a legislator has introduced a bill, he very frequently wants to see something happen to it. He therefore spends valuable time rounding up support in and out of Congress, and additional time badgering committee clerks and Congressional colleagues in an attempt to get action.[7]

As was shown earlier, 95.6 percent of legislators rated researching legislation as either important or very important in terms of the ideal role of the assistant. This would seem to indicate that they considered this function valuable to them and would be at least indirect evidence that Bailey and Samuel's criticism has some merit.

An impressionistic evaluation of their assertion would tend to be supportive also. I personally spent a great deal of time on a number of projects which were the special interest of the representative for whom I worked. I very quickly got the impression that they truly were *his* special interests and his alone after discussing them with committee heads and members. One quickly acquired the feeling of tilting at windmills. Again, on an impressionistic basis, I feel many aides with whom I was acquainted had similar experiences.

One should exercise caution, however, in being overly critical of this. Legislation which *is* of special interest to a legislator can also be valuable legislation which eventually becomes law. Even if the legislation is only pertinent to a special interest of the legislator's district, the instructed delegate theory of representation behooves him to act upon it if he considers it worthwhile.

A variation of this criticism was voiced by Bertrand Gross:

> But it must be kept in mind that the man who tries to do a better job often turns out to be one who sees that the better job is really a bigger job. Moreover, imaginative staff aides often uncover new problems, new opportunities, and new challenges. They tend to create—or at least attract—heavier burdens.[8]

I'm not certain that this is a valid criticism. Life *is* complex, as is government. It would be my assumption that it takes complex legislation to deal with complex problems. Any support that staff can give in improving the quality of legislation should be appreciated. Again, the fact that such a high percentage of legislators approved of such activity would appear to indicate that aides serve their *intended* function. Unless aides are viewed as errand runners, which this study shows they are *not,* this would seem to be a valid function.

Gross's criticism is similar to another of Bailey and Samuel's that the increased complexity of legislation caused by aides elevated it above the comprehension of the public. Repeated studies have shown, however, that a small percentage of the general public follows legislation with any regularity, and that their level of knowledge does not extend beyond the superficial. It is assumed that special interests would have a good grasp of and appreciate the complexity of the issue.

What of aides actually initiating legislation peculiar to *their* interests? Again, the high rate of approval supports this possibility. It must be kept in mind, however, that the chances are great that an aide may be a more qualified expert on legislation of a certain type than is the legislator. It might be asserted that the greater the length of service of the legislator, the greater this likelihood.

In summary, it is my belief that aides must be viewed as essentially a tool of the legislator. Like any tool, they achieve their purpose in the hands of the user. Their potential for use or abuse lies primarily with the legislator and, ultimately, with the people who elect him or her.

NOTES

1. William Lambert, "The Murky Men from the Speaker's Office," *Life,* October 31, 1969, pp. 52-58.

2. Bruce J. Biddle and Edwin J. Thomas, *Role Theory: Concepts and Research* (New York: John Wiley, 1966), p. 4.

3. The following definitions from Biddle and Thomas are utilized in this presentation: role—a set of standards, descriptions, norms, or concepts held (by anyone) for the behavior of a person or position; role consensus—sameness or commonly held norms; and

role conflict—inconsistent prescriptions held for a person by him- or herself or by one or more others.

4. Source: Personnel Offices, Florida Senate and House of Representatives.

5. Florida, the Florida Legislature, Joint Legislature Planning Committee, *Uniform Personnel Policies* (Tallahassee, 1969), pp. II-8 and II-9.

6. Kenneth Kofmehl, *Professional Staffs of Congress* (West Lafayette, Ind.: Purdue Research Foundation, 1962).

7. Stephen K. Bailey and Howard D. Samuel, *Congress at Work* (New York: Henry Holt, 1952), p. 8.

8. Bertrand M. Gross, *The Legislative Struggle* (New York: McGraw-Hill, 1953), p. 422.

LEGISLATIVE STAFFING:
A VIEW FROM THE STATES

A L A N P. B A L U T I S

INTRODUCTION

The recent decline in prestige of legislative bodies has prompted searching self-appraisal and substantial reform efforts in Congress and in a number of state legislatures. Dissatisfaction with the traditional organization and pro-cedures of legislative bodies has grown among the public, political scientists, and legislators themselves. As was noted earlier (see my earlier contribution), one of the most critical factors identified as essential to allow legislative leaders, committees, and individual members to respond to their growing responsibilities is staff.

If one were to visit any of a number of capitol buildings in the United States and ask someone there what has been the most important change in the legislature during the last few decades, the likely response would be a single word—staff. Walking about the building, an observer would get a number of visual confirmations from the plethora of staff offices. Staff members today are inexorably involved in all aspects of the legislative process.

Yet, staffing as a factor in the process of legislation has been, until fairly recently, almost completely ignored by political scientists. Moreover, to the extent that professional staff has been a subject of study, the utility of this research for students of legislatures has been limited by a major perceptual bias. That is, that legislative scholars have seemed to believe that Congress, and Congress alone, is worthy of study. Alan Rosenthal touched upon what might be termed "the Washington bias" in existing studies in his recent article on contemporary research on state legislatures.[1] In terms of both material and intellectual resources, Rosenthal argued, "state legislatures are neglected institutions of American government. Compared to Congress, for example, they are ignored by the public and are given little attention by political scientists.[2]

The purpose of this chapter is threefold. First, to briefly survey current trends in the movement for modernization and improvement of our state legislatures. Second, to examine from a number of perspectives the backgrounds, norms, activities, functions, and effects of professional staff members in one state legislature, that of New York. Finally, to analyze the direction of current reform efforts in the states and to speculate about the most appropriate research strategies for the future.

LEGISLATIVE REFORM IN THE STATES

A wide variety of aides currently services our legislatures and the use of the generic term "staff" conceals their diversity. Jewell and Patterson have noted two broad types of legislative staffs for American legislatures: the housekeeping staff and the specialist or professional staff.[3] The housekeeping staff performs various clerical, secretarial, and service tasks and includes the Clerk of the House, the sergeant-at-arms, the parliamentarian, and a wide variety of other aides, from attendants in the mailroom to Xerox machine operators. The professional staff performs policy-related tasks and may be characterized in terms of several subtypes: research, bill-drafting, investigating, subject matter expert, and political.[4] Moreover, staffs may serve individual legislators, committees, committee chairmen, the leadership, an entire chamber, or the whole legislature and may be either partisan or nonpartisan.

In the face of such a wide array of staff aides, it becomes necessary to . conceptualize some classificatory scheme to begin to cope with their diversity. Norman Meller once suggested that legislative service agencies could be arranged along two axes, the horizontal one oriented to "clientele" and "graduated from facilitating the whole legislature at one extreme to individual legislator service at the other."[5] The vertical axis was to measure personal identification, and was similarly graduated from "personal involvement" at one pole to "anonymous objectivity" at the other. Four quarters of the matrix were delineated by crossing the "clientele" and "identification" axes at their midpoints.

The advantage of this schema is, as Meller notes, "that both service agencies and individual legislative aides may be placed within the same

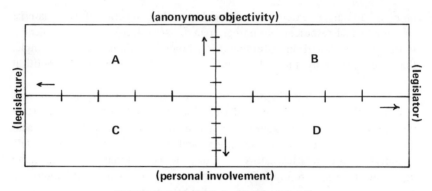

FIGURE 1. Legislative Service Matrix

meaningful categories."[6] For example, the Congressional Research Service or a Legislative Reference Library, providing basic information on request to all members, would be placed in block A, close to the total legislature—anonymous objectivity perimeter. The chief clerk of a legislative body and his staff, owing allegiance to their political mentors and seeking to further party ends to the extent permissible within the legislative rules, fits within block C, oriented to total legislature-personal involvement, and probably close to the midpoint on the clientele axis. The legislative aide or administrative assistant, intent on the reelection of his or her patron, would be placed at the juncture of personal involvement and single legislator identification in block D.

The staffing reforms advocated as offering a means of solving the legislatures' ills seem, in the main, to be of a nature as to be classified above the midpoint along the vertical identification axis in their tendency to anonymous objectivity, and oriented more toward service to the legislature rather than to individual legislators.[7] Of the roughly 100 or so permanent state legislative service agencies created during the period 1963-1973, seventy-four percent appear to be oriented more toward the legislature as an institution than to individual members. In addition, sixty-five percent of the total were nonpartisan (which would seem to indicate a tendency to anonymous objectivity), while twenty-nine percent were partisan appointments (indicating some personal involvement with the fate of their employer, be it the party or an individual member). Six percent were not classified or classifiable.[8] In terms of plotting on the Legislative Service Matrix, then, current reform efforts in the states would seem to encompass blocks A and B, and usually only A.

Yet, several observers have noted that legislative staffs of all types have grown fairly steadily in recent years. A survey conducted by the Citizens Conference on State Legislatures revealed that more respondents noted changes in the areas of staffing and services—mainly improvements—than in

any other category. Questionnaires from forty-three states (eighty-six percent) reported changes in staffing and services. Reports from thirty-nine
states noted increases in professional staffing; twenty-three of those also
noted expansion of clerical staffs.[9] In fact, as the size and number of
legislative staff offices have grown, a number of states have felt the need to
develop a coordinated approach to legislative operations and created management or administrative committees. Included among the functions performed
by such agencies are preparation of the legislative budget, employment of
legislative personnel, procurement of supplies and equipment, and the coordination of operations of legislative service agencies and committees. Legislative
management committees or other special mechanisms have been established
in twelve states.

The development of legislative management committees can be related to
the evolution of those legislative agencies providing research and policy
analysis services. Until fairly recently, virtually all research and policy analysis
in state legislatures was conducted by legislative reference bureaus or by
legislative councils. In the 1960s and the early years of the 1970s, however,
more and more states have developed other specialized research agencies. In
Connecticut, for example, a bipartisan office of legislative research com-
prising eleven professionals and three clerical personnel has been established.
The research function seems to be passing increasingly to professional staff
assigned exclusively to the leadership caucus and to standing and interim
committees. Nearly three-quarters of the states responding to the Citizens
Conference survey reported an increase in professional assistance for standing
committees since 1965.[10]

In surveying current trends in the movement for modernization and
improvement of our state legislatures, Karl Kurtz noted that "the most
substantial efforts toward legislative improvement have been made in the area
of improving the legislatures' ability to make independent judgments concerning taxation and spending by state government."[11] One of the most
important aspects of the modernization of state legislatures has been the
creation of specialized agencies to provide a capacity for independent analysis
and review of the budget. Thus, in 1972-1973, fiscal staffs were added in
Idaho, where the legislative council had some responsibility for budgetary
analysis in the past; in Alabama, which had authorized such positions in
1971; and in Louisiana, which had previously borrowed staff from the
executive branch. Ohio also established a Legislative Budget Office, which
will staff both parties.[12]

There has also been a movement toward placing the post-audit function
under legislative control as legislatures place greater emphasis on their responsibility for oversight of the executive branch. There are now twenty-eight
states where the auditor is selected by the legislature, and in five other states

the auditor is at least partially responsible to the legislature. Moreover, following the lead of New York, a number of legislatures have established separate committees, independent of the post-audit function, with responsibility for program review and evaluation.[13]

Of those states reporting professional staff additions in the Citizens Conference survey, six said there was now professional staff assistance attached to legislators as such or by virtue of their office. Michigan and Wisconsin respondents, for example, reported that professional aides have been authorized for all senators. Reports from Iowa and Tennessee indicated professional help was available to leaders and some committee heads. In Alabama, professional aides were made available to the presiding officers; in Nebraska, to committee heads.

The direction of the current trend in legislative modernization efforts seems clear, then. As Kurtz concludes, "The early 1970's appear to be a period for the diffusion of the innovations of the 1960's in staff services to a larger number of States and for the expansion of existing staffs."[14] Given this marked increase in the size and variety of legislative service agencies, there seems to be a very real danger that legislators and legislative reformers may have come to regard staffing as a panacea.[15] If a little staffing is good, it does not necessarily follow that a lot is much better. As Norman Meller has pointed out, indiscriminate staffing "could well lead to the institutionalizing of the legislator, and eventually to each legislator becoming the captive of his own staff. . . . For this reason, flat recommendations for larger staff fall short of the mark."[16]

Senator Earl Brydges, former majority leader of the New York State Senate, expressed this point well when he said: "To help us in decision making, we need not just more staff, not just full-time staff, not just better-trained staff, so glibly urged by the traditional reformers." Even more important, he continued, "We need to know what kinds of staff we need."[17] It seems quite possible that a particular staffing arrangement may result in some alteration in the balance of power in the legislature.[18] While this is not necessarily harmful, legislators and legislative reformers should be aware of the ramifications of various staff changes and consider the distinctive natures of the expert staff with which they would equip the legislature. In other words, the probabilities of who gets what when and how should be considered before a legislature decides on one type of staff rather than another.

The only adequate test of the validity of the many diverse and often conflicting perceptions of legislative staffs is how they have worked in practice. Since a number of state legislatures now have been operating with a sizable professional staff for some time, it would be desirable to examine the nature and working of these staffs. This is what this chapter proposes to do in an exploratory way in one state legislature.

THE SCOPE AND FOCUS OF THE STUDY

Neither legislative modernization or professional staffing is new in New York. On a comparative basis to the other states, it was the first to establish a state library, legislative reference section, and a bill drafting commission. This series of agencies was created over a period of some ninety years as the need arose and as the legislature itself matured. The cumulative effect was to give to the individual New York legislator access to one of the best collections of first-order information in the country.[19] Professional staffs have since been accepted, made permanent, and expanded.

This paper concentrates on four major components of the New York legislative staff: the Senate Finance Committee staff, the Assembly Ways and Means Committee staff, Assembly Central Staff,[20] and the leaderships' staff.[21] Of the 493 full-time employees of the legislature, forty-one percent are employees of these four staffs. Preliminary interviews with legislative correspondents, several legislators, and legislative staff members indicated that these staffs are the most closely knit elements of the legislative staff, perform the bulk of the staff work on legislation and in the oversight of administration, and comprise a large share of the professional staff members.[22] Their selection also allows us to examine three distinct types of staffs—personal staff, committee staff, and a central staff serving the entire chamber—and to begin to determine whether there are differences among the various expert staffs serving the legislature.

The major source of data for this paper is a body of 148 interviews conducted by the author with individuals involved in the legislative process in New York State. Most of the interviews used in this study were conducted in Albany between July 1971 and February 1972 as part of a larger study of legislative staffing in New York. Of the 148 interviews, 62 were with members of the professional staffs of the Assembly Ways and Means Committee, the Senate Finance Committee, Assembly Central Staff, and the legislative leaders (speaker, president pro tempore of the Senate, and the minority leaders), 51 were with legislators, 20 with members of the executive branch, 10 with lobbyists, and 5 with journalists. The interviews were of the focused type. Certain key questions, all open-ended, were asked of all respondents holding similar positions. But the interview was kept very flexible in order to permit particular topics to be explored with those individuals best equipped to discuss them. Notes were not taken during the interview but were transcribed immediately afterwards. Unattributed quotations in the text, therefore, are as nearly verbatim as the author's power of immediate recall could make them.[23]

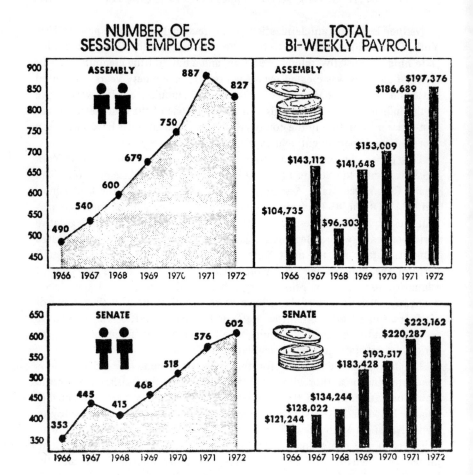

SOURCE: *Albany Times-Union,* February 20, 1972, p. B-1.

FIGURE 2. Legislative Staff Personnel and Bi-weekly Payroll, 1966-72

BACKGROUND, NORMS, AND CONSTRAINTS

Legislative staffs in New York have grown fairly steadily in recent years, as Figure 2 shows.

The number of full-time Senate employees increased from 135 in 1966 to 223 in 1972. Full-time employees in the Assembly, although under Democratic and then Republican control, climbed from 194 in 1966 to 270 in 1972. So-called "session" employees have increased by nearly seventy percent. In the Assembly, for example, the average number of session employees increased from 490 in 1966 to 887 in 1971, although this dropped to 827 for the beginning of the 1972 session. Of course, many of the employees of the legislature are secretarial or clerical personnel. But the professional staffs have also grown markedly since 1966.

Yet little is known about the role of professional staff in the legislative power structure. As Ralph K. Huitt has noted, "[The staff person's] influence has been both underrated and overrated. Surely he is more than a facilitator, more than extra hands to relieve the legislator of errand-running, more than a trained research mind to end legislative dependence on bureaucrat and lobbyist. Surely he is less than the real power behind the throne, as the frustrated lobbyist, and even the staff man himself, sometimes thinks he is."[24] Huitt goes on to raise an interesting question: "What is he like, this bright and ambitious man who submerges his own career aspirations in those of another? What does he want, what does he think he can get? How does he perceive his role, its satisfactions and limitations?"[25] It is to a consideration of these questions that we now turn.

CHARACTERISTICS OF THE LEGISLATIVE STAFF

A survey of the educational backgrounds of the professional staff of the New York State Legislature indicates that their educational qualifications compare favorably with those of corresponding employees in the executive branch or outside government service. Of the roughly representative sample of sixty-two professional staff aides interviewed, all had B.A.s or B.S.s; thirty-three, M.A.s or M.S.s; twelve, L.L.B.s,[26] and three Ph.D.s. This information is broken down by level, field, and type of staff in Tables 1 and 2.

A legal education was seen as particularly valuable by members of the leadership staffs. Eighty-two percent of the staffers serving the leadership pointed out the helpfulness of a legal background in mastering the art of bill-drafting and preparing bill analyses, briefs, opinions, and other legal memoranda. Their opinion was that a legal education inculcated the staffer

TABLE 1

EDUCATIONAL LEVEL OF NEW YORK STATE LEGISLATURE'S PROFESSIONAL STAFF MEMBERS, BY TYPE OF STAFF
(in percentages)

Education	Finance Committees' Staffs	Central Staff	Leadership Staffs
B.A. or B.S.	10	13	23
Some graduate work	13	7	——
M.A. or M.S.	67	66	18
L.L.B.	3	7	59
Ph.D.	7	7	——
	100	100	100
	(n = 30)	(n = 15)	(n = 17)

TABLE 2

EDUCATIONAL FIELD OF PROFESSIONAL STAFF MEMBERS, BY TYPE OF STAFF
(in percentages)

Education	Finance Committees' Staffs	Central Staff	Leadership Staffs
Public administration	33	53	——
Political science	23	27	6
Law	3	7	59
Economics	7	7	6
Journalism	——	——	12
Business administration	3	7	6
Miscellaneous	17	——	6
Unspecified	13	——	6
	99	101	101
	(n = 30)	(n = 15)	(n = 17)

with a propensity to adopt a client-counsel attitude in his relationship with the legislators, equipped her to be a generalist, facilitated learning parliamentary procedures, and was useful in handling casework and other kinds of legislative oversight duties involving technical points of law. It was their view that being of the same profession and knowing the vocabulary and mind-set of legal practicioners is an asset in dealing with the many lawyer-legislators.

In fact, several leadership staff members expressed a feeling of inadequacy because of a lack of legal training. One said that he had decided on his present work as a permanent career and was, therefore, taking a leave of absence to attend law school. He stated, "The [law] degree gives you not only the technical training and background, but it confers a certain status in the legislature." This opinion of the value of a legal education was not shared by members of the other staffs surveyed. Only ten percent of the staff members of the finance committees and twelve percent of the members of Central Staff interviewed mentioned a legal background as being helpful in the performance of their work. This may be due to the fact that, as Alan Hevesi has noted, the character and recruitment of the staff of an individual legislator or a legislative leader bear, to a large extent, the imprint of the personality and background of the leader himself.[27] The fact that three of the four legislative leaders in the 1971-1972 sessions were lawyers seems to be a major factor in the recruitment of the members of their staffs. The only non-lawyer in the leadership group (the speaker of the Assembly) had fewer lawyers on his staff than any of the others. While the evidence is weak, it does point in the direction of the legislator's previous background influencing staff recruitment and background.

In terms of previous political or governmental experience, twenty-five of the professional staff members surveyed had been employed in the executive branch of the state government; nineteen in the same general field as their legislative work. Fifteen had had prior legislative staff experience. Four had had experience as federal or local government employees. Two had been newspapermen. Nine had been (or still were) practicing lawyers. Three had held responsible positions in private business concerns. One had taught in college, and one in high school. This information is presented by type of staff in Table 3.

Previous legislative staff experience and prior employment in the executive branch were viewed by senior staffers in charge of recruiting and staffing as being very valuable to a legislative aide. Previous legislative staff experience familiarized an individual with the unique environment of the legislature and helped him or her to gain an appreciation of the political factors that members of the legislature have to take into account in performing their work

TABLE 3
EXPERIENTIAL BACKGROUD OF STAFF MEMBERS,
BY TYPE OF STAFF
(in percentages)

Education	Finance Committees' Staffs	Central Staff	Leadership Staffs
Executive branch	43	53	23
Legislature	33	20	12
Federal or local government	7	7	6
Newspapers	---	---	12
Law offices	7	7	35
Student	7	13	6
Miscellaneous	3	---	6
	100	100	100
	(n = 30)	(n = 15)	(n = 17)

and to learn the other items included in the term "political savvy." Prior employment in the executive branch often had been a primary source of the aide's substantive knowledge of his specialty on the legislative staff. Also, from such experience, a legislative staff member gained an understanding of how the administrative agencies operate, a knowledge of where and how to obtain most readily various kinds of services, and usually a network of personal acquaintances that made securing such assistance easier.

Again, the emphasis on a legal background for the members of the leadership staffs revealed itself. Where seventy-six percent of the finance committees' staffers and seventy-three percent of the members of Central Staff had experience in the legislature or in the executive branch before assuming their current position, only thirty-five percent of the leadership staffers had held such positions. An equal number (thirty-five percent) came directly from law offices to the legislative staff. In each case, they were a member of the leader's law firm, an associate from the home district, a friend from law school, and some similar relationships. They had usually worked with the legislator they served in his first campaign for office and had joined the staff upon his election. Because of these early campaign ties, the work of these staffers often had some overtly political content, and they usually continued to be involved in elections.

The legislative recruitment process in the United States tends to select the middle-aged—men in their forties and fifties—for careers as legislators.[28] A comparison with the age range of the members of the staff surveyed is instructive (see Table 4).

TABLE 4
AGE OF NEW YORK STATE LEGISLATORS AND STAFF MEMBERS
(in percentages)

Age	Legislators	Staffers
21-29	2	21
30-34	10	24
35-39	14	16
40-44	24	8
45-49	20	10
50-54	15	13
55-59	9	8
60-69	6	––
	100	100
	(n = 104)	(n = 62)

SOURCE: Robert Jennings and Michael Milstein, *Educational Policy Making in New York State with Emphasis on the Role of the State Legislature* (U.S. Department of Health, Education, and Welfare, Office of Education, Bureau of Research, 1970), Appendix B, p. 4.

The staffers seem to be quite a bit younger than the legislators they serve. There are also differences within the three types of staff. The mean average age for members of the staff of the Ways and Means Committee is thirty-one; for those serving the Senate Finance Committee, it is forty-one; for Central Staff, thirty-six; and for the leadership staffs, forty-six.

The hoary adage has been that politics is a man's game. While male domination continues to be the rule in the legislature, women are making inroads in certain of the legislative staffs. The Ways and Means Committee and the leadership staffs continue to be bastions of male hegemony, with no women employed at the professional level during the period covered in this study. Two women were serving as budget analysts with the Senate Finance Committee, one with the Democrats and one with the Republicans. On Central Staff, however, six of the fifteen researchers were women. Both the director and assistant director of Central Staff were women.

Professional staff members as a group are well paid. The salaries of the staffers interviewed ranged from $9,540 for a beginning research assistant with Central Staff to $38,850 for the secretary of the Ways and Means Committee. The mean average salary for members of Central Staff was $17,000; for those working for the Ways and Means Committee it was $21,117; for Senate Finance, $22,719; and for the leadership staffs, $27,432.

Because many of the professional staffs of the New York State Legislature are relatively new, it is difficult to determine whether a career pattern exists for professional staffers. However, there seems to be developing an increasing desire to make work with the legislature a career. Of the fifty-seven aides who responded to a question concerning their future plans, thirty-four stated that they would like to stay on in legislative staff work. There were marked differences among the three types of staffs in their career aspirations (see Table 5).

TABLE 5
CAREER ASPIRATIONS OF STAFF MEMBERS BY TYPE OF STAFF
(in percentages)

Career Aspirations	Finance Committees' Staffs	Central Staff	Leadership Staffs
Legislative staff	70	67	18
Executive branch	17	20	6
Private research firm	––	7	––
Interest group	7	7	12
Career identified with legislator	––	––	47
Not responding	7	––	18
	101	101	101
	(n = 30)	(n = 15)	(n = 17)

The members of the finance committees' staffs and Central Staff were the most oriented toward a legislative career, as the figures in Table 5 indicate. As we noted earlier, many of the professional staff members had been employed in the executive branch or in private research groups in the same general field as their legislative work. Often they expressed a desire to move back to the administrative establishment after leaving the legislature.

Among those individuals serving the leadership, the staff members identified their careers with those of the legislators they were working for. "Who you know" rather than "what you know" was more important in their original decision to join the legislative staff. Among those staff members interviewed, all except one knew the legislators they were working for in some capacity before they were hired. They knew him as a friend, a college classmate, a business associate, a law partner, or in some similar capacity. He was their "sponsor" when they initially came to Albany, and it is around him that their careers are oriented. They view their service in Albany, not as a possible career, but as a temporary interruption in some other career.

Party also seems to be a definite factor in staff career plans. Of the twelve Democratic aides responding, only two expressed any interest in staying on with the legislature. As one of these staffers put it, "Some people make their career staying with the Legislature, but more of these people are Republicans than they are Democrats. I think most of us want to move on because Democratic control of the legislature is such an infrequent thing."

In fact, because of the long Republican control of the legislature, an element of doubt pervaded the future plans of a number of those staff members interviewed. The feeling was expressed by one aide in this way:

> I can see this as a career position if things go on as they are. The head of our staff has assured us that it would be a nonpartisan staff, never asking in an interview what party anyone belonged to. The senior people here view it as a potential career. I say potential because we have · an unknown situation—what happens when the Democrats take over. We have no guarantees, but we expect, or at least hope, that if party control changed we'd be kept on.

There seem to be important differences in educational and experiential background, career aspirations, age, sex, and salary among the three types of staffs under examination. The average member of the finance committees' staffs is a male with an M.A. in public administration or political science and prior governmental experience in the executive branch or with the legislature. He is thirty-six years old, makes approximately $22,000 a year, and wants to make his career in legislative staff work.

The average member of Central Staff also is an M.A. in political science or public administration with prior executive or legislative experience. Either a man or a woman, (s)he is thirty-six years old, makes approximately $17,000 a year, and would like to make work with the legislature a career.

The average member of the leadership staff is a man with an LL.B. and little or no previous governmental experience. He came to Albany to work with one of the leaders after having known him personally earlier. He identifies his legislative staff career with that of the legislator he is working for and views it as a temporary interruption in some other career. He is forty-six years old and makes about $27,400 a year.

What differences, if any, do these differences make in the way in which the staffer perceives his role, its satisfactions and limitations? It is to a discussion of this that we now turn.

NORMS AND CONSTRAINTS

Donald Matthews, in his description of the "folkways" of the U.S. Senate, stated that every group of human beings has "its unwritten rules of the game, its norms of conduct, its approved manner of behavior."[29] Legislators and staff members in New York State were asked, "Would you say there are unofficial norms, rules, expectations among members of the staff, i.e., certain things staff members must do and things they must not do if they want the respect and cooperation of legislators and fellow staff members?" If the response was affirmative, they were also asked, "What are some of these 'rules

TABLE 6
"RULES OF THE GAME" PERCEIVED BY TYPES OF STAFF AND LEGISLATORS
(percentage of respondents naming rule)

Rules of the Game	Finance Committees' Staffs (n = 30)	Central Staff (n = 15)	Leadership Staffs (n = 17)	Legislators (n = 46)
1. Legislative norms	83	100	73	52
2. Limited advocacy	77	80	40	30
3. Loyalty	83	60	100	91
4. Deference	73	73	47	26
5. Anonymity	47	47	20	19
6. Specialization	97	100	53	11
7. Partisanship	43	33	100	13
8. Apprenticeship	50	30	7	9
9. Institutional patriotism	30	33	7	7
10. Legislative work	70	60	7	39

NOTE: Percentages total more than 100 since most respondents named more than one rule.

of the game' that a staff member must observe?" Every legislator and every staff member responding to the questions (eighty-eight percent and ninety-seven percent of those interviewed, respectively) said there were unwritten rules of the game that governed a staffer's behavior. The staff norms identified were: legislative norms; limited advocacy; loyalty; deference; anonymity; specialization; partisanship; apprenticeship; institutional patriotism; and legislative work.[30] The frequency with which each rule was mentioned by members of each of the three types of staffs and by legislators is indicated in Table 6.

Legislative Norms

Legislative staffers tend to adopt the norms and orientations of the members of the committees (or the leaders) for whom they work. Thus, staff members of the Assembly Ways and Means Committee and the Senate Finance Committee tend to accept the budget-cutting orientations of the committees. Since the normative integration of committees varies fairly widely, accepted goal orientations on the part of committee staffs also vary. Two of the general legislative norms which staff members seem to feel are most relevant are courtesy[31] and reciprocity.[32]

A cardinal rule of legislative behavior is that political disagreements should not influence personal feelings. Personal attacks, unnecessary unpleasantness, and such are all thought to be self-defeating. Reciprocity is also pervasive in the legislative system. While legislators are trading votes, staff members are trading information, favors, and expert insight.

Limited Advocacy

The staff norm of limited advocacy implies that the staff member will not press his or her own policy too far; that he should be sensitive to limitations on the presentation if his own conclusions and proposals.

Loyalty

The norm of loyalty is a crucial one, and the sanctions for violations of this norm are likely to be immediate and fatal. It was the norm mentioned most frequently by the legislators interviewed. The chairman (or the leader) is the major figure in the staff member's employment relationship, in promotion and continued tenure. In a variety of ways, staff members interviewed reflected their loyalty to the chairman (or the leader).[33] There were marked differences among the three types of staff both in the frequency with which they mentioned this norm and in the object of their loyalty. Every member of the leadership staffs interviewed mentioned loyalty as one of the "rules of the game" for staffers. Moreover, their loyalty is to the boss and they identify with his career. They use their expertise and experience not as part of a "profession" or a "career," but for "the boss." If he moves (is elected to the upper house or to Congress), they will go with him. If he stays in the legislature, they will stay with him. If he is defeated, their legislative careers will also end and they will return to the law firm, business, etc., from whence they came. Not only did these staffers mention loyalty as a norm more frequently than other staff members surveyed, but it was almost invariably the first norm they mentioned[34] —providing, in some way, a crude indication of its importance. A Senate staff man said, "It's hard to distinguish between what the Senator thinks and what I think. My job is to enhance the position of the Senator."

The object of other staffers' loyalty varied—the head of the committee, "the committee," the speaker, or "the legislature."

Deference

The norm of deference to legislators is very strong, and is often reflected in comments by staff members that the staff "should be on tap, not on top," that "the staff shouldn't be bigger than the Senator they serve."

Anonymity

The norm of anonymity is also strong, and probably more difficult for staff members to live with. The norm was expressed by one aide this way: "The job of the staff is to help the legislators do their jobs better. They make the decisions. We're the anonymous assistants. They're supposed to get all the glory." This behavior makes possible closer relationships with the legislators they serve.

Specialization

Committee staff people and members of Central Staff are expected to specialize and develop a subject-matter expertise. The confidence which committee members have in the staff is dependent upon their demonstrated expertise. Only through specialization can the staff member come to know more about a subject than the legislators or other staff aides—and thus make a positive contribution to the operation of the chamber.

Among members of the leadership staffs, specialization is a less important norm than among the other staffers surveyed. Only fifty-three percent of those interviewed mentioned it as a norm, compared to ninety-seven percent of the members of the finance committees' staffs and all the members of Central Staff. Leadership staff members stated that attempts have been made to develop generality and interchangeability of staff competence. The senior staffers often have sought to rotate the staff "so that a back-up man will always be available." Moreover, those serving on leadership staffs, as we pointed out earlier, often were hired less on the basis of "what they knew" and what their background and expertise were than because of "who they knew." Subject area specialization, then, seems less important for members of the leadership staffs.

Partisanship

An extremely powerful norm among the leadership staffers was partisanship. Every member of the leadership staffs interviewed mentioned this as a norm of behavior. Moreover, four of the fifteen questioned mentioned partisanship first as one of the "rules of the game," and the others mentioned it second. Legislative leaders sought staff personnel whose party affiliation coincided with their own, and this type of agreement was universally viewed as essential by legislative leaders and staff members.

Forty-three percent of the members of the finance committees' staffs, and thirty-three percent of the members of Central Staff also mentioned partisanship as a behavioral norm. Most went on, however, to stress that what they meant by "partisanship" was not political partisanship, but rather partisanship in the broad sense that a sympathetic political philosophy is sought in staff members regardless of party affiliation.[35] Some of the staff members serving the Republican majority were, in fact, Democrats.

Apprenticeship

Legislators are usually expected to serve an apprenticeship.[36] It seems that most staff members feel that other staff members need not serve an apprentice period. Only one member of the leadership staffs and three members of Central Staff mentioned this as a norm. Among members of the finance committees' staffs, half of those interviewed felt that new members of the staff were expected to serve a proper apprenticeship period.

Institutional Patriotism

About a third of the members of Central Staff and the finance committees' staffs felt that, at least most of the time, they should defend the legislature and members against outsiders and that they should not do anything to reflect on the legislature as a body. Only one member of the leadership staff mentioned institutional patriotism as a norm. Again, the majority of leadership staffers see their first loyalty as being to "the boss." Given such an individual devotion, there is little room for any loyalty to the legislature as a whole.

Legislative Work

Staff members are expected to devote a share of their time, energy, and thought to what are sometimes characterized as highly detailed, dull, and unrewarding tasks. As Table 6 indicated, legislative work is seen as one of the most important rules of the game by the members of the legislature. Yet, only one member of the leadership staffs mentioned this as a norm. Again, this may be due to the manner of their recruitment and their reasons for staying (or alternatively, the reasons for their being kept on).

Summary

Normative rules of conduct are seen to exist by staff members in the New York State Legislature. Marked differences in emphasis exist, however, between staff members serving on different staffs and between staffers and legislators.[37] Table 7 lists the difference in relative emphasis upon the various rules between members of the three staffs and legislators.

Thus, while all staffers and a majority of legislators adhere to various general legislative norms, differences exist in degree of emphasis on other

TABLE 7
DIFFERENCES IN EMPHASIS ON VARIOUS RULES OF THE GAME BETWEEN LEGISLATORS AND STAFF (percentage change)

| Rule | Difference Between Proportion Naming Rule Among Legislators and Proportion Naming It in: | | |
	Leadership Staffs	Central Staff	Finance Committees' Staffs
Legislative norms	+21	+48	+31
Limited advocacy	+10	+50	+47
Loyalty	+ 9	−31	− 8
Deference	+21	+47	+47
Anonymity	+ 1	+28	+28
Specialization	+42	+89	+86
Partisanship	+87	+20	+30
Apprenticeship	− 2	+11	+41
Institutional patriotism	0	+26	+23
Legislative work	−32	+21	+31

rules of the game. Members of the finance committees' staffs emphasized specialization, loyalty, limited advocacy, and deference. Central Staff members stressed specialization, limited advocacy, and deference, while members of the leadership staffs mentioned most loyalty and partisanship as rules of the game. Legislators viewed loyalty and legislative work as the most important norms of behavior. In most cases, the members of the leadership staffs were closer to the members in their perceptions of the norms of behavior than they were to their fellows on Central Staff or the committees. Only in the area of legislative work, where they downplayed it as a norm, and in the case of partisanship, where they emphasized it much more than even the members, were there noticeable differences. The reasons for the existing differences have been suggested in the text where it was deemed appropriate and where enough information existed to do so.

While direct inferences from knowledge about staffers' educational and experiential background, career aspirations, norms, and so on, to their actions and behavior would certainly be simplistic, knowing something about the composition of these staffs helps us to understand the recruitment of legislative staff aides in our political system and to map the structure of the legislative careers of professional staffers. An important area is the vital functions that staff members perform for the legislative system. It is to an examination of these that we now turn to determine whether background characteristics of staff members have any bearing upon staff behavior.

THE FUNCTIONS OF THE STAFF[38]

Intelligence

One of the visible capabilities of the staff involves the intelligence function of the legislature. The whole legislative procedure "is built around the process of acquiring information and intelligence with respect to particular conditions and situations, and the application of that information to the fashioning of laws."[39] Information provides the premises for decision or action. By one definition, decision-making is simply "the process of converting information into action." Information—intelligence, news, facts, data—is essential to all phases of the process. It is a common assumption that "bad" or "wrong" decisions in politics as in business stem from insufficient or improperly processed information,[40] and increased legislative staffs are often justified on the basis of providing more complete and more accurate information.[41]

Research on Congress has found that the legislative staff is a major source of information,[42] and recent research on the New York State Legislature resulted in similar findings.[43] Staffers are "facts-and-figures" men, and

they spend a great deal of their working time engaged in processing information and supplying it to legislators (see Table 8).

Staffs investigate, research, schedule, edit, compile, and distribute much of
the information on which legislative decisions are based. The staff network, in
fact, is the only organization with sole responsibility for directing and
filtering the flow of information to the legislature.

TABLE 8
INTELLIGENCE FUNCTION PERCEIVED BY
LEGISLATIVE STAFF MEMBERS
(in percentages)

Activity	Proportion of Staffers Naming Each Activity in		
	Finance Committees' Staffs (n = 30)	Central Staff (n = 15)	Leadership Staffs (n = 17)
Planning and conducting hearings: selecting witnesses; notifying interested groups and executive agencies; setting room and time; balancing witnesses; preparing questions; briefing legislators; writing summaries.	80	80	47
Bill-drafting: drafting bills; drafting amendments; preparing memoranda to accompany bills; writing committee reports.	73	100	88
Participation in executive sessions: attending executive sessions to explain bill or report; drafting amendments; marking up bill; discussing technical provisions; pointing up policy questions; keeping track of decisions.	97	67	88
Preparing for and assisting during floor action: drafting bill manager's opening statement; preparing memoranda to use on floor; sitting with legislator to aid him; aiding other legislators.	83	40	47
Oversight of administration: conferring with top departmental officials; investigating; handling casework; examining agency reports; reviewing administrative actions and changes in advance.	43	87	24

NOTE: Percentages total more than 100 since most respondents named more than one
activity.

Integration[44]

Legislative staffs contribute to the integration of committees, they contribute to intercameral integration, and they contribute to legislative-executive integration. Staff members interact with other participants in the political subsystem—members of the governor's staff, executive agency staffers, budget personnel, interest group representatives, other staffers in the same chamber and in the other house, rank-and-file legislators, and the legislative leadership (see Table 9). These relationships provide much of the cement that holds the legislature together and binds the legislative and executive branches together. This network of staff interactions helps to establish lines of communication to and from the legislature through which staff members can obtain information and oversee administrative action. Personal friendships, previous work relationships, and membership in the same professional organizations are crucial elements in this network.

TABLE 9
CONTACTS NAMED BY STAFFERS (in percentages)

	Proportion of Staffers Naming Each Contact in		
Contacts	Finance Committees' Staffs (n = 30)	Central Staff (n = 15)	Leadership Staffs (n = 17)
Governor's staff	23	67	82
Executive agency staffs	90	100	30
Division of the budget	57	7	——
Interest groups	70	60	35
Staff counterparts in other chamber	67	33	24
Staff of other committees in same chamber	33	47	35
Rank-and-file	7	27	30
Leadership	17	13	82
Miscellaneous (OLR, Legislative Reference, Bill Drafting Commission)	7	7	6

NOTE: Percentages total more than 100 since most respondents named more than one contact.

Innovation

Legislative staff members see themselves as having innovative capabilities (see Table 10). One of the reasons members of the legislative staff like their work is that they have the opportunity to innovate, to initiate public policy, or to see it initiated.

TABLE 10
PROPORTION OF STAFFERS NAMING
INNOVATION OR INITIATION AS FUNCTIONS

Staff	Percentage of Staffers Naming Functions
Finance committees (n = 30)	53
Central Staff (n = 15)	67
Leadership staffs (n = 17)	29

Innovation and initiation are somewhat slippery concepts to be sure, but a number of staff people and legislators described projects which the staff was undertaking at their own initiative, and many staffers described legislation on which they themselves were working. Staff members, especially those with long tenure in key staff positions, are about as likely to initiate legislation as are legislators themselves.[45]

Influence

Staff members see themselves as important participants in the legislative process and are seen as being influential by legislators, lobbyists, and members of the executive branch (see Table 11). There were, however, differences among the staffs in terms of their perceptions of their own importance (see Table 12).

Moreover, among the staffers interviewed, there were differences in the reasons given for their influence (see Table 13).

TABLE 11
VIEWS OF LEGISLATIVE STAFF INFLUENCE

Group	Percentage Viewing Legislative Staff as		
	Very Influential	Influential	Not Influential
Legislators (n = 51)	44	52	4
Executive personnel (n = 20)	55	40	5
Lobbyists (n = 10)	20	70	10
Staffers (n = 62)	27	64	8

TABLE 12
VIEWS OF LEGISLATIVE STAFF INFLUENCE, BY TYPE OF STAFF

Group	Percentage Viewing Legislative Staff as		
	Very Influential	Influential	Not Influential
Finance committees (n = 30)	27	63	10
Central Staff (n = 15)	20	67	13
Leadership Staffs (n = 17)	35	65	——

TABLE 13
REASONS GIVEN FOR STAFF INFLUENCE BY TYPE OF STAFF
(in percentages)

Responses	Finance Committees' Staffs	Central Staff	Leadership Staffs
Knowledge of field (expertise)	67	87	29
Tenure with legislature	10	7	35
Personal abilities	27	33	12
Specialization	63	87	35
Heavy burden on legislators	37	47	76
Information filter	60	73	24
Other	7	13	6

NOTE: Percentages total more than 100 since most respondents named more than one reason.

Summary

As was the case in the backgrounds and the perceived behavioral norms of the three types of staffs under examination, there were differences in the way in which staff members perceived their functions. Members of the finance committees' staffs viewed themselves as performing an important intelligence function for the legislature, though both staffs remained dependent on sources of information in the executive branch and the private sector. Staff members stated that they spent a considerable amount of time planning and conducting committee hearings, participating in executive sessions, preparing for and assisting during floor action, and in bill-drafting. Staffers also engaged in oversight of administrative agencies, although only forty-three percent of the staff members interviewed noted this as a part of their function.

The staffers serving the finance committees were frequently in contact with executive agency staffers, especially people in the Division of the Budget, interest group representatives, and each other. As we noted earlier, legislative staffs are widely recruited from among executive branch employees, and occasionally legislative staff people are appointed to major administrative positions. Such an intertwining of people is very marked between the Division of the Budget and the finance committees. When the legislature was not in session, members of the staffs of Ways and Means and the Senate Finance Committee often combined their trips to the field to study agency operations. Few stated that they had contact with members of the governor's staff, staffers serving other committees in their chamber, the leadership, or rank-and-file legislators.

While spending a great amount of time processing proposals that came from outside the legislature and drafting bills and amendments at the request of various legislators, staff members of the finance committees also felt that they had a role in initiating legislative proposals of their own. This orientation was accepted by more members of the Ways and Means Committee staff (sixty-two percent of those interviewed) than by those serving the Senate Finance Committee (forty-three percent of those interviewed). Members of the Ways and Means staff particularly saw themselves as committed to a continual "search" for policy gaps and opportunities and actively involved in initiating and innovating legislation. They seemed to approach issues with the idea of exposing the practices of some groups and stimulating the interest of others, pointing up executive inertia, formulating legislative remedies, and stimulating legislative activity.[46] One of the members of the Ways and Means Committee staff discussed the innovative function of the staff in these terms:

> Oh, there's always been this talk about staff being "on tap, not on top" and "staff only advises, it doesn't decide," etc. But that's not our role here. We're not here like some encyclopedia that one has on hand and refers to occasionally. We're not just fact gatherers. We see it as part of our job to present alternatives to the legislator, to lay out things before him that he might want to do, to remind him sometimes of past promises and what he stands for, and, sometimes, to convince him of the worth of particular objects. That doesn't mean that we tell him what to do or that he's some kind of robot, with us in control. But a good staffer can point out executive inertia, formulate legislative remedies, and stimulate legislative activity.

Finally, members of the finance committees' staffs saw themselves as influential figures in the legislative process and emphasized expertise, specialization, and the staff's role as a filter of information to the legislature in explaining staff influence. These staff members also seemed willing to use their positions and influence to implement their own policy preferences and to let political considerations determine the role they assumed.

Members of Assembly Central Staff also viewed themselves as performing an intelligence function for the legislature. The staffers interviewed mentioned bill-drafting (one hundred percent of the sample), oversight of administration (eighty-seven percent), and participation in executive sessions (sixty-seven percent) as prime functions. Staffers also aided assembly members by preparing for and assisting during floor action, though fewer of those interviewed (forty percent) mentioned this as a part of their work. Members of Central Staff, then, were more involved in bill-drafting and administrative oversight than those staffers serving the finance committees, and less involved in executive sessions and actions on the floor.

As was the case with members of the finance committees' staffs, members of Central Staff were frequently in contact with executive agency staffers (though not as often with budget officials) and with interest group representatives. They were in communication with members of the governor's staff, the rank-and-file legislators, and other staffers in their chamber more often than the finance committees' aides and had about the same amount of contact with the legislative leaders. Those staffers serving the finance committees were more often in touch with their counterparts in the other chamber than were the members of Central Staff.

Members of Central Staff did share an innovative orientation with the finance committees' staffers, but there seemed to be a significant difference in emphasis. Innovation or initiation for members of Central Staff did not mean the staff originating a legislative proposal as often as it meant helping an assemblyman work out a legislative idea or helping him amend, or in some way modify, a proposal emanating from the executive branch or an interest group. As one member of Central Staff put it:

> It's not part of our job here to sit around thinking up pieces of legislation and then to go to the assemblymen and tell them, "I think this is a good idea. I drew up this bill and I think you ought to introduce it." Sometimes, when you're examining a bill, you may find a problem in it, or a defect, and, in that case, we'd say, "You have a problem here and this is a way to take care of it," but whether the assemblyman does it or not is up to him. Sometimes if an assemblyman comes up with an idea for a bill, but it's just in a seminal stage, we'll work with him on it to make it a developed piece of legislation. But the idea comes from the legislator. We react to his ideas and suggestions.

A look at one of the legislative ideas that could claim Central Staff parentage points up the staff's role further and reveals the manner in which "professionalism" is linked to a role free of advocacy. In 1970, then-Assemblyman John Terry (Rep.–Syracuse) began to develop a bill that would guarantee the public's right to scrutinize records of nearly all state and local governmental agencies. Terry dropped the so-called "Freedom of Information Bill" when he was elected to Congress later that year. Central Staff continued to refine the measure and, in 1972, its sponsorship was taken over by

Assemblyman Donald L. Taylor (Rep.—Watertown) and Senator Ralph J. Marino (Rep.—Long Island). The member of Central Staff who worked on the measure described his role:

> The "Freedom of Information Bill" wasn't a matter of the staff going to Terry and setting him on to the idea. I worked on the bill, but it was at Terry's direction. Our job here isn't to go around manipulating legislators like a bunch of puppets. We react to legislators' wishes, sentiments, etc. We don't get involved in politics, in working on matters from the district, etc. We're here to serve all the members of the Assembly, and if you start feeding ideas to one assemblyman or another, you get away from the ideal of being nonpartisan. It might get you into trouble.

Legislatively initiated projects like the "Freedom of Information Bill" displayed Central Staff ingenuity and revealed the importance of their skills to those assembly members who sought to initiate legislation, but the staff could rarely be credited with the instigation of legislation.[47]

Members of Central Staff also saw themselves as having influence in the legislature, but were quite frequently self-effacing in describing their importance and anxious to deny that they "took sides" on legislative issues. They attributed their influence to their knowledge of the field, specialization, and their role as a filter of information to the legislature.

Members of the leadership staffs often participated in executive sessions (often in the capacity of the leader's representative at committee meetings) and drafted legislation, according to their responses in the interviews. They engaged in work on legislative hearings, action on the floor, and administrative oversight less frequently than the other staffers surveyed. Their main contacts were with the governor's staff and the leadership, often meeting with members of the governor's staff prior to meetings between the legislative leaders and the governor to identify areas of real agreement and disagreement. More often, the principals themselves did not actually meet, but rather the differences were resolved by the relevant staff personnel. They had slightly more contact with the legislative members themselves than did members of Central Staff, and substantially more than the finance committees' staffers. In fact, a number of leadership staff members saw their role as serving as "buffers" for the leaders, performing some of the more unpopular tasks and "taking the heat" from the rank-and-file for unpopular decisions, strategic errors, and so on. They functioned as a channel of dissent from members who were reluctant to bring their complaints to their leaders personally. They served as the "eyes and ears" of the leaders, informing them of the mood of the rank-and-file members, letting them know when things were going smoothly or when storms were brewing among the rank and file, and advising them as to who needed attention and encouragement to back the party's position.

While the leadership staff members interviewed did not seem to play much of a role in initiating legislation (only twenty-nine percent of those interviewed saw this as part of their function), they did view themselves as having influence. In fact, they were more likely to see themselves as "very influential" and less likely to see themselves as having "no influence" than either of the other staffs examined. They noted the increasingly heavy load on legislators as a factor in staff influence. A staff member serving an Assembly leader stated:

> Legislators would be hopelessly bogged down in detail and trivia without staff to relieve them of the routine tasks given them by constituents, other legislators, the governor, etc.

> The assemblyman can only deal with bills with major implications statewide or those that directly impact his district. We're his extra hands, arms, legs, etc. to deal with the other 10,000 or so bills that are introduced each year.

Interest group representatives in New York go where power is, or where they think power is, and the leadership staff is not shortchanged when it comes to contacts with lobbyists. As a lobbyist pointed out:

> A lot of lobbyists would rather talk to the staff than try to get in to see the leaders themselves. Staff members are more accessible than the leaders. They're going to be gathering the information anyway, so why not talk to them at the beginning. They're more expert in the subject matter, therefore they're more likely to understand your argument. And besides, the leaders and their staff people are so intertwined that talking to a staffer is just like talking to the legislator.

This, of course, raises the problem that large and efficient staffs may be a mixed blessing. Critics of large legislative staffs fear that they may develop into independent power centers in the legislative process. They may develop cozy relationships with legislators, agency personnel, and interest group representatives that are difficult for both the executive and the legislature to control. As a Republican assemblyman said, there is an "inevitable tendency of all busy persons to get rid of routine tasks which they think staff assistants will be competent to perform. Sometimes it turns out that the tasks are not routine at all but are in fact policy determining." It is this fact that alarmed an assistant budget director:

> Certain staff members have become too influential. Last year, when we were discussing the tax program for New York City, we were dealing with [a Ways and Means staffer] and [an aide to the Senate Majority

Leader]. They were acting as if they had a personal stake in the thing. They represent themselves as just staff of their bosses, the legislative leaders. But they were dealing on their own; their own views were very much evident. I think the legislators are assuming a certain neutrality as the legislative leaders should have the facts presented to them. The legislators are being manipulated by the staff. Some of the staff members are acting like they're legislators.

SUMMARY AND CONCLUSIONS

The members of the three types of staffs examined—the leadership staffs, the finance committees' staffs, and the Central Staff serving the entire chamber—differ in several important ways. They differ in their background, their career aspirations, their norms of behavior, and their perceived functions. While these findings are based on the *perceptions* of legislative staff members, they do lend weight to the hypothesis that different types of staff may have different types of effects. Further weight is provided by the recent finding of Alan Rosenthal in Wisconsin.[48]

While the evidence is sketchy and somewhat impressionistic, it does seem that a particular staffing arrangement may result in some alteration in the balance of power in the legislature. Given the thrust of current reform efforts in the states, especially in creating "nonpartisan professional" staffs oriented toward service to the legislature rather than to individual legislators or standing committees, this fact merits further attention. It has not been unusual, as Meller noted years ago, for the advocates of staff augmentation to ignore the "distinctive natures of the expert staff with which they would equip the legislature, and correspondingly, to base their recommendation upon unexamined assumptions whose questionability goes far to undermine the advisability of staff expansion."[49] As we stated earlier, the probabilities of who gets what when and how should be considered before a legislature decides on one type of staff rather than another. Legislative staffers serving individual members, specialists serving standing committees, and political aides serving legislative leaders may have different effects. The first group may enhance the capability of individual legislators, the second may add to the strength of the committees, and the third may increase the power of the leadership.

For example, a number of legislators interviewed felt that increased leadership staffs had helped to solidify the position of the leaders. The staff publicized leadership positions and activities, giving them increased coverage in the press. They also served, as was noted earlier, as buffers to absorb pressures which the leadership wanted to avoid or divert. This was variously labeled in interviews as "taking the heat," "acting as fall guy," "getting him off the hook," and so on. Thus, increased leadership staffs were seen as tools to increase the leaders' influence over the legislature. Further research on this matter certainly is warranted.

As was argued earlier, state legislatures provide an ideal location to examine the effects of professional staffs. Unfortunately, many legislative scholars have ignored this rich area of research and, in addition, have deprived themselves of the lessons that could be learned and the benefits derived from an examination of the alternative paths the states have followed in managing and developing their new staff capabilities. It is recognized, of course, that Congress' requirements for staff systems and services differ from those of the state legislatures, just as the requirements vary from state to state. But the author would contend that further state legislative research could point up the benefits and limitations discovered in the use of professional staff by state legislatures. As Larry Margolis of the Citizens Conference on State Legislatures argued:

> Although there are similarities between State legislatures and Congress, there are many, many differences which make it difficult to apply the experience of one set of institutions to the other.
>
> We can, however, look to particular practices and forms of organization, in certain legislatures, or to the beginnings of trends which are developing in the State legislatures which may have application to the Congress.[50]

Much more, obviously, remains to be done.

NOTES

1. See Alan Rosenthal, "Contemporary Research on State Legislatures: From Individual Cases to Comparative Analysis," in American Political Science Association, *Political Science and State and Local Government* (Washington, D.C.: The Association, 1973), pp. 55-85.

2. Ibid., p. 55.

3. Malcolm E. Jewell and Samuel C. Patterson, *The Legislative Process in the United States* (New York: Random House, 1973), p. 250.

4. Ibid., p. 251.

5. Norman Meller, "Legislative Staff Services: Toxin, Specific, or Placebo for the Legislature's Ills," *Western Political Quarterly*, Vol. 20 (June 1967), p. 383.

6. Ibid.

7. This is based on an analysis of information presented in the Book of the States Series in their review of legislative modernization efforts. Volumes from 1963 through 1973 were reviewed to determine what agencies were created, who they were intended to serve, how staff members were chosen, whether they were to be partisan or nonparti-

san, and so on. While admittedly a crude index, the direction of current reforms in state legislatures seems clear.

8. See the Council of State Governments, *The Book of the States* (Chicago, Ill., and Lexington, Ky.: The Council), Vols. 9-19.

9. Citizens Conference on State Legislatures, "Legislatures Move To Improve Their Effectiveness," Research Memorandum No. 15 (Kansas City: The Conference, April 1972).

10. Ibid.

11. Karl T. Kurtz, "The State Legislatures," in *The Book of the States* (Lexington, Ky.: The Council of State Governments, 1974).

12. These findings represent a summary of the efforts reported by Kurtz, ibid., and the Citizens Conference on State Legislatures, "Legislatures Move To Improve Their Effectiveness," p. 10.

13. New York was the first state to establish such an agency with the creation in 1969 of the Joint Legislative Commission on Expenditure Review.

14. Kurtz, "The State Legislatures."

15. See Meller, "Legislative Staff Services," pp. 381-389.

16. Ibid., p. 388.

17. Earl W. Brydges, "New Frontiers in Legislative Staffing," *State Government,* Vol. 39 (Autumn, 1966), p. 227.

18. See Alan Rosenthal, "The Consequences of Legislative Staffing," in Donald Herzberg and Alan Rosenthal, eds., *Strengthening the States: Essays on Legislative Reform* (Garden City, N.Y.: Doubleday Anchor, 1971), pp. 75-88.

19. George C. Littke, "The Role of the Joint Legislative Committee in the New York State Legislative System" (unpublished Ph.D. dissertation, New York University, 1970), p. 33.

20. A recent step to professionalize the work of the New York State Assembly standing committees was the creation in 1969 of a Central Staff Office. While recognizing that four of the twenty-one committees (Rules, Ways and Means, Judiciary, and Codes) handled, on the average, some seventy percent of the Assembly bills, the leadership concluded that the other legislative committees needed better staff services. The Central Staff idea created teams of two research experts to be assigned to three related committees. Eighteen of the twenty-one standing committees were served by Central Staff. Those excluded were the Ways and Means Committee, which had its own staff, the Rules Committee, which is controlled by the leadership and served by leadership staff, and the Ethics Committee. Under the direction of committee and subcommittee heads, this staff provided legislative analysis and research and set up and assisted in conducting hearings and meetings. The nonpartisan staff members were hired by the director, who was directly responsible to the speaker. The recent change in party control in the Assembly has made doubtful the survival of Central Staff in its current form, however.

21. For purposes of analysis, the staffs of the leaders (the speaker and minority leader of the Assembly and the majority and minority leaders of the Senate) are considered together.

22. See Joseph Picchi, "Cost of Legislators' Favors Soars," *Albany Times-Union,* February 20, 1972, p. B-2.

23. See Alan P. Balutis, "Professional Staffing in the New York State Legislature: An Exploratory Study" (unpublished Ph.D. dissertation, State University of New York at Albany, 1973). Unless otherwise indicated, quotations in the text are taken from this study.

24. Ralph K. Huitt, "Congress, the Durable Partner," in Ralph K. Huitt and Robert L. Peabody, *Congress: Two Decades of Analysis* (New York: Harper & Row, 1969), p. 226.

25. Ibid., pp. 226-227.

26. Some political scientists have suggested that there are too many lawyers and not enough social scientists on the professional staffs of legislatures. See, for example, Gladys Kammerer, "The Record of Congress in Committee Staffing," *American Political Science Review,* Vol. 45 (December 1951), esp. p. 1130. A number of senior legislative staffers in New York said that a conscious attempt had been made to bring in social scientists, economists, etc., to broaden the perspective of the legislature.

27. Alan G. Hevesi, "Legislative Leadership in New York State" (unpublished Ph.D. dissertation, Columbia University, 1971), p. 134. Donald Matthews suggests in his study of the U.S. Senate that "the way a senator staffs and organizes his office is a kind of political Rorschach test which, when studied with some care, tells a great deal about him as a man, what his problems and preoccupations are, and how he defines his role." See Donald R. Matthews, *U.S. Senators and Their World* (New York: Vintage Books, 1960), p. 83.

28. David Walker examined the hypothesis that "middle-agedness is part of the electorate's image of a Congressman" and found that the age of the candidate may be independently significant in the selection process. A similar phenomenon may occur at the state level. "The Age Factor in the 1958 Congressional Elections," *Midwest Journal of Political Science,* Vol. 4 (February 1960), pp. 1-26. See also Frank Sorauf, *Party and Representation* (New York: Atherton Press, 1963), p. 66.

29. Matthews, *U.S. Senators,* p. 92. For a further description of the concept of "norm," see George Homans, *The Human Group* (New York: Harcourt, Brace, 1950), pp. 123-124 and John Wahlke, Heinz Eulau, William Buchanan, and LeRoy Ferguson, *The Legislative System* (New York: John Wiley, 1962), esp. pp. 141-143.

30. For a more complete treatment of these norms, see Samuel C. Patterson, "Congressional Committee Professional Staffing: Capabilities and Constraints," in Allan Kornberg and Lloyd Musolf, eds., *Legislatures in Developmental Perspective* (Durham, N.C.: Duke University Press, 1970), esp. pp. 412-426.

31. The rules mentioned that defined this norm were respect for other staffers' rights, impersonality, self-restraint in discussions with other staff members, courtesy, advance notice of changed stance, restraint in opposition to other staffer's views, gracefulness in defeat, non-venality, and avoidance of trickery.

32. The rules mentioned that defined this norm were negotiation, willingness to cooperate, compromise, conciliation, willingness to share and exchange information.

33. The question staffers were asked if they mentioned loyalty as a norm was: "To whom or what does the staff member owe his first professional loyalty? The rest of the staff, the committee, the chairman (or leader), the party, or what?"

34. Of the fifteen members of the leadership staffs responding to this question, ten mentioned loyalty first in their listing of "rules of the game."

35. Ten of the thirteen finance committees' staffers and three of the five members of Central Staff went on to make this distinction.

36. See Matthews, *U.S. Senators,* pp. 92-94 and Malcolm C. Jewell and Samuel C. Patterson, *The Legislative Process in the United States* (New York: Random House, 1966), pp. 366-367 and p. 375.

37. It is significant that not a single respondent suggested the existence of conflicting sets of rules, each with its own set of respondents; nor did any respondent suggest any of the rules he named conflicted with other rules he named or rules which might be

mentioned by other staff members or by legislators. All seemed to accept the fact that rules of the game are the same rules for all staffers. The differences in proportions of staffers and legislators mentioning the various rules, therefore, can be interpreted not as indicating different degrees of legitimacy or acceptance of these rules but as possibly reflecting different degrees of emphasis on them.

38. The discussion will center around four staff capabilities—intelligence, integration, innovation, and influence—suggested by Samuel C. Patterson, "The Professional Staffs of Congressional Committees," *Administrative Science Quarterly,* Vol. 15 (March 1970), pp. 22-38. Although these functions overlap, each is of sufficient importance to warrant separate consideration.

39. H. Alexander Smith, "Information and Intelligence for Congress," *Annals of the American Academy of Political and Social Science,* Vol. 289 (September 1953), p. 114.

40. John S. Saloma, III, *Congress and the New Politics* (Boston: Little, Brown, 1969), p. 209.

41. For a further discussion of this point, see William J. Siffin, *The Legislative Council in the American States* (Bloomington: Indiana University Press, 1959), pp. 218-223.

42. See Lowell Hattery and Susan Hocheimer, "The Legislator's Source of Expert Information," *Public Opinion Quarterly,* Vol. 15 (Fall, 1954), pp. 300-303.

43. Robert E. Jennings and Michael Milstein, *Educational Policy Making in New York State with Emphasis on the Role of the Legislature* (U.S. Department of Health, Education, and Welfare, Office of Education, Bureau of Research), Appendix B, p. 92.

44. Integration is here defined as the degree to which there is a working together or meshing together of mutual support among legislative and executive subgroups.

45. See Robert Sherrill, "Who Runs Congress?" *New York Times Magazine,* November 22, 1970.

46. For an interesting discussion of staff orientations in Congress, see David E. Price, "Professionals and 'Entrepreneurs': Staff Orientations and Policy Making on Three Senate Committees," *Journal of Politics,* Vol. 33 (May 1971), pp. 316-336. The views expressed by Ways and Means staffers conform closely to Price's "policy entrepreneurs."

47. This is not to say that the particular innovative orientation of Central Staff was not a considerable legislative asset. It in fact enabled the Assembly to rewrite a number of bills introduced during the session and to get its concerns taken into account by the governor's staff and executive agencies at the formulation stage. And those assembly members who sought to initiate legislation found the skills of Central Staff indispensable to their efforts.

48. Alan Rosenthal, "Professional Staff and Legislative Influence in Wisconsin," in James A. Robinson, ed., *State Legislative Innovation* (New York: Praeger, 1973), pp. 183-225.

49. Meller, "Legislative Staff Services," p. 385.

50. Testimony of Larry Margolis before the Select Committee on Committees, U.S. Congress, House, *Panel Discussions Before the Select Committee on Committees,* 93rd Congress, 1st Session (Washington, D.C.: Government Printing Office, 1973), Vol. 2, part 2, p. 371.

CONGRESSIONAL STAFFS AND CONGRESSIONAL CHANGE

HARRISON W. FOX, JR.
and
SUSAN WEBB HAMMOND

Research on the U.S. Congress has recognized that the congressional structure is composed of various elements—leaders and followers, chairpeople, sub-committee heads, rank-and-file, and committee and personal staff.[1] One of these elements, congressional staffs, particularly personal office staffs of Senators and Representatives, will be the major focus of this chapter. We are concerned primarily with several aspects of congressional staffing—activities of individual staff aides, office organization patterns, and communication networks, describing and analyzing them in relation to several variables.[2] Various types of change in Congress are discussed, and some trends in staffing patterns identified. Overall, we are especially concerned with the impact of staff on the legislative process, and more broadly, on the congressional system, and with the interrelation of congressional change and congressional staffing.

How important are congressional staffs? Saloma, for example, says, "The issue of congressional staff is pertinent to all congressional functions."[3]

AUTHORS' NOTE: The authors wish to express their appreciation to the following persons for support and encouragement during our research and for valuable comments on earlier drafts of this paper: Carl Akins, the American University; Roger H. Davidson, University of California (Santa Barbara); Lewis A. Dexter, Fellow, Woodrow Wilson International Center for Scholars, Washington, D.C.; Bruce F. Norton, the American University; Robert L. Peabody, the Johns Hopkins University; and Morley Segal, the American University.

Evans argues that "of all the sources of power in Washington today, the most nearly invisible—yet in some ways the most influential—is the congressional staff. . . . A staff of professionals is no less essential to the care, feeding, and orderly operation of Congress than Merlin was to King Arthur or Cardinal Richelieu to Louis XIII."[4] Our data indicate that personal staffs perform important legislative and policy functions in addition to the constituent-related work widely acknowledged by congressional observers.

Generically, "congressional staff" subsumes a number of different kinds of staff. The General Accounting Office, the Congressional Research Service, committee staffs, and the personal staffs of Senators and members of the House, as well as other employees on Capitol Hill are all, technically, congressional staff. During July 1974, they totaled 36,619, at a monthly cost of $43 million for salaries (see Table 1).

Staffs function as important points of linkage between Congress and the outside environment, as well as between the congressional office and other groups or individuals of the congressional subsystem. At many points in the congressional policy process, the staffs exchange information. In some instances, staff itself is exchanged, as, for example, when a Congressional Research Service specialist is loaned to a Senate or House Committee. Staff assist the congressperson in all aspects of his or her work, from greeting constituents to researching emerging national issues.

Our research was conducted during the Ninety-Second Congress. The Senate research was based mainly on two questionnaires sent to all or subpopulations of professionals on the personal staff of Senators. In addition, semi-focused interviews were later conducted with a dozen of the respondents. Both questionnaires and interviews focused on office organization

TABLE 1
PERSONNEL EMPLOYED BY THE LEGISLATIVE BRANCH DURING JULY 1974, AND PAY FOR JUNE 1974[a]

	Personnel	Pay (in thousands)
Legislative branch:		
Congress:		
House of Representatives	10,400	11,709
Senate	5,673	6,733
Architect of capitol	1,931	1,922
Botanic garden	66	62
Cost Accounting Standards Board	43	84
General Accounting Office	5,264	7,785
Government Printing Office	8,574	9,772
Library of Congress	4,475	4,710
Total	36,426	42,777

a. Data from Joint Committee on Reduction of Federal Expenditures, *Federal Personnel and Pay,* July 1974, U.S. Government Printing Office, Washington, D.C., 1974, p. 12.

patterns, sources of information, and who communicated with whom and how often. The central focus of the research, conducted by Harrison Fox, was on role-taking, activity, attributes, interpersonal relations, values, and attitudes of professional staff members. The research in the House consisted of seventy-two semi-focused interviews with virtually all professional staff and most House members in twenty-five randomly selected House offices.[5] The research, conducted by Susan Hammond, was directed at whether or not professional staffs impact on the policy process, and, if so, what variables affect that impact. Interviews yielded data on office organization, job specifications, staff background, and activities of staff, including information sources and communication channels.

Each author did separate research, and, hence, topics were not always approached in the same way. However, we were struck by the many points of similarity in our findings, and in some instances found that the analysis illuminated differences between the houses.

In relating our studies of staffs to change, we might note that personal staffs of congresspeople have been an obscure element of the congressional process. A book, a few articles, and a number of journalistic accounts that touch on various aspects of congressional staffing exist (see note 1). In addition, congressional records of clerk-hire allowances, salary, and staff numbers are available, and using congressional records, it is possible to trace changes in staff salaries and numbers, and to some extent, to trace qualitative changes over time.

CONGRESSIONAL CHANGE[6]

A number of factors may lead to congressional change affecting personal staffs. Some change, often based on the congressional work schedule, is cyclical, and occurs regularly every Congress or even every session. Variation in demand from constituents is one of the most obvious. Constituents tend to correspond most heavily with Representatives during the "visible" days of each congressional session. This is generally early in the year, during the time of committee organization and the President's State of the Union Address, and after a national or local issue focuses attention on the Congress. Staff members are under great pressure during these times to keep up with the mail, receive delegations from the state in their congressperson's name, answer "urgent" phone calls, and so on.

Great flurries of legislation, requiring specialized staff assistance, are introduced near the beginning of each Congress. The end of the fiscal year brings demands for assistance in gaining grants and funding programs and projects before the authority to allocate budget outlays runs out. End-of-session activity also brings a sharp increase in the workload and staff pace. Adjournment-recess periods often are times for staff vacation, getting caught up, and spending time on that special activity that "I never get around to." In some offices, this may lead to particular research projects or investigative, oversight activities.

In addition to calendar-related change, changes may occur in the situation of individual Senators or House members. A different committee assignment, newly acquired control of committee staff, or, especially in the case of House members, advancing seniority which in some instances appears to trigger a reassessment of the Representative's role, may result in staff changes.

Changes in the congressional system itself may occur, often a result of changing forces within the larger political system; in turn, personal staff are affected. Stressful experiences may bring about changes in the organizational functioning of the Congress.[7] For example, the establishment of the Joint Study Committee on Budget Control in October of 1972 and the Subcommittee on Budgeting, Management, and Expenditures of the Senate Government Operations Committee, in January 1973, was a reaction to a presidential challenge, causing great stress, to the Congress' "power of the purse." Staffs were quickly formed for each of these budget organizations; hearings were held, legislation produced, and congressional response to the challenge generated.

Changes in the congressional system also can result in additional activities for staffs. For example, as the Congress moves toward being a more complex organization, staff members are being recruited who have higher educational attainment, greater professional training, and are specialized in various technical areas.[8] Nelson Polsby has written of the institutionalization of the House.[9] One aspect of this appears to be larger and more expert staffs which are increasingly highly organized. A concomitant change is the heavier and more complex congressional workload, generated both by forces outside Congress (more "aware" constituents, and a more complicated economy, for example), and to some extent by Congress itself with passage of more numerous and detailed legislative programs.

Will growth of congressional staffs be accompanied by decreased efficiency? This question has been of concern to various scholars.[10] Growth of staffs is very much influenced by uses of technological advances within the Congress. For instance, the Senate Computer Center essentially provides a mailing list depository for most Senators. One Senator has hired a staff member to utilize the Senate computer facilities to its fullest extent. This staff member has developed a document indexing system and specialized mailing lists for his Senator. Thus, increased staff, in this instance, enhances the efficiency with which documents are handled within the office and the mailing list operation is utilized.

Conversely, staff changes may affect the congressional system. Personnel turnover, at the staff level, is one change in the congressional system that helps to keep the Congress in touch with the "constituents back home." Turnover is especially noticeable among staff professionals and, in the House, among staff below the administrative assistant (AA) level. An indicator of this rapid turnover is that nearly half the Senate personal staff professionals are under thirty-five years of age. In the House, well over half the professional aides below the AA level are under thirty in the offices surveyed. Often when a personal staff member leaves a congressperson's office, a replacement is brought in from the home state or district; nearly two-thirds of Senate staff professionals have legal residences in their Senator's home state. These trends in personnel turnover and recruitment have helped to counterbalance the movement toward institutionalization and less change in the congressional system, as many Senators or Representatives make serving in the Congress their career.

Movement of staff between House or Senate offices and, a less common occurrence, between the houses of Congress, also brings change. Occasionally, a Congress member continues in office but institutes wholesale changes in his or her staff. The office structure and some of the processes change in this type of reorganization; a result may be a different impact on policy formation.[11] Senators Scott of Virginia and Griffin went through this type of change in their offices during the Ninety-Third Congress. There is evidence that, in the House, some Representatives reassess their own congressional roles after several terms, on occasion determining to devote more attention to certain issues or areas, with resulting staff changes. Finally, newly elected congresspeople may bring wholly new staffs to the Hill. Senator Bellman, a former governor of Oklahoma, brought his own home state organization to the Senate. During the Ninety-Second and Ninety-Third Congresses, he decentralized his staff. Many staff members returned to Oklahoma, including his administrative assistant, and now function out of his state offices. In the House, the data make clear that changes in staff organization and function may occur when a Representative changes committee assignment.

We might summarize by saying that a number of factors presently contribute to staffing change. These include cyclical changes of congressional activity as well as certain trends and pressures which derive from the political system as a whole. We turn now to a discussion of House and Senate personal staff.

HOUSE OF REPRESENTATIVES STAFFS

The House presently functions in an environment which has been rapidly changing both externally and internally, and it appears that this will continue for the immediate future at least. Externally, the number of constituents in each congressional district has increased, and there are many more federal programs. Representatives say that constituents are "more aware" than they used to be, and, hence, mail volume—on issues, cases, and projects—has increased, too. The legislative-executive confrontation during the Ninety-Third Congress, brewing during the Ninety-Second, has illuminated the congressional role, and, it might be added, the significance of staff.

Types of Activities Offices Perform

Within every office individuals perform certain types of activities: administrative; legislative; research; oversight; constituency service such as casework; federal project assistance;[12] and press and publicity. Offices vary, however, in the emphasis placed on each activity. Seniority and party affect legislative, press, research, and oversight work; most senior (highest quartile) members of the majority party use personal staff only for the most routine work in these areas, for example. Other factors which are significant are the congressperson's perception of his or her role, his perception of the type of district he serves; her training and experience and her view of the function of Congress.

In House offices there are not enough staff for each type of activity to be performed by a different individual. Hence, House personal staff jobs are basically generalist in nature.

Administrative work is generally handled by a congressperson's administrative assistant who supervises the personnel of the office, coordinates and assigns workload, oversees hiring, payroll, and use of office allowances, and also handles duties within a specific area of expertise—most generally press and federal projects. In sixteen percent of the offices surveyed there was no administrative assistant. Routine administrative work (office procedures, ordering of supplies, for example) was handled by an experienced executive secretary. The more policy-oriented administrative duties were handled primarily by the legislator, in some cases with some assistance from a political aide in the district. Most typically, however, the AA functions as the Representative's alter ego, and has long-time ties of his or her own with the district. He or she talks with constituents and lobbyists, attends meetings for the House member, tries to anticipate information needs, and filters communications through a perceptual screen attuned to the Representative's views.

Legislative functions of the office are typically handled by a legislative assistant (LA). In the few offices (twenty-eight percent of the sample) where there is no legislative assistant, Representatives handle legislative matters themselves and obtain some fairly routine data from staff assistants working under close supervision of the House member, or devote their major attention to committee work and use committee staff exclusively for this. In most offices, however, one legislative assistant handles legislative matters in all issue areas: briefing, drafting floor statements, researching data and drafting amendments, and often also handling legislative mail—i.e., letters from constituents about pending legislation or current issues. A few offices have more than one legislative assistant, or are appointing legislative secretaries to handle legislative mail or research assistants to work with the LA. Among Representatives with high activity in the legislative area (large number of bills introduced, co-sponsored, and/or staff engaged in extensive committee work) there appears to be a trend toward further specialization of legislative duties.

The research looks particularly at the type of legislative work performed in offices by personal staff. Fully eighty-four percent of the offices surveyed (all but four) used personal staff for committee work, much of it fairly extensive. It is clear that personal staffs are supplementing the work of committee staffs in substantive input on committee legislation: doing initial research and data gathering on issues, briefing for hearings, drafting amendments and individual views for reports, and on occasion handling (committee) correspondence and drafting press releases. Unless a House member controls committee staff appointments, he often feels he must rely on his own personal staff for major assistance in committee work. According to our data, this is true whatever policy position the member may take (as for example, whether a member has a low or high score on the Congressional Quarterly Conservative Coalition Scale) and whether or not the committee staff is considered nonpartisan.

The major reason for using personal rather than committee staff is that the congressperson can be sure her own attitudes and interests will be reflected. Interview comments indicate congressional thinking: a seventh-term Democrat who serves on two committees and chairs a subcommittee said, "Committee staff can be inside lobbyists for certain things. You have to watch this." A senior Republican said, "The key guys (on a committee staff) reflect the chairman. Therefore, I do my own work. You can't even use minority staff if you want to do something which is against the minority (ranking) member who controls it." Except for chairpeople and ranking minority members, personal staffs of a large majority of legislators are deeply involved in substantive committee matters.

Staff also give major assistance on legislative work not related to their boss' committees.[13] Depending on the Representative's interest and the office organization, staff input may be an important force in legislative policy-making.

Also important is the linkage made by some offices between individual casework, administrative oversight, and legislation. Some legislators use a constituent complaint regarding an individual problem with a federal program as a method of agency oversight. In addition to facilitating solution of the individual situation, the congressman and his staff will also examine agency administration of the law in general, and on occasion will bring about changes in agency procedures. Constituent casework may also lead to legislation. One congressman, for example, was alerted by a constituent to problems in the payment of Medicare claims. After investigation, an amendment remedying the situation was drafted and subsequently approved by the Ways and Means Committee and passed by the Congress.

Evident from the data are the growth in recent (particularly in the past five) years of staff involvement in planning and execution of strategy, and the increase in bipartisan cooperation (both member and staff) around a specific issue. On the SST issue, for example, staff played a major role, devising floor strategy, assigning jobs, and presenting a total plan to their bosses.

Press matters are, in many offices, handled by the AA, who also takes responsibility for federal project assistance and often is a close adviser on district matters. But the number of offices appointing press assistants is increasing—sixteen percent of the sample in the Ninety-Second Congress. The press function includes the preparation of regular news releases, newsletters, columns for local newspapers, and radio and TV tapes. In offices with a staffer titled "Press Assistant," all these are done frequently and with a certain planned professionalism. In addition, many press assistants double as writers—drafting speeches and floor statements or testimony for the congressperson. Press assistants in the House are essentially generalists with some chance to use specialized expertise.

A few offices hire research assistants, who perform a variety of research: collecting data for a speech or working on issues which eventually may result in legislation. These are not necessarily related to matters under the jurisdiction of the committee on which the legislator serves. Very often research is related to district problems. In one office, a staff man hired to do special research developed legislation on gas pipeline safety after a pipeline explosion in the district. The initial impetus for office concern was district-oriented, but the output was national legislation.

Most offices do not do original research, but rely on data from a wide range of sources.[14] Staff gather and synthesize factual and analytical material. There is heavy reliance on the executive departments for data, as well as on lobby groups and, increasingly, on expert consultants and advisers. One office sent the legislative assistant out-of-state to use archives and to interview on an issue of concern to the district; this type of basic research, however, is extremely rare.

Federal project assistance now occupies a good deal of staff and often House members' time. Although the major effort involves contacts with Washington agencies, a number of offices are prepared to assist district groups at all stages of grant application, even giving advice on how to prepare the application. Top staff, most often the AA, generally perform this function. In a very few offices, a federal projects assistant helps the top staffer, performing an information function and making initial contact with both district groups and federal agencies.

Typologies of Office Organization

Related to staff function is office organization. The way an office is organized—in terms of, for example, supervision, communications channels, and division of workload—affects the specific duties of all aides as well as the general work milieu. More importantly, organization patterns may ultimately affect policy output. Does a rigidly hierarchical office with one aide supervising all other staff limit the number of issues with which the office can deal? Does increased number of staff bring pressure for more "layered" organization, possibly isolating congresspeople to some extent? Are these situations functional or dysfunctional for legislative output?

Three patterns of staff organization, from most to least hierarchical, are present.[15] (See Table 5 for a schematic chart.) In "hierarchical" offices, one senior staff aide (usually the title is administrative assistant) coordinates the work of the office, in terms of both workload and work content. Virtually everything crosses the AA's desk on its way to and from the Representative; in addition, he or she may have responsibilities for some aspects of the substantive work of the office—legislative, press, or federal programs, for example.

Another method of organization might be labeled "individualistic." Here, professionals with certain loosely defined functions operate independently, working directly with the congresspeople on matters within their purview, coordinating among themselves primarily for information and to avoid overlap—and clearing certain things with a coordinating AA when tasks for which they are responsible fall in the areas which he or she oversees.

A middle pattern is that of a loosely organized hierarchy; this can be termed "coordinative." An administrative assistant clearly coordinates the work of the office, but operates more as an adviser than as a "clearance person" for most professionals on the staff. The professionals have independent, and often frequent, access to the legislator. Within this pattern there are two major variations: Most usual is the office where the AA and the LA work as a team, dividing responsibility according to expertise, but at least apprised of, it not involved in, each other's work. The AA is the senior member of the team and top aide in terms of ultimate responsibility. But for most matters where the professional staff are concerned, the office is similar to an "individualistic" office, with each professional working with the congressperson in areas which are his or her specialty. This arrangement is most prevalent when there are only two professionals in the office; in offices with more than two, more overt coordination apparently becomes necessary, and formal coordination, if not clearance procedures, are put into effect. Less usual is the other variation, with the AA as both coordinator and adviser for the work of other professionals in the office, who nevertheless may have direct access to the Representative themselves.

Democrats split evenly on type of office organization. No Republicans had individualistic offices; they appear to prefer some lines of authority, even if only loosely delineated. Party is probably not the primary causal factor, however, Other variables, which may contribute to choice of party, of course, would appear to be more significant. These would include professional training and experience, as well as delegation advice and example. More complete data on all House Republicans and Democrats might shed light on the causal factor involved.

As Table 2 indicates, seniority has a bearing on office organization. All Representatives in the most senior quartile have hierarchical offices; no Representatives in the least senior quartile do. Almost without exception, Representatives in the least senior quartile expressed a wish to be involved in legislation and policy analysis on issues which were not necessarily related to committee assignment. Less senior Representatives also have larger professional staffs. It is presumably more difficult to limit professionals' access to legislators and to channel the work of professionals through one top-level staff supervisor.

TABLE 2
SENIORITY AND OFFICE ORGANIZATION
(n = 25)

Seniority	Type of Office		
Quartile	Hierarchical	Coordinative	Individualistic
Most senior	100[a]	0	0
Second most senior	29	43	29
Third most senior	43	43	14
Least senior	0	67	33

a. Percentage of quartile.

Identifying office organization patterns offers insight into congressional processes. Other variables might well be analyzed for correlation with such organization patterns. Further, do office patterns tell us anything about the Representative him- or herself? Do Representatives with several legislative assistants and a nonhierarchical office have ambitions which differentiate them from their colleagues? Is the office different because of a different perception of the congressional role and function? What about the impact of differently organized offices on the legislative output of Congress?

If present trends continue, it may be that, over time, the patterns of office organization will change,[16] affecting congressional processes and output.

Communications Nets

Communication is central to congressional functioning, and professional staffs play a key role in establishing and maintaining communications networks. The quality of information can affect congressional decision-making. Information on substantive issues and on strategy are both important, and staff are often actors in obtaining and analyzing it. Staff aides are also links to other actors in the congressional system, and to those outside.

Externally, staff seek out and cultivate interest groups, maintain ties with expert constituents, and nourish linkages to the executive branch. Internally, formalized communications channels which stem from the organizational apparatus of the House function as system maintainers and coordinators, and in some instances are trusted sources of expertise which may influence the content of legislation or its passage. These include the whip notice, leadership cues, party, regional groups, state delegations, and issue groups such as the Democratic Study Group and the Wednesday Group. In addition, previous staff experience and contacts, similarity of attitude on issues, congressional class, and office geography are significant factors in establishing and maintaining communications links.

Staff communicate with other House personal staff, with Senate personal staff (usually of their own state, less frequently with other Senators' staffs with whom there is a similar issue interest), with committee staff, with members of the House and Senate and other congressional actors. Communication content ranges from pro forma information on matters such as the date of hearings to discussion of legislative substance and strategy.

One freshman congressman from the Midwest hired a staff fairly evenly balanced between district and Hill professionals. Those staff people who joined the staff from other jobs in Washington had contacts in and detailed knowledge of a number of other offices, having worked previously for two other Senators (one from the congressman's home state), a very senior mid-western liberal congressman, a conservative eastern congressman, and a moderate western congressman.

On the basis of similar interest in and attitude toward issues, the congressman and his staff worked frequently with another Democrat of the state delegation and both of the state's Senators. The new congressman's staff relied heavily on the staff of the delegation colleague, through them developing ties with the staff of a western congressman of similar policy attitude for advice on tax issues, and the staff of another midwest congressman for assistance on social security issues. They also established links to staffs of Democrats from the region who had a similar rural district, and on some matters (primarily agricultural) cooperated with staff of rural Republicans facing similar district problems. This is not an atypical example. The milieu of the House, where reciprocity, courtesy, and assistance are accepted norms, appears to facilitate the establishment of communications nets.

Class and office location interact, in that House members of similar seniority often have offices in the same general area. Many freshmen are in Longworth House Office Building (HOB), particularly on the top and ground floors. Because they share socialization experiences, they often come to rely on each other for information and advice. These bonds continue as members gain seniority and move to more desirable offices. One AA to a senior member noted that the architectural arrangement of the Rayburn HOB was not really conducive to getting to know other offices, but that everyone on the corridor had known each other for many years, so it really did not matter. Information exchange crosses party lines as staff of congresspeople sharing nearby offices attend each other's research presentations or consult on issues. In most instances, information exchange does not extend to legislative strategy, but in some issue areas where bipartisan groups are formed, it of course does.

State delegations are extremely important to House staff communications nets. AAs, and occasionally LAs or press assistants, of the delegation meet on a regular basis and exchange press releases, newsletter items, and background data. Staff of delegation members, if expert in a field, are considered particularly useful information sources, as they are perceived to base judgment and advice on commonly shared considerations.

Staff organizations, informal social occasions (such as regular Friday get-togethers for all House staff, and congressional ball games) and staff orientation and briefing sessions serve to widen the area of communications and the number of linkages available. But much of the information exchange which occurs is haphazard, and based, within certain general structural constraints, on personal staff contact and predilection. On administrative matters, AAs do not know how other offices are organized: the hours required of staff, the division of jobs, the salaries paid. Staff would find a compilation of administrative data helpful. On legislative matters, there is increasing coordination of information and strategy, but also a great deal of duplicated work. Groups such as the Democratic Study Group are filling some gaps; the trends toward staff involvement in substance and strategy, and staff organizations paralleling those of Members are also useful to Hill coordination. But at present, there seems little substitute for staff aggressively attempting to widen communication nets.

Intraoffice communication, as in Senate offices, is generally verbal. With fewer professionals, channels of communication need not be as formalized, but coordination and exchange are necessary. One staff aide noted, "The key is to have communication among each other." In another office, an aide left because of a personality clash with the administrative assistant. The need for coordination and reciprocity among staff was frequently stressed by both staff aides and Representatives.

Staff, of course, control much of the communication between the office and the outside environment in activities such as interpreting interest group positions to the congressperson and handling "Dear Colleague" letters. Staff communications nets are particularly crucial in those offices—and they appear to be increasing—where staff opinion and judgment are wanted, and where staff serve as sounding boards and initiators for ideas, opinions, and legislative content and strategy.

SENATE STAFFS

U.S. Senators have the most extensive staffs within any legislative body in the world. Senators are able to hire secretaries, administrators, and experts to support the activities in which they wish to engage.

In this section, the types of activities Senate staff members perform, typologies of office organization, and external and internal staff communication networks will be discussed. Senate personal staff professionals comprise 467 out of the 2,141 Senate personal staff members. Some of the observations made are colored by this focus, but the characterization of the Senate office that follows has a general import.

Types of Activities Staff Perform

As staff members perform a great number of the activities that a Senator receives credit for, they are under certain constraints. In their activities, staff members are guided by the "politician's philosophy, his ethics, his relationship with other Senators, the realities of his home state, other irons he has in the fire,"[17] and the realization that Senators are human and have families. In addition, it should be made clear that the activities of top assistants may vary widely. "Some assistants perform little more than routine responsibilities; others are in every sense advisors and assistants."[18]

The full Senate professional staff population was asked to identify their activities.[19] For example, nearly nine of ten staff professionals handle at least once a week such constituent projects as sewage systems, urban renewal, water systems, dams, roads, airports, health grants, and educational assistance. These types of projects are important to the development of each Senator's state and thus in most offices receive a great deal of staff attention. Constituent casework also receives the professional staff member's attention. But casework is often handled in Senate offices by staff who have been excluded, for the purposes of this study, from the professional category. Thus, casework is of much more active concern within each Senate office than the data indicate (Table 3 notes this).

A concern with pressure and opinion mail, visiting with constituents, and work on various forms of correspondence are other activities in which professional staff members actively engage.

The staff professional's general role is defined by one or more of the recurrent staff activities within the total set of interdependent Senate office activities. General staff roles give an indication of the dimensions of work in a Senate office. These dimensions provide a framework for discussion and analysis of staff activities. The range of activities in any particular office can be defined in terms of these dimensions and thus organizational "pictures" can also be constructed for individual congressional offices.[20]

Five meaningful factors were empirically identified by taking the inter-correlations among the responses of staff members to the activity items and subjecting them to a factor analysis utilizing the Varimax method. These factors have been designated as general professional staff roles. In the following paragraphs each of the general staff role types is identified. A list of the activity items that identify each type is also included along with the factor loading of each item on the role type (factor).

Role I: Interactor. A staff member scoring high on this factor interacts with individuals who have political problems or issues to push. For those in this role category, a great deal of time is spent handling constituent problems, interacting with lobbyists, and reacting to political mail. More specifically the staff member performs the following set of activities:

With lobbyist and special interest groups (.63)
Handling constituency problems: projects (.76)
Handling constituency problems: casework (.70)
Visiting with constituents in Washington (.69)
On pressure and opinion mail (.48)

TABLE 3
PROFESSIONAL STAFF ACTIVITIES PERFORMED WITHIN
THE SENATE OFFICE
(in percentages; n in parentheses)

Question: Please note how often you engage in the activities below.					Response				
Activities	Once Each Hour	Once a Day or More	Once a Week or More	Once a Month or Less	a Year More or Less	Not at All	Missing	Mean[a]	Total
With Senator in committee	1.6 (3)	17.0 (32)	29.8 (56)	18.6 (35)	12.3 (23)	19.7 (37)	1.0 (2)	9.51	100.0 (188)
Writing floor remarks and speeches	3.2 (6)	20.3 (38)	35.7 (67)	16.0 (30)	5.3 (10)	18.1 (34)	1.6 (3)	8.97	100.2 (188)
On legislative research, bill-drafting, and reading and analysing bills	8.0 (15)	37.2 (70)	20.2 (38)	11.1 (21)	3.7 (7)	17.0 (32)	2.7 (5)	8.24	99.9 (1880)
With lobbyist and special interest groups	2.1 (4)	36.7 (69)	39.3 (74)	13.3 (25)	0.5 (1)	6.4 (12)	1.6 (3)	7.70	99.9 (188)
Investigation and oversight	9.0 (17)	25.6 (48)	22.9 (43)	18.1 (34)	4.3 (8)	12.8 (24)	7.5 (14)	8.35	100.2 (188)
Handling constituency problems: projects	33.0 (62)	34.1 (64)	19.7 (37)	7.9 (15)	1.1 (2)	2.7 (5)	1.6 (3)	6.22	100.1 (188)

							Mean	Total
Handling constituency problems: casework	17.6 (33)	23.4 (44)	25.0 (47)	10.6 (20)	6.9 (13)	14.4 (27)	2.1 (4)	8.08	100.0 (188)
Visiting with constituents in Washington	10.1 (19)	35.1 (66)	36.2 (68)	10.1 (19)	2.6 (5)	4.3 (8)	1.6 (3)	7.28	100.0 (188)
On pressure and opinion mail	22.3 (42)	39.9 (75)	21.2 (40)	5.8 (11)	2.6 (5)	5.9 (11)	2.2 (4)	6.71	99.9 (188)
On letters of congratulations and condolence	4.3 (8)	23.9 (45)	22.8 (43)	19.7 (37)	3.2 (6)	25.0 (47)	1.0 (2)	9.29	99.9 (188)
On correspondence other than described	19.1 (36)	43.6 (82)	20.3 (38)	5.8 (11)	1.6 (3)	5.9 (11)	3.7 (7)	6.74	100.0 (188)
On request for information	14.9 (28)	36.7 (69)	21.8 (41)	10.1 (19)	2.7 (5)	11.7 (22)	2.1 (4)	7.56	100.0 (188)
On opinion ballots	1.1 (2)	8.5 (16)	18.7 (35)	23.4 (44)	15.5 (29)	28.7 (54)	4.3 (8)	10.64	100.2 (188)
On press work, radio, TV	16.0 (30)	26.6 (50)	26.6 (50)	13.3 (25)	2.2 (4)	13.3 (25)	2.1 (4)	7.85	100.1 (188)
Mailing government publications	2.7 (5)	5.8 (11)	12.7 (24)	20.2 (38)	16.4 (12)	48.4 (91)	3.7 (7)	11.41	99.9 (188)
Campaign	8.0 (15)	20.2 (38)	16.5 (31)	5.9 (11)	11.8 (22)	26.0 (49)	11.7 (22)	9.53	100.1 (188)
Write magazine articles, books, and speeches other than those for Senate floor use	3.2 (6)	6.9 (13)	16.0 (30)	27.1 (51)	13.8 (26)	30.9 (58)	2.1 (4)	10.62	100.0 (188)

a. Mean calculated on basis of the following values: once each hour, 4: more than once a day, 5: once a day, 6: more than a week, 7: once a week, 8: more than once a month, 9: once a month, 10: more than once a year, 11: once a year, 12: less than once a year, 13: and not at all, 14.

A staff member who assumes the Interactor role has been given considerable responsibility for one of the more important clusters of activities performed in a Senate office. Often the administrative assistant or other senior professional member is given responsibilities for performing these tasks.

Interacting with lobbyists and special interest groups is shared to some extent with the Investigator (Role V), who has a factor loading on this activity of .41. The Interactor may also be engaged in campaign activities on occasion (the factor loading is .35 for this activity).

Role II: Supporter. Role type II, the Supporter, provides legislative and journalistic support for the Senate office. The activities most often engaged in by this role type are:

With Senator in committee (.54)
Writing floor remarks and speeches (.91)
On legislative research, bill-drafting and reading and analyzing bills (.70)
Writing magazine articles, books, and speeches other than those for
    Senate floor use (.56)

It is the Supporter who is found writing floor remarks and speeches, very likely engaging often in these activities. These activities load higher than any others within the set of activities on a specific role type.

The Supporter shares the activity, "Writing magazine articles, books, and speeches other than those for Senate floor use," with role type IV, the Advertiser. This activity also loads moderately (.51) on the Advertiser role type.

Legislative assistants and staff assigned to cover substantive issue areas are the most likely staff members to be acting within this general role.

Role III: Corresponder. Secretaries, clerks, and those who spend much of their time in the Senate office sitting before a typewriter are identified with this role type. The Corresponder provides an informational service to the constituent and produces the letter or telegram as output. Activities on which this member scores high follow:

On letters of congratulation and condolence (.63)
On correspondence other than described (.34)
On requests for information (.68)
On opinion ballots (.66)
Mailing government publications (.57)

The activity, "on correspondence other than described," is shared to some extent with most of the other role types but most especially, the Advertiser (.32). Corresponders may also be found helping out "on pressure and opinion mail" (.31).

Role IV: Advertiser. Press aides and assistants advertise the Senator through the media—press, radio, and television. Staff members in this role are likely to engage in campaign activity also. The activities included within this role are:

On press work, radio, television (.64)
Campaign (.58)

Advertisers also may write "magazine articles, books, and speeches other than those for Senate floor use" (.51) and work "on correspondence other than described" (.32).

Role V: Investigator. The Investigator actively oversees the activities of the executive or judicial branches of government. A staff member in this role scores high on the following item:

Investigation and oversight (.59)

Two other activities may be performed by the Investigator: "on legislative research, bill drafting, and reading and analyzing bills" (.41); and "with lobbyists and special interest groups" (.41).

Very few staff members perform this role exclusively. Usually another set of activities is performed in addition to this activity.

Typologies of Office Organization

No two Senate offices are organized alike. Each is a little bureaucracy that lends support to one person—the Senator. Factors that underlie the wide range of staff office organization are: the Senator's seniority, legislative responsibilities and committee assignments, office location, demands and needs of the constituents, the Senator's political ambition and vulnerability, quality of available staff, the staff's own view as to proper office procedure, the Senator's personality,[21] priorities and responsibilities.[22]

Three major types of Senate office work hierarchies have been identified by professional staff members—hierarchical, coordinative, and individualistic. These office work hierarchies are indicators of office organization. Office organization is a key indicator of lines of authority and channels of influence.

Over forty percent of Senate staff members perceive their office as lacking an organization hierarchy. This type of office is identified as individualistic. An aide describes this type of office:

Organization doesn't make any difference in this office. The Senator talks to each of us. There are twelve or so individuals that the Senator can talk to. Whom he talks to depends on the issue. [In this type of office,] each staff member may go directly to the Senator. [Also, there is a feeling in this type of loosely organized office that] we must protect the Senator from being overwhelmed. Sometimes we must act in his name.

TABLE 4
STAFF ORGANIZATION IN SENATE AND HOUSE OFFICES

Type of Organization	Senator or Representative Hierarchical (Type I)	Senator or Representative Coordinative (Type II)	Senator or Representative Individualistic (Type III)	Other (Draw own)	None or missing	Total
SENATE (n = 188 staff Members)						
Respondents	32.9[a] (62)	14.4 (27)	31.4 (59)	18.6 (35)	2.7 (5)	100 (188)
Respondents (With "others" redistributed)	35.6 (67)	18.1 (34)	43.7 (82)		2.7 (5)	100 (188)
HOUSE (n = 25 offices)[c]						
Democrats	33.3 (5)	33.3 (5)	33.3 (5)			100 (15)
Republicans	50.0 (5)	50.0 (5)	0			100 (10)

a. In percentage.
b. Number of staff members or offices in this category.
c. Type II exhibits some qualitative differences with Senate offices. See text.

In hierarchical (35.6%) offices, the administrative assistant is seen as being the "most directly related to the Senator on a line basis." Many of the large staff operations by necessity have this type of line organization. "We are one of the biggest staffs on the Hill. Maybe we are too large—eighty-five people, twenty-seven are professional (including personal and committee staff)." A former administrative assistant in an office similar to the one above noted that he was replaced by an individual who was a known "organization man." He felt that his former office had grown too big for him to handle, and that after the new administrative assistant arrived the office seemed to be better organized.

Large offices tend to have expertise in many areas. But there are drawbacks to this type of office. A staff professional in a hierarchical office notes, "We have expertise in many areas. We have known the trees but have not seen the forest."

The coordinative office (18.1%) has two staff members through whom direct access to the Senator is funneled. In this type of Senate office, the two staff leaders would tend to be the administrative assistant or executive assistant and the legislative assistant or press secretary. Nearly one-fifth of the responding population felt that their office was organized along these lines.

A recent trend noted in at least four Senate offices is the decentralization of staff with certain activities—primarily casework—moved from Washington to state offices. "We are trying to get all our nonlegislative work back to our home state. We have moved [staff member] back recently and [staff member] spends half his time there. I will be going back in a few months." An administrative assistant notes, "We have the largest contingent of staff outside our office of any Senator. . . . Sixteen staff members operate out of five major [urban] centers in our state. Seventeen staff members are in this office."

Communication Networks

U.S. Senators' professional staffs come in contact with a wide variety of individuals. Within each Senate office, professionals communicate with their Senator, other professional staff, nonprofessional staff, volunteers, and interns. Interaction on the extraoffice level with constituents, executive department personnel, committee staff(s), other parts of the legislative bureaucracy, lobbyists, newsmen and commentators, and citizens who are not from the home state are common occurrences.

Communication at the intraoffice level tends to be verbal. A professional staff member notes that verbal communication is common when a staff member interacts with a Senator.

The primary means of communication is by voice. Usually any memo or any piece of written matter that runs more than two pages they balk at. You haven't got a lot of academicians or scholars up here—they want to get it quick and fast. The one I work for now [Senator Frank Church], he's a real reader and very studious and well-read, but for the most part it's on the fly, it's cursory. Lots of things go by them that they catch in the corner of the eye, like a quarterback.[23]

Interoffice and extraoffice communication is both verbal and written with an emphasis on the written. Letters and memos pass quite regularly between staff members and the Congressional Research Service, constituents, and the executive departments.[24]

Professional staff communicate with various types of people. Most obviously, they talk to those within their office. The significance of internal communication is noted in an administrative assistant's statements, "The important thing is that we get along. One bad apple can ruin a staff operation."

Communication networks can be influenced by the professional staff member's perception of the quality of his or her working relationship with fellow senate actors. The vast majority of senate actors perceive that they have a good working relationship with other persons in the Senate. In this case, by equating staff perceptions of interpersonal relations with the quality of communication within the Senate, it can be concluded that there is on the whole positive, conflict-free communication among Senate actors.

Communication with staff in other Senate offices is not quite as frequent as intraoffice contact. An interesting and illuminating comment was made by a professional staff member about interoffice communication patterns of those in senior positions on Capitol Hill.

Staff on the Senate side are more pompous than those on the House side. You have a system of layers here—the Senators only talk to Senators, the administrative assistants to administrative assistants, the legislative assistants to legislative assistants, etc. On the House side, you could find out what was going on in forty-five minutes by going from group to group in the cafeteria. Over here, I go down to the cafeteria and eat alone.

Communication with committee staffs is important with regard to legislation in the Senate. A former House administrative assistant, now a Senate administrative assistant, compares Senate and House legislative communication patterns:

If you wanted to find out about some piece of legislation on the House side there was always a Congressman who knew all about it. You could get him aside and he would go down the list of political as well as practical matters. Here in the Senate the Senators are not experts. You have to go to the staff. First, I call the office and find out as much as possible. Then they usually refer me to a committee staff person. Committee staff many times know the practical but not the political issues. You have to know both to make a decision on the bill.

Staff communication with their Senators is perceived as being fairly frequent (see Table 5). Nearly all staff professionals perceive that they have contact with their Senator each day. The administrative assistant is often the staff member who is most often in communication with the Senator. "At first I went to him on every problem," comments an administrative assistant. "He told me to stop it. He was being overwhelmed. On the issues I knew what he thought, I went ahead and did it."

The general communication patterns among U.S. Senate staff professionals are of three types: personal-promotional, administrative, and legislative. These types emerge out of a combination of formal and informal role relations between the professional staff member and persons with whom he or she may come in contact.

What are the basic dimensions describing the general communication patterns of professional staffs? To answer this question, a factor analysis was performed.[25] Three types of general communication patterns are identified for staff members. These types give a general indication of the nature of professional staff communication networks even though no staff member's communication pattern is characterized exactly by any one of the general types. The three types are generated for parsimony, description, and theory development.

Type I, the personal-promotional, comes in contact most often with the Senator and outside journalists. This type of person would most likely handle the press and promotional activities of the office. She would be in contact with the Senator nearly every hour, possibly to clear with him the press releases that she would communicate to journalists.

The administrative type, type II, is in contact with constituents, staff in other Senate offices, staff in House offices, the bureaucracy, and staff in the executive offices of the President. This type would most probably handle constituent problems—casework and projects—and be involved in the "political" activities of the office.

The third type, legislative, is in communication with the various committee staffs of House committees, Senate committees that the Senator sits on, and those that he does not. Since all communication for this type is with congressional committees, we would expect most of the role behavior to be related to legislative research and drafting, and possibly a certain amount of legislative casework.

TABLE 5
COMMUNICATION PATTERNS:
PROFESSIONAL STAFFS OF SENATORS
(in percentages; n in parentheses)

	Frequency							
	Once an Hour or More	Once a Day or More	Once a Week or More	Once a Month or More	Once a Year More or Less	Not at All	Missing	Total
Senator	45.7 (86)	47.8 (90)	4.8 (9)	0.5 (1)	0 (0)	0 (0)	1.0 (2)	99.8 (188)
Constituents	35.1 (66)	42.6 (80)	16.5 (31)	3.7 (7)	0.5 (1)	0 (0)	1.6 (3)	100.0 (188)
Journalists	14.4 (27)	33.0 (62)	35.1 (66)	10.1 (19)	2.1 (4)	2.1 (4)	3.2 (6)	100.0 (188)
Staff in your Senate office	93.1 (175)	4.3 (8)	0.5 (1)	0 (0)	0 (0)	0 (0)	2.1 (4)	100.0 (188)
Staff in other Senate offices	10.6 (20)	64.3 (121)	20.3 (38)	1.0 (2)	0.5 (1)	0.5 (1)	2.7 (5)	99.9 (188)
Staff in House offices	.5 (1)	18.1 (34)	44.7 (84)	29.8 (56)	3.7 (7)	2.1 (4)	1.0 (2)	99.9 (188)
Bureaucracy	21.8 (41)	46.3 (87)	21.8 (41)	5.9 (11)	2.7 (5)	0 (0)	1.6 (3)	100.1 (188)
Committee staff (Senator's committee)	13.3 (25)	49.5 (93)	27.7 (52)	6.4 (12)	0.5 (1)	1.6 (3)	1.0 (2)	100.0 (188)
Committee staff (other committees)	2.7 (5)	25.6 (48)	45.2 (85)	19.7 (37)	2.7 (5)	2.7 (5)	1.6 (3)	100.2 (188)
Committee staff in House	0 (0)	5.4 (10)	21.3 (40)	45.2 (85)	14.9 (28)	11.2 (21)	2.1 (4)	100.1 (188)
Staff in Executive Office of the President	1.1 (2)	16.5 (31)	23.9 (45)	34.6 (65)	14.4 (27)	8.5 (16)	1.0 (2)	100.0 (188)

SUMMARY AND CONCLUSIONS

Both Senate and House personal staffs perform similar functions. Senate staffs are larger, more bureaucratized, and more specialized. But House staff members, while more generalist in terms of job content, perform activities which are similar to those of their Senate counterparts. The intensity of staff activity is high in both the House and the Senate. Compared to other organizations, the specificity of staff activity in the congressional office is quite low.[26] Congressional staff at the professional level are fairly free to pursue activities they think are supportive of their legislator in a fashion similar to that of other professionals.[27] Also, the support staff—secretaries, etc., if so motivated—may in addition to their regular duties occasionally help to formulate legislation, identify and define pressing policy issues, or serve the Senator or Representative in various social capacities.

Ranking committee members' personal staffs in the House perform primarily nonlegislative activities, whereas in the Senate personal professional staff members are often engaged in legislative and committee activities.

Senators, even freshman Senators, are more likely to have access to committee staffs. Thus the total number of staff "working for" a Senator may actually be considerably larger than the number specified by clerk-hire records. This enables Senators to have a flexibility denied their House counterparts, where seniority and majority or minority party status appear to affect personal staffing arrangements significantly.

Common organizational patterns are noted for each house. In the Senate most offices are perceived as either individualistic (43.7%) or hierarchical (35.6%) with a minority of offices operating under the coordinative type (18.1%). In the House, however, a typical office organizational pattern is coordinative. Office organization tends to be a function of the size of staffs, personality of the congressperson, and the nature of staff activities.

In both houses, it is clear that larger staffs are accompanied by somewhat more formal communication and coordination channels. The larger and more specialized Senate staffs generally have administrators at their head; administration of the smaller House staffs is handled by an AA with substantive as well as administrative duties.

Well-developed communication networks are essential to carrying out the congressional functions. In the smaller House staffs, intraoffice communication depends to a large extent on staff activity, staff and the legislator's personalities, and working habits. Most often staff and Representatives are housed in the same office suite; thus, communication is facilitated. In the Senate, larger staffs are spread out in a variety of rooms and offices. Greater specialization in the Senate tends to bring about somewhat more fragmented intraoffice communication patterns.

Our data appear to indicate that there is more interoffice communication within the House than within the Senate. Staff assistants in the House exchange information and data more frequently and actively seek out coordinative mechanisms. In the Senate, there appears to be more frequent communication with actors outside the Congress. We are hesitant, however, to draw any firm conclusions at present without additional research.

Demands for more manpower are heard all over Capitol Hill. With the recent establishment of the Office of Technological Assessment and the staff increases provided the General Accounting Office and the Congressional Research Service, the legislative bureaucracy continues to grow. In fact, the establishment of a Congressional Budget Office and Budget Committees in both houses lends credence to the observation that the legislative branch (and personal and committee staffs in particular) appear to be undergoing further rapid staff expansion.

In the future, Senators' staffs are likely to become less personal and even more bureaucratic. The small staff of eight to ten will be found only in the offices of Senators from the least populated states. Today a few Senators have fifty to eighty staff members, including both personal and committee, that they can call their own. This appears to be a continuing trend. As Senate staffs expand, there will be much less of an emphasis placed on hiring personal staff from the home state, although the receptionist and a few other staff members will continue to be recruited from the home state. More staff members will be recruited on merit, regardless of geographic origin.

House staffs too are likely to increase in size, although they will not be as large as Senate staffs. In addition, a number of House members are aware of what they consider dysfunctional consequences arising from large staffs, and hope to achieve a workable balance which allows specialization and professionalism without overbureaucratization. Recruitment of additional legislative aides and research assistants can be expected. It seems likely that many Congress members will continue to hire personal staff from the home state, although we might predict that there may be fewer staffs with only home state personnel. Furthermore, the skills of professionals with a home state background will continue to be important.

In the House, it is evident that personal staff have a substantial and increasing role in legislation and policy-making, and trends toward improving professional staff capability and interoffice coordination of staff resources are clear. Staff have been important to recent congressional reforms—assisting, for example, in background research and coordinating strategy on seniority changes. The apparent emphasis on legislative capability by more junior House members, combined with the seniority reforms and recorded teller vote changes, may mean that even the most senior Representatives of both parties will maintain policy-oriented personal staffs. The way the House handles minority staffing on committees will also affect personal staffs.

Previous changes in personal staffing have resulted, to some extent, from the failure of reform efforts. In the House, for example, what Representatives perceive as inadequate minority committee staffing has led to additional issue research and staff support by personal staff. Office staffing will be affected by future reforms, and personal staff will participate in bringing these about—without, possibly, assessing consequences for personal staffs.

The resources available to congressional staffs may well expand at a fast pace over the next few years. Computer systems, expanded work space, and additional data sources can provide the staff member with capabilities that few current staff professionals have foreseen. For example, presently in the Congress there are three pilot tests under way. A legislative status system and keyword indexing system are currently being tested by the Computer Services Subcommittee of the Senate Rules Committee. Also an up-to-date teletype summary of floor activity in both houses is being tested by the Joint Committee on Congressional Operations. These changes, when adopted generally, coupled with recent changes in the Senate clerk-hire system, the group efforts of the forty-three freshmen Senators (classes of '69, '71, and '73), as well as the various coordinative group efforts in the House and Senate, have brought and will continue to bring about significant changes in the modus operandi of congressional staff members.

Other possible sources of change are an expanded Congressional Research Service (CRS) and added capability, and use, of the GAO. CRS has already undergone significant change pursuant to the 1970 Legislative Reorganization Act, for example.

A significant problem facing the Congress is the lack of office space. Congressional staff working conditions are as bad as any in the civilian side of the federal bureaucracy. Most staffers are crowded together three, four, five, or more to a room. Increases in personal and committee staffs in many cases can be justified only if office space is readily available. For instance, the Senate Watergate Committee was housed in the Senate Auditorium—the only space of necessary size remaining in the Senate Office Buildings. Perhaps the short-term solution to the space problem is for Congress to rent office space, as needed, in close proximity to Capitol Hill and provide shuttle bus transportation between these locations and the congressional office buildings. In the long run, more Senate and House office space will be needed.

As staffs grow and modern technology is utilized in the Congress, the question remains of whether these changes will result in a variety of officialism, or, as we have so often been promised, in a more responsive and responsible Congress.

NOTES

1. We found during the course of our research that the following works on Congress and staffs were particularly helpful: Charles L. Clapp, *The Congressman* (Washington, D.C.: Brookings Institution, 1963); Lewis A. Dexter, *The Sociology and Politics of Congress* (Chicago: Rand McNally, 1969); Malcolm E. Jewell and Samuel C. Patterson, *The Legislative Process in the United States* (New York: Random House, 1973); Kenneth T. Kofmehl, *Professional Staffs of Congress* (West Lafayette, Ind.: Purdue University Press, 1962); Donald R. Matthews, *U.S. Senators and Their World* (Chapel Hill, N.C.: University of North Carolina Press, 1960); John S. Saloma, *Congress and the New Politics* (Boston: Little, Brown, 1969); Samuel C. Patterson, "Congressional Committee Professional Staffing: Capabilities and Constraints," in Allan Kornberg and Lloyd Mulolf (eds.), *Legislatures in Developmental Perspective* (Durham, N.C.: Duke University Press, 1970), pp. 391-428; James A. Robinson, "Staffing the Legislature" in Ibid., pp. 366-390; Warren H. Butler, "Administering Congress: The Role of the Staff," *Public Administration Review,* Vol. 26 (March 1966), pp. 3-13; James D. Cochrane, "Partisan Aspects of Congressional Committee Staffing," *Western Political Quarterly,* Vol. 27 (June 1964), pp. 338-348; Norman Meller, "Legislative Staff Services: Toxin, Specific, or Placebo for the Legislature's Ills," *Western Political Quarterly,* Vol. 20 (June 1967), pp. 381-389; Samuel C. Patterson, "The Professional Staffs of Congressional Committees," *Administrative Science Quarterly,* Vol. 15 (March 1970), pp. 22-37; David E. Price, "Professionals and 'Entrepreneurs': Staff Orientations and Policy-Making on Three Senate Committees," *Journal of Politics,* Vol. 33 (May 1971), pp. 316-336; Eugene Eidenberg, "The Congressional Bureaucracy," unpublished Ph.D. dissertation, Northwestern University, 1966; Cynthia Thomas and Lynda Carlson, "Interaction Among Staff Members in the Indiana Delegation: A Preliminary Study," unpublished paper presented at the annual meeting of the Southern Political Science Association, Gatlinburg, Tennessee, November 11-13, 1971; and four working papers on House Committee Organization and Operation produced for the U.S. House of Representatives' Select Committee on Committees during June 1973 by Samuel C. Patterson, "Staffing House Committees," James A. Robinson, "Committee Staffing," John S. Saloma, "Proposals for Meeting Congressional Staff Needs," and Walter Kravitz, "Improving Some Skills of Committee Staff."

There have been few studies of staffing per se. Kofmehl's is the major study, and recently, Patterson (1970, 1973) and Price (1971), have had published studies of committee staff role and function. Otherwise, most studies deal with staffing as incidental to the major focus of the study. For example, Donald G. Tacheron and Morris K. Udall, *The Job of the Congressman* (Indianapolis: Bobbs-Merrill, 1966); Leroy N. Rieselbach, *Congressional Politics* (New York: McGraw-Hill, 1973); Richard F. Fenno, Jr., *The Power of the Purse* (Boston: Little, Brown, 1966); and John F. Manley, *The Politics of Finance* (Boston: Little, Brown, 1970).

2. These were chosen as aspects basic to staff function. Further analysis of these and additional aspects of staffing can be found in Harrison Fox, "Personal Professional Staffs of U.S. Senators," unpublished Ph.D. dissertation, the American University, 1972, and Susan W. Hammond, "Personal Staffs of Members of the U.S. House of Representatives," unpublished Ph.D. dissertation, the John Hopkins University, 1973.

3. Saloma, *Congress and the New Politics,* p. 160.

4. Rowland Evans, Jr., "The Invisible Men Who Run Congress," *Saturday Evening Post,* June 8, 1973, p. 13.

5. In the Senate, professionals were defined primarily as staff members with an annual salary of $15,000 or more per year (n = 468). In the House, professionals were defined primarily by function—e.g., those staff members who performed professional press, legislative, administrative or other duties; a $15,000 salary cutoff in the House would mean that a number of House staff who in fact perform professional duties would be excluded from a study of professional staff members.

6. The following texts were of particular assistance in the conceptualization of this section: Robert L. Kahn et al., *Organizational Stress* (New York: John Wiley, 1964); Daniel Katz and R. L. Kahn, *The Social Psychology of Organizations* (New York: John Wiley, 1966); J. Eugene Haas and Thomas E. Drabek, *Complex Organizations* (New York: Macmillan, 1973); and Wilbert E. Moore, *Social Change* (Englewood Cliffs, N.J.: Prentice-Hall, 1963).

7. Haas and Drabek, *Complex Organizations.*

8. See for example, Frank Ryan, "Information Systems Support to the U.S. House of Representatives," *Working Papers on House Committee Organization and Operation,* Select Committee on Committees, June 1973. Our data also support this conclusion.

9. Nelson W. Polsby, "The Institutionalization of the U.S. House of Representatives," *American Political Science Review,* Vol. 62 (March 1968), pp. 144-168.

10. Haas and Drabek, *Complex Organizations,* n. 18, p. 270; and Kofmehl, *Professional Staffs.*

11. See Polsby, "Institutionalization," for example.

12. Assistance to district groups for grants such as those from HUD, or for model cities, water pollution control, etc.

13. Staff work of this type should be viewed in the overall context of other cue-giving groups and individuals. See, for example, studies by David B. Truman, *The Congressional Party: A Case Study* (New York: John Wiley, 1959); Alan Fiellin, "The Functions of Informal Groups in Legislative Institutions: A Case Study," *Journal of Politics,* Vol. 24 (February 1962), pp. 72-91; Julius Turner, *Party and Constituency: Pressures on Congress* (Baltimore: Johns Hopkins Press, 1951); and Warren E. Miller and Donald E. Stokes, "Constituency Influence in Congress," *American Political Science Review,* Vol. 57 (March 1963), pp. 45-56.

14. Problems of data collection and reliance on outside sources have been of concern to congressional scholars and commentators. See, for example, essays by Kenneth Janda and James A. Robinson in Alfred de Grazia (ed.), *Congress: The First Branch of Government* (Washington, D.C.: American Enterprise Institute for Public Policy Research, 1965) and Saloma, *Congress and the New Politics.*

15. These patterns are based on the organization of the professional staff members and their relationship with the legislator. For secretarial staff, all offices are hierarchical. The similarity to Senate offices should be noted; Patterson found somewhat similar patterns among committee staffs. See "The Professional Staffs," esp. pp. 32-33.

16. It may be that variables such as seniority and year of first election affect interest in non-committee-related policy matters, and that as these most junior legislators gain seniority, their interests and the type of staff employed will change and will eventually resemble most closely the present seniors. It seems more likely however, that they will retain to some degree the type of office staff they now have, as the present most senior congresspeople come from a different congressional tradition. Proposed congressional reforms such as adequate minority staffing on committees and lessened control of committee staff by ranking members may also affect staff-seniority relationships.

17. Robert Sherrill, "Who Runs Congress?" *New York Times Magazine,* November 22, 1970, p. 52.

18. Clapp, *The Congressman,* p. 71.

19. These activities were suggested by Saloma, Butler, Meller, Patterson, Dexter, Sherrill, Matthews, Jewell and Patterson, Thomas and Carlson, and Haynes Johnson, "Congressional Staffs: The Third Branch of Congress," *The Washington Post,* January 18, 1970, 1A and 17A.

20. For a full discussion of how staff members "fit" in these roles, see Fox, "Personal Professional Staffs," Chapter 6.

21. Clapp, *The Congressman,* p. 71; and Matthews, *U.S. Senators,* p. 83.

22. Butler, "Administering Congress," p. 4.

23. Sherrill, "Who Runs Congress?" p. 68.

24. Thomas and Carlson, "Interaction Among Staff Members," pp. 11 and 25.

25. Responses made by 172 staff members to 11 questions about their frequency of contact with other persons were intercorrelated and a factor analysis using the principal axes method was performed. Three factors thus obtained were blindly rotated utilizing the Varimax method. These three factors indicate that three general communication patterns can be discerned among staff professionals.

26. Kahn, *Organizational Stress,* Appendix M.

27. Douglas J. Snyder, "The Components of Professionalism: A Conceptual Clarification," unpublished paper presented at the annual meeting of the American Sociological Association, September 1970.

LEGISLATIVE BEHAVIOR AND LEGISLATIVE STRUCTURES: A COMPARATIVE LOOK AT HOUSE AND SENATE RESOURCE UTILIZATION

NORMAN J. ORNSTEIN

USING STAFF RESOURCES: THE HOUSE AND SENATE COMPARED

When political scientists previously studied legislative decision-making behavior, they generally looked at how legislators interact with one another. Whether they cluster in voting by party or ideology,[1] whether committee heads or state delegations are important influences,[2] are questions which assume that legislators rely heavily on their colleagues on the legislative floor. The recent focus on "cue-taking" as a process model of decision-making underscores this point.[3] Only John Kindgon's landmark book, *Congressmen's Voting Decisions,* tries to systematically examine the relative importance of a range of possible influences other than legislators' colleagues upon their votes.[4]

Presumably, legislators have a number of alternative resources to draw upon for information and assistance in their legislative work. We know little, though, about how these resources, such as floor and cloakroom personnel, committee staffs, or office staffs, are used by congresspeople. If they are used as primary information sources for some members, it is important to know how, why, and with what effect. Beginning in 1969, I focused largely on one such resource, personal staffs, and how they were utilized by House and Senate members.[5] The backbone of my research was a series of interviews with professional staff members from samples of twenty House and ten

Senate offices, as well as a handful of legislators, a total of sixty interviews, conducted while I was a Congressional Fellow in 1969-1970. This article focuses on comparison of the House and the Senate: How do Representatives differ from Senators in their use of staff resources, and why do those differences exist?

My chief analytic concern is how legislators direct their staff resources; are they utilized in any proportion for legislative as opposed to clerical or constituency-related purposes, in either the House or the Senate? I explored the relative use of staff resources within the two institutions, as well as the broader House-Senate comparisons. Both intra- and inter-institutional foci yielded interesting results, though perhaps the most interesting finding was that personal staffs perform entirely different functions for legislators in the two houses of Congress. Largely utilized for constituency and clerical purposes in the House of Representatives (with some definite exceptions among House members; their characteristics are described below), personal staffs are in contrast an integral part of the Senate decision-making process. The in-depth staff interviews permitted a definition of the relative utilization of staff resources in terms of the number of individual staff members working full time in areas related to legislation.[6] Using similar definitions for both House and Senate, Table 1 demonstrates the striking intercameral differences.

TABLE 1
**EXTENT OF STAFF RESOURCE LEGISLATIVE UTILIZATION—
HOUSE AND SENATE COMPARED**

	House	Senate
High	20	90
Medium	20	0
Low	60	10
TOTAL	100	100
n =	20	10

Other data confirmed these differences. Using information on personal staffs provided by the *Congressional Staff Directory* [7] and the biannual *Report of the Secretary of the Senate,* [8] I computed for ninety-eight Senators in 1973 and a sample of one hundred 1972 House members, the number of full-time staff members whose titles indicated the performance of legislative duties.[9] While these data are not terribly reliable indicators in and of themselves, they are enormously useful for comparative purposes, particularly since there are two independent sources. The average number of such legislative aides in the House was 1.35; the Senate average, 3.85.

These basic interchamber differences will underlie the analyses which follow. It might be useful, though, to first explore the characteristics manifested by the legislators in both bodies who utilize their staff resources most heavily for legislative duties—to do a bit of intra-institutional analysis, in other words. The nature of these characteristics can tell us much about House and Senate institutional constraints upon legislative actors.

The 1970 interview data strongly indicated that, *within* the House and *within* the Senate, the heaviest legislative staff utilization came from the more ideologically liberal, legislatively active, junior legislators. These are largely northern Democrats.[10] In addition, in the House, those members tended to come from urban districts—especially large cities; in the Senate, they were found among Senators from the most urban, industrialized states.[11] The more recent data, on average number of personnel with legislatively defined jobs, handsomely bear out these findings in most respects.

As Table 2 indicates, the average number of legislative staff, in both the House and the Senate, is greatest for northern Democrats, followed by Republicans, with southern Democrats at the low end. Within the party groupings, in Tables 3, 4, and 5, the more junior, ideologically liberal, and urban-based members use more of their staff resources for legislative purposes. To some extent, the impact of seniority in both houses is an artifact of the ideological distribution, as Table 6 shows.

It is quite interesting that, in spite of the overall House-Senate differences, the characteristics which distinguish the greatest legislative staff reliers in each house are nearly identical. Why is this the case? In both House and Senate, ideological liberals have more work cut out for them than do their colleagues. Committed to social solutions which involve alterations of the existing governmental structure, they must formulate their ideas into legislation—this involves initial research and a subsequent translation into legal terminology. Moreover, and much more important, they are the legislators most likely to disagree with, to challenge, the legislative recommendations of the standing committees. With the vast and complex array of bills voted upon in House and Senate chambers, it is much less effort for legislators to cast ballots in

TABLE 2

AVERAGE NUMBER OF STAFF WITH LEGISLATIVE DESIGNATIONS, BY PARTY AND REGION, HOUSE AND SENATE, 1972, 1973[a]

	House of Representatives (1972)			Senate (1973)		
	Northern Democrats	Southern Democrats	Republicans	Northern Democrats	Southern Democrats	Republicans
Average # of Legis. Staff	1.7	1.1	1.2	4.4	3.1	3.7
n =	33	21	46	37	18	43

(Sample totals 100 in House, 98 in Senate)

a. For definitions, see note 11.

TABLE 3

AVERAGE NUMBER OF STAFF WITH LEGISLATIVE DESIGNATIONS, FOR PARTY GROUPS, BY SENIORITY, HOUSE AND SENATE, 1972-1973

	House of Representatives							
	Democrats					Republicans		
	Seniority (#terms)							
	0-3	4-6	7+			0-3	4-6	7+
Average # of Legis. Staff	1.8	1.3	1.2			1.3	1.4	0.7
n =	18	20	16			23	17	6
	Senate							
	Democrats					Republicans		
	Seniority (#years)							
	1-5	6-12	13+			1-5	6-12	13+
Average # of Legis. Staff	5.1	4.6	3.0			4.1	3.8	3.2
n =	16	11	28			20	10	13

(Sample totals 100 in House, 98 in Senate)

TABLE 4

AVERAGE NUMBER OF STAFF WITH LEGISLATIVE DESIGNATIONS, FOR PARTY GROUPS, BY ADA RATINGS, HOUSE AND SENATE, 1972-1973[a]

	House of Representatives							
	Democrats				Republicans			
	ADA Rating (1973)[b]							
	0-25	26-49	50-74	75+	0-25	26-49	50-74	75+
Average # of Legis. Staff	0.7	1.4	1.7	2.1	1.0	1.4	1.7	2.0
n =	18	5	11	15	25	7	3	1
	Senate							
	Democrats				Republicans			
	ADA Rating (1973)[b]							
	0-25	26-49	50-74	75+	0-25	26-49	50-74	75+
Average # of Legis. Staff	2.4	3.4	3.2	4.8	3.4	3.9	4.6	5.5
n =	7	8	9	25	22	11	5	2

a. ADA, or Americans for Democratic Action, rates legislators on selected roll calls; the higher the rating, the more "liberal" the legislator.

b. Because of the unavailability of ratings for newcomers to the Senate, six Democrats and three Republicans, all freshmen, are not included in the table. For similar reasons, for the House, five Democrats and ten Republicans are not included in the table.

TABLE 5

AVERAGE NUMBER OF STAFF WITH LEGISLATIVE DESIGNATIONS, FOR PARTY GROUPS, BY URBANIZATION OF DISTRICT, HOUSE AND SENATE, 1972-1973

	House of Representatives						
	Democrats				Republicans		
	% Central City & Suburb in District						
	0-49	*50-75*	*76+*		*0-49*	*50-75*	*76+*
Average # of Legis. Staff	0.8	1.4	1.8		1.1	1.1	1.4
n =	12	16	26		17	9	20
	Senate						
	Democrats				Republicans		
	% Central City & Suburb in State						
	0-49	*50-75*	*76+*		*0-49*	*50-75*	*76+*
Average # of Legis. Staff	3.3	4.0	5.1		3.2	3.8	4.2
n =	25	17	13		17	10	16

TABLE 6

AVERAGE NUMBER OF STAFF WITH LEGISLATIVE DESIGNATIONS, BY SENIORITY AND ADA RATINGS, HOUSE AND SENATE, 1972-1973[a] (Democrats only)

	House of Representatives			
	Seniority (# terms)			
	Under six terms		Six terms or more	
	ADA Rating		ADA Rating	
	0-49	*50+*	*0-49*	*50+*
Average # of Legis. Staff	0.7	2.4	1.0	1.4
n =	9	15	13	12
	Senate			
	Seniority (# terms)			
	Under two terms		Two terms or more	
	ADA Rating		ADA Rating	
	0-49	*50+*	*0-49*	*50+*
Average # of Legis. Staff	4.3	4.1	2.5	3.4
n =	4	18	11	17

a. For explanations of ADA ratings and missing members, see Table 4.

accordance with the positions of the ranking members of the relevant committees. For one who is predisposed otherwise, additional information on the legislation is required before a vote can be cast—and, if a full-scale challenge is mounted, the legislators involved need additional resources for information-gathering and preparation of materials for debate, as well as for mounting collegial support for the effort.

Beyond ideology alone, the extent to which a legislator emphasizes *legislative* tasks will have an impact upon the decision on how to allocate his limited staff resources. Fenno has outlined several possible goals for legislators, among them getting re-elected and implementing public policy.[12] For a member who emphasizes the latter, more of his or her own efforts—and his or her limited resources—will be invested in the area of legislating. Table 7, taken from the 1970 research, and Table 8, using 1970 staff title data, show a strong direct relationship between degree of legislative activity (defined here as number of bills co-sponsored in a session) and the use of staff resources. The most legislatively active members have more legislative staff.

It is no accident that legislators such as those described above come from urbanized districts and states. Two factors might be postulated to be involved. One is a recruitment process in constituencies of this type which tends to pick liberal and activist candidates. Second, these urbanized locales

TABLE 7
LEGISLATIVE USE OF STAFF, BY NUMBER OF
BILLS CO-SPONSORED BY CONGRESSMEN

Use	Number of Bills Co-sponsored (one session)			
	0-20	21-49	50-99	over 100
High	(0) 0%	(1) 25%	(1) 13%	(2) 67%
Moderate	(0) 0%	(0) 0	(3) 38	(1) 33
Low	(4) 100	(3) 75	(4) 50	(0) 0
TOTAL	100%	100%	101%	100%
n =	4	3	4	3
				Tb = .541

TABLE 8
AVERAGE SIZE OF LEGISLATIVE STAFF, BY NUMBER OF
BILLS CO-SPONSORED BY SENATORS (one session)

Number of Bills Co-sponsored	Mean Staff Size	N
0-50	3.4	26
51-74	3.7	26
75-99	4.7	17
100-149	4.7	22
150+	5.9	7
		98

are likely to have small but articulate and vociferous collections of individuals (who in all likelihood either contribute heavily to the candidates' campaigns, or would, if necessary, labor for their defeat), who prod their legislators on in a liberal and activist direction. In addition, the possible role of ambition (with many urban Representatives trying to move to the Senate, and urban Senators to the White House) should not be ignored.

Partly because they come from districts of this type, these legislators have not accumulated a great deal of seniority relative to their colleagues (though this situation is changing rapidly). Hence, the availability of many other legislative resources, such as committee staffs, is quite limited. Committee staffs are allocated quite differently in the two houses but still end up heavily concentrated among senior members. Regardless, my interviews suggested that young, liberal active Senators and Representatives are quite predisposed to utilize whatever resources they have available to them to carry out their legislative work—and these resources include, of course, their own clerk-hire allowances.

DEFINING LEGISLATIVE WORK

If we were to break down "legislative" work into its various components— floor behavior, information-channeling, policy initiation, coalition-building— the much-enhanced role of Senate personal staffs in each would become apparent. Here, we will concentrate on only one aspect of legislative behavior—obtaining information for floor voting.

For the House of Representatives as a whole, personal staffs play a relatively insignificant role in providing information for floor-based voting. Without the necessary floor access, and given the availability of a multitude of collegial sources, staffs in the House are severely restricted in this area.[13] For controversial matters, they may screen lobbyists, acting as information filters for their bosses, and hence having an input into the gathering of constituency-political information. But a systematic and consistent overview of upcoming legislation—in other words, a regular role as information source—is virtually nonexistent among House personal staffs. Only one of twenty sampled staffs, for example, would fit in this category.

For the Senate, on the other hand, there is not the plethora of collegial sources present in the House. There are no large state delegations, and the number and availability of committee "cues" is more limited. Thus, the potential of Senators as information sources for their colleagues is considerably less than that of Representatives. And, correspondingly, the role of Senate staffs is considerably larger. The great importance of Senate staffs in this area is best illustrated with comments from the legislators themselves. In 1973 and early 1974, Professors Robert L. Peabody, David W. Rohde, and I conducted interviews with more than forty U.S. Senators. In response to a question on sources of information for floor decisions, the first response given by all but two of the Senators was, "my staff." The question posed, and some representative responses, are given below.

[Question] There were 955 roll call votes in the Ninety-Second Congress. You are well ahead of that pace in the Ninety-Third. With all these roll calls, how do you get the information you need to make your decisions?

It is difficult. I have two bright young men on my legislative staff that try to keep me briefed as to what is coming up from time to time.
(Senior southern Democrat)

Someone on my staff is supposed to be following the floor. Depending on what it is one of the members of the legislative staff is following it. When you get these unprinted amendments I go over there blind and try to find out what the hell is going on.   (Junior southern Democrat)

I get it from my staff. I've got every committee covered by my legislative staff in addition to the committees I'm on. Every other committee has a person assigned to it or to a part of it. It is their responsibility to prepare me with the memoranda or information on the floor battle. To be here every day and to have material on it.
(Junior moderate Republican)

I would presume that other offices do it the way I do. We take all of the committees that there are and divide them between the staff members, the legislative assistants that we have, and then we ask them to study the bills that are coming out and to brief us on them before they hit the floor.   (Senior conservative Republican)

I depend more on my staff than anything else. I have my legislative staff instructed to know at all times what is going on on the floor. They come up with two- or three- or four-page memoranda on what the subjects are, pro and con, and how they think I probably should vote. I don't always go that way, but at least I have a brief summary of what the matters are and the likely amendments and how they feel I should vote.   (Middle-seniority northern Democrat)

These responses contrast markedly with those expressed by House members to a similar question. To quote some of Stevens' respondents:

On those bills on which I have doubts, I depend on friends whose views I can trust. Sometimes when I don't know the content of a bill or amendment, I look to see how others vote.

You get to know committee members and people who agree with you ideologically and go to them for information. Frequently we go to the floor not knowing what bill or amendment is up, find out, then remember who is on the committee and talk to those with whom we agree.[14]

Perhaps a better contrast is provided by Kingdon's respondents, when asked directly about the legislative role of their staffs:

I don't have a staff like that. I'm the only expert in this office.

I never listen to them. They don't know me well enough. They read the mail, they watch how I vote, but that's all.

I do the legislating here.[15]

It is by now evident that the nature of information-processing for floor-based decision-making is distinctly different for the two bodies. House members rely most heavily upon their colleagues for all information types. Senators, in contrast, will often turn first to other sources, especially their own staffs, for their immediate information needs.

A small proportion of House members *do* use their staffs (though irregularly) as information sources in this manner, and it often has a significant impact on their actions, and on the decision-making process in the House. These members are young, liberal, and predisposed to activity, and a use of staff in this manner can spur behavior on their part which liberalizes (in the sense of challenging the "status quo" of committee recommendations) their votes, and perhaps those of many of their colleagues. If staff are actively engaged in this function for a wide variety of pending legislative matters, they may delve more deeply into committee reports or statements than legislators who do not utilize staff in this fashion and who rely on their committee colleagues. Such staff behavior can stir up a battle where none would ordinarily exist, or at least bring a proper organization to the cause. For example, a legislative assistant interviewed in the House, while researching a military authorization bill, came upon a recommendation of the committee head to give surplus military hardware to Taiwan and to Greece—acts with major foreign policy significance. These transactions had been written into the bill largely unnoticed, in a massive committee report and complex bill text. The actions of the staff aide, however, spurred his superior to engage in a vigorous legislative battle to delete these authorizations from the bill. The resultant activities, while ultimately unsuccessful, drew a great deal of national publicity, and provoked a long and heated debate on the House floor (as well as two teller votes). The aide noted,

Every once in a while, while researching these bills, I'll come across something hidden but controversial. I'll go to [the Representative] and point it out to him, and if it hits him, he'll follow through, or at least activate some of the others. This was one instance where he followed through himself, and created a major battle with the chairman.

In the Senate, where a much higher proportion of legislators turn to their staffs for legislative information, such consequences are undoubtedly more frequent, though the varied mass of legislation that hits the floor and the chronic unavailability and late publication of committee reports and hearings, limits the occurrence of such battles led by non-committee members.

Overall, the widespread reliance on staffs for floor-related information in the Senate probably means, at the macro-level, a lessened influence by committee heads and senior members and by party leaders. Hence, the weight of committee recommendations is less than it is in the House, and, up to now, more liberal vote outcomes have occurred. Should liberals, over the long run, take over the senior positions and committee chairs, the nature and impact of staff utilization might change as well, and perhaps reverse this process.[16]

House-Senate Differences: Why They Exist

Having established the broad contrasts in information-gathering for floor decisions between members of the House and of the Senate, the next task is to step back and systematically compare the structural characteristics of the two legislative bodies. Why do these behavioral differences exist? Other characteristics of the House and the Senate must, in interrelationship, provide environments which encourage different decision-making patterns on the part of Representatives and Senators.

Size

One structural contrast which probably has a greater impact on House-Senate differences than any other single variable is size of membership. Since their formation, the differences between the House and Senate sizes have remained large; as Table 9 shows, the House of Representatives started with 65 members, growing to its present-day 435. The original Senate of 24 members expanded more slowly as new states were added, but the gap in size between the two bodies steadily increased.

This factor has an impact on every aspect of legislative life. In a direct sense, the difference in membership size means especially a difference in the size of committees, and the number of committee assignments and heads. It also has a great influence on the nature of floor rules and procedures—

limitations on debate, and scheduling of legislation—which of course bears directly on the role of information in legislative decision-making.

The U.S. Senate had in 1974 twenty-three committees (seventeen standing and six select) for 100 members, while the House of Representatives' 435 members sat on twenty-six (twenty-one standing and five select), with nine joint committees. It is easy to see that, numerically, Senators would have either to reduce the size of their committees or increase their average number of assignments.

To an extent, the Senate has done both of these things. Standing committees in the House range in size from nine to fifty-five with an average size of thirty, while Senate standing committees range from seven to twenty-five members, with an average size of fifteen. And, as Table 10 shows, a typical Senator has twice as many committee assignments as his or her House counterpart.

Senate Democrats and Republicans have an average of 3.5 and 3.2 committees, respectively; House Democrats and Republicans average but 1.7 and 1.6 committees.[17] The same general results hold true for subcommittee assignments in both bodies, as Table 11 demonstrates. Senate Democrats and Republicans hold an average of 10 subcommittees each, while House Democrats and Republicans average but 3.6 and 3.4—an even more dramatic contrast than committee assignments.

While these differences are a direct result of the size factor, they have profound implications themselves for the behavior of legislators in both bodies. First, of course, they mean a difference in workloads and time commitments. A larger number of committee or subcommittee assignments for a legislator does not per se mean more work. But House members who serve only on the busy Ways and Means Committee, for example, can be contrasted with Senate members who not only sit on the equivalent Finance Committee, which handles the same legislation, but also have two, three, or even four additional assignments. In addition, an increase in committee and subcommittee assignments will in most cases mean an increase in time commitments—there are more committee and subcommittee meetings and hearings to attend. While one reaction to this overload of commitments in the Senate might be to reduce the average attendance at these meetings and hearings, the more important effect is that it decreases the amount of time that a Senator has available to spend on the floor—or in the cloakroom—communicating with colleagues on legislation outside of his or her specialties.[18] Nearly every Senator I interviewed recently commented spontaneously on this problem. This lack of contact of course reduces the effectiveness of colleagues as a direct source of information for voting. It also means that any regularized and direct communications networks between

TABLE 9

GROWTH IN SIZE OF MEMBERSHIP FOR HOUSE AND SENATE,
1789 to 1970

	House	Senate
1789	65	24
1790	106	26
1810	186	34
1830	242	48
1860	243	66
1890	357	88
1910	435	92
1970	435	100

TABLE 10

FREQUENCIES, NUMBER OF COMMITTEE[a] ASSIGNMENTS,
HOUSE AND SENATE, BY PARTY, 1970

Number of Committees	Proportion of House Members		Proportion of Senate Members	
	Dems.	Reps.	Dems.	Reps.
1	42.3%	47.3%	0.0	0.0
2	48.1	46.2	17.3%	19.0%
3	7.1	6.0	43.1	54.8
4	2.5	0.5	22.4	14.3
5	0.0	0.0	10.4	9.5
6	0.0	0.0	6.9	2.4
TOTAL	100.0%	100.0%	100.1%	100.0%
n =	241	188	58	42

a. Includes standing, select, and joint committees.

TABLE 11

FREQUENCY, NUMBER OF SUBCOMMITTEE ASSIGNMENTS,[a]
HOUSE AND SENATE, BY PARTY, 1970

Number of Subcommittees	Proportion of House Members		Proportion of Senate Members	
	Dems.	Reps.	Dems.	Reps.
0	9.5%	6.9%	0.0	0.0
1, 2	25.4	31.9	3.5%	7.1%
3, 4	30.7	35.1	1.7	0.0
5-7	29.9	23.4	20.7	16.7
8-10	3.3	2.2	37.9	31.0
11+	1.2	.5	36.2	45.2
TOTAL	100.0%	100.0%	100.0%	100.0%
n =	241	188	58	42

a. There are some inconsistencies here, for both bodies, due to the ex-officio assignment of committee heads and ranking minority members to all subcommittees on their particular committees. Ex-officio memberships were not included here. Also, it should be noted that many committees with heavy workloads, such as Ways and Means and Rules in the House, have no subcommittees.

Senators are quite difficult—locating individuals at a given point in time can be impossible. In describing the "typical" day of a Senator (Mike Monroney of Oklahoma), Bibby and Davidson comment, "Task follows task and Senator Monroney is able to check in at his office only sporadically."[19] Thus the roles of Senate *staffs* as both sources of legislative information and as communications links between Senators are enhanced, as other possible information sources become less readily available.

The nature of committee and subcommittee assignments has an impact in addition on the nature of membership expertise and specialization. In the House, as Asher notes, members generally have and are expected to have a relatively narrow area in which they are deemed "specialists." This area almost always hinges upon one's committee assignments, and is crucial to a cue-taking model. House members, with relatively few committee and sub-committee assignments, can specialize rather easily.[20]

In the Senate, two opposing forces are at play. By virtue of smaller membership and a more flexible application of seniority, most Senators are head or ranking minority member of at least one standing, select, or joint committee, or a subcommittee. In 1969, twenty-one Senate Democrats and fifteen Republicans, or thirty-six percent of the body membership, chaired or were ranking members of committees; a remarkable ninety percent (fifty Democrats and forty Republicans) headed up at least one subcommittee. House-Senate comparisons are set out in Table 12.

Each Senator would normally be expected to be an "expert" in his or her areas of committee leadership. But, on the other hand, Senators have an average of over three committee and ten subcommittee assignments, each of which requires an investment of time and energy, leaving precious little time for Senators to examine closely even the bills under their committee and subcommittee jurisdictions. Thus, individual expertise is diluted when com-pared to the House.

TABLE 12
DISTRIBUTION OF COMMITTEE AND SUBCOMMITTEE
CHAIRMANSHIPS AMONG DEMOCRATS IN HOUSE AND SENATE, 1969

Number of Committees and Subcommittees Chaired by Each Member	Senate	% of Democrats	House	% of Democrats
6+	2	3.5%	1	0.4%
5	5	8.8	0	0.0
4	10	17.5	1	0.4
3	8	14.0	7	2.9
2	14	24.6	28	11.7
1	11	19.3	77	32.2
0	7	12.3	125	52.3

This diffusion of Senate committee-based power also results in a diffusion of committee staff resources. Committee personnel are less centralized and less controlled by the person chairing the committee. Instead, many staff members will be hired by and responsible to subcommittee ranking members, or high-ranking full committee members other than the head. This fact—that committee staff personnel are directly responsible to a very broad range of legislators—combined with a frequent habit of placing committee staff people in the offices of their Senators rather than in the committee suites, enhances the importance of committee staffs as sources of legislative information. The recent House reform spreading out subcommittee staffs might, over the long run, have a similar effect.

The impact of membership size on the nature of committees in the legislative system may also affect the overall work milieu in the two bodies. The smaller size of Senate committees fosters, overall, a more informal, "club-like" atmosphere within the committees. Every Senator on a committee, even a freshman, knows the chairperson and ranking minority member, and fewer committee members means more opportunity to participate fully in committee activities. Of course, the fact that nearly all Senators hold subcommittee chairs or ranking minority memberships enhances this relationship. Most likely, Senators on the whole feel more efficacious legislatively than their House counterparts. Two other factors contribute to this interinstitutional contrast. First, the overconcentration on the Senate by the mass media means that considerably more attention is paid to Senate proposals than to those that are initiated by House members. A good example of this is the television coverage extended to two very innovative health care proposals, introduced in 1969 by Rep. Martha Griffiths (Dem.–Mich.) and Sen. Abraham Ribicoff (Dem.–Conn.). The Ribicoff bill was mentioned on national news broadcasts of all three networks; the earlier Griffiths bill, on none, though differences in content were slight.

A second factor contributing to a greater sense of legislative efficacy among Senators is the probability of individual legislative success—i.e., having your name attached to a successful legislative proposal. In the House, a bill introduced by a junior member has little chance of being reported out of the committee, even if he or she is a member of the committee; a Senate bill has a much better chance if it is pushed strongly by the Senator, and even freshmen can accomplish much legislatively (as Birch Bayh's successfully implemented Twenty-Fifth Amendment to the Constitution demonstrates).

In short, for a variety of reasons related to institutional and committee sizes, legislative power and influence are widely dispersed in the Senate, and are tightly controlled in the House, and hence a much greater proportion of

Senators are likely to *feel* powerful and efficacious. In all likelihood, a greater sense of legislative effectiveness among Senators means that Senators will invest more of their limited resources into the legislative arena while most Representatives, in contrast, will see such an investment as having a distinctly limited payoff.

RULES AND PROCEDURES

The size factor also directly influences the nature of the legislative rules and procedures, especially for floor actions. As a body's membership increases, the ability to loosely and informally coordinate debate and voting decreases correspondingly, and the complexity of regulatory rules increases. Thus, the House rules consume 241 pages of its Manual, while the Senate rules occupy only 49 pages. It is interesting to compare, for the House of Representatives, the relationship between the size of membership and the dates of major rules changes.

This is not to suggest that in every case the membership increase resulted directly in a rules change—that assertion would be particularly hard to defend in terms of the 1910 changes, which had numerous causes. However, that is the only rules revision noted above which did not in some fashion limit debate. In the other instances, the dual pattern is clear—the size of House

TABLE 13
**SIZE OF MEMBERSHIPS AND MAJOR RULE CHANGES,
U.S. HOUSE OF REPRESENTATIVES**

Size of Membership		Rules Changes	
Year	Size	Date	Change
1789	65		
1790	106	1798	First debate limitations; right to speak only once in debate
1810	186	1812	Previous question rule
1840	232	1841	Hour rule
		1847	Five minute rule
1880	332	1880	Debate limitations—relevancy and forty minutes
		1883	Rules Committee jurisdiction over special bills
1890	357	1890	Reed rules ending filibustering
1910	435	1910	Limitations on Speaker

membership steadily rose, and each new rule limited debate in some further fashion. As MacNeil comments, "The larger the membership of the House grew, the smaller became the significance of the individual member of the House and the more difficult the House found its task of functioning effectively."[21]

The Senate, on the other hand, has revised its rules only four times: in 1806, 1820, 1868, and 1884—with no general revisions since then. What Henry Cabot Lodge wrote in 1893 is as true today: "The rules of the Senate are practically unchanged from what they were at the beginning."[22] Attempts in the Senate (and there admittedly have been many) to limit debate in the same manners as the House have always been defeated, with the exception of the 1917 cloture rule requiring a two-thirds vote to end debate. The heavier workload in the Senate of the 1970s and activist Majority Whip Robert Byrd (Dem.–W. Va.), *have* brought about increasing informal restrictions on debate via unanimous consent agreements, but no formal rule changes have been precipitated.

These differences in procedure have a strong impact on legislative behavior. The complexity of the rules in the House of Representatives means a much greater need on the part of its members for procedural-technical information. The limitations of debate and amendment procedures in the House as opposed to the Senate decrease the relevance of floor debate in providing information necessary for voting, and thus increase the necessity for House members, in noncontroversial, non-committee matters, to turn to an already knowledgeable source. And one other rules difference—the prohibition in the House of individual office staff members from the floor, clearly related to the size of the House—means that for the most part staffs are not accessible at the moments when information is most required. Thus, the complex rules of the House enhance the role of colleagues as direct information sources for decision-making.

On the other hand, while free debate in the Senate increases the potential relevance of the debate in providing necessary information for Senators, most Senators are rarely on the floor to listen to it. Since staffs are allowed access to the floor, it is common practice when debate on a complex bill is taking place, to send a staffer to the floor to gather information on upcoming votes for the Senator. Better than half the legislative assistants interviewed did this with some regularity.

A key variable for utilization of an information source is access. A lack of floor access by staffs in the House strictly limits their potential for assistance on floor voting, while freedom of floor access by Senate staffs enhances their potential use as information sources. And it is size of membership, more than anything else, which has created these differences in floor access.

GENERALIZED ROLE EXPECTATIONS

One other variable which ought to be mentioned here is the broad difference in role expectations for Representatives and Senators—expectations which I would posit are almost universally held. Very simply, Representatives are viewed and view themselves in terms of their constituencies and constituents—the congressperson as ombudsman—while Senators are viewed and view themselves in terms of national issues and national leadership—the Senator as diplomat. This is obviously an overdrawn and simplistic description, and each individual Representative and Senator fits either role to some degree. But we can pinpoint distinct differences overall. The electorate "write their Representatives" for casework proportionally more than they do their Senators; when national crises occur, the legislative spokespeople are nearly always from the Senate side. These expectations are held to a large degree by the legislators themselves, and shape their behavior. Representatives narrow their areas of expertise, often in a field relating in some close way to their districts, and at the same time utilize their staffs for constituent service and casework. Of the non-freshman Representatives contacted by Asher, eighty percent felt that congresspeople should specialize in a field rather than try to be generalists.[23] The widespread acceptance of this norm of course leads to an expectation of deferring to the specialist and enhances the probability of some form of cue-giving and -taking on low-information votes.

Deviants from this norm—i.e., Representatives who prefer to be generalists—are most likely the ones whom we have identified as high staff users in the legislative area. And indeed, Asher's findings, though dealing only with freshmen, provide some evidence—his "deviants" were liberal, ideologically activist Democrats.[24]

Senators, on the other hand, feel some obligation to be knowledgeable in every major issue area of national import; the sharing of this expectation by journalists and other mass media makes it imperative for Senators to use their resources for generalized knowledge, rather than remaining narrow specialists.

Why do these broad role expectations and their attendant behaviors differ between House and Senate? Obviously, the structural consideration of constituency nature and size is an important factor. Congressional districts are generally homogeneous, in most respects, while states include urban and rural areas, varied economic interests and social groupings. Hence, constituent pressures are likely to be more localized in nature for House members. Electoral differences are also relevant—a Representative is vulnerable every two years, and hence must be more concerned with immediate constituency needs than the Senator, who has a six-year "cushion."

Other more internalized factors are important as well. The importance of journalists and their expectations cannot be neglected. The Senate has long had more "prestige" among newspersonnel than has the House. Some structural factors contribute to this difference—particularly, as we shall note, the provision in the Senate, in contrast to the House, to televise committee hearings.[25] And, undoubtedly, it is more prestigious to represent a whole state rather than merely a segment of it (a fact recognized by the large number of Representatives who leave their seats to run for the Senate).

For journalists, though, the extra concentration on the Senate has most likely been due to two facts. First, it is easier to choose a legislative spokesperson, for either a state-related, national, or international issue, from the stable of Senators—there are fewer of them. This, of course, is especially true of the larger states. For a California newspaper reporter, the task of choosing a representative legislative spokesperson is extremely difficult if one has to choose from among forty-three Representatives, while there are of course only two Senators. In general, it is easier for journalists to remember, know, and keep tabs on a core of Senators.

Second, the relative openness of Senate proceedings is also important. The long tradition of free and open debate in the Senate chamber has lent it a more reflective, statesmanlike aura. And the open amendment procedures of the Senate (contrasting with the House particularly on legislation from Appropriations and Ways and Means/Finance Committees, which always go through the Senate last), focus much attention on the Senate—the 1969 Tax Reform legislation provides a good example. Moreover, the twin factors of Senate advice and consent on presidential appointments, and open and televised hearings, also focus national media attention on the Senate and Senators—as the hearings on such potential Nixon appointees as Walter Hickel, Clement Haynsworth and L. Patrick Gray, and the Ervin Committee hearings, demonstrate.

At any rate, if journalists turn to Senators for response on the wider range of issues, local to international, the Senators must be prepared to respond and hence must keep abreast of the world and national situations, beyond their state responsibilities.

So, we can see three sets of actors who hold these general role expectations—the electorate, the journalists, and the legislators themselves. There is little doubt that the three groups mutually reinforce these views— media overconcentration on the Senate reinforces its position as the "body of statesmen" for the public and for the Senators whose universal employment of full-time press secretaries ensures continuous media coverage—though it would be difficult to pinpoint the origins of these relationships. The role expectations themselves also may reinforce other behavior patterns. For example, Senators, as relative celebrities and national figures, have additional time commitments, are more inaccessible and less able than their House colleagues to spend time on the floor or personally study legislation. This both enhances their need for information resources, and at the same time makes collegial resources less likely because of their relative inaccessibility.

It should be noted that there are deviants from this broad Senate role as well. These legislators, who for the most part are more interested in narrower state interests, would be more likely to fit in the "low" or "medium" categories for staff legislative utilization; in our sample, these are the Senators from southern and western rural states, with large farming or mining interests. However, because of the other structural variables mentioned above, they are still much heavier legislative staff users than nearly all House members.

THE CAUSAL NETWORK

Figure 1 graphically displays some of the interrelationships which have combined to cause this marked interinstitutional difference.

The figure's most striking element is the suggested importance, almost primary importance, of size, which is directly or indirectly related to every other variable. While it overstates the direct importance of membership size, Figure 1 nevertheless is correct in its portrayal to the extent that size indeed contributes to each of the intercameral differences outlined.

The importance of size as an explanatory variable has been emphasized many times in organizational theory literature,[26] and it is perhaps worthwhile to try to relate this prior research to Congress, which itself can be considered in organizational terms.[27] For the most part, organizational theorists have directly related organizational size positively to innovation; Victor Thompson, Mansfield, Eisenstadt, and others have suggested this pattern.[28] Mohr, however, suggests a more complex pattern—that it is the impact of size on availability of resources which is important, rather than size per se.[29] The concept of "innovation" as it is used in organizational theory is not particularly relevant for us here. What is more important in examining the Congress is the relationship between size and available resources. With organizations for the most part, size is directly and positively related to availability of resources—but, "resources" are usually defined in terms of money.

Looking at the Congress, things are a bit more complex. First, of course, the definition of "size" must be clarified. While we make a distinction here between *members* and *staff*, such a distinction is meaningless for a firm.[30] In addition, we may look at "resources" in terms of either overall monetary allotments, or number of personnel.

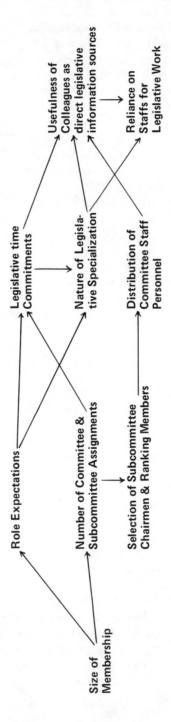

FIGURE 1

In an aggregate sense, the relationships are clear—the larger body, the House of Representatives, has more staff resources available to it for legislative work. Why, then, does the smaller Senate utilize its more limited resources much more heavily in this area?

The relationships are much clearer if we look at the individual legislator, rather than the overall legislative body. Relatively speaking, the staff resources available to the average Senator are greater than for the average Representative. Thus, in fiscal 1970, the Senate was allocated $25 million for staff personnel, an average of $250,000 per senator, while the House received $47 million, a greater overall amount but an average of only $108,000 per legislator.[31] One could argue that Senators represent more territory and more people and hence have more direct constituency demands eating away at their resources, but, as we have already shown, additional constituent demands do not account for all of the increment in staff resources, which Senators are free to put into other areas (especially press and legislation).

Looking at size as number of members, we can also examine its relationship to a host of other variables affecting legislative decision-making. We have already examined the phenomenon of role expectations, and the impact on institutional size. The existence of these broad role expectations—the Senator as statesman, the Representative as ombudsman—in turn means that Senators have more time commitments than House members (press conferences, speaking engagements around the country, etc.). This means that Senators spend very little time on the floor, or even in their offices; they are always on the go. And this limited accessibility limits their usefulness as legislative information sources for their colleagues.

In addition, the image of a Senator as national spokesperson (enhanced by the smaller size of the Senate) requires a Senator to broaden his base of expertise, retaining some knowledge in a very wide range of issues, which limits his depth in any one area (and also limits his usefulness as a "cue"). As collegial resources diminish in importance, their place is taken up by other legislative resources—in this case, staffs.

Membership size also has a direct impact on the average number of committee and subcommittee assignments for the legislators in the two bodies. As we noted previously, the Senate's much smaller size combined with a total number of committees and subcommittees comparable to that of the House, means that Senators will have many more committee and subcommittee assignments than House members. This one fact, in turn, has massive implications for other aspects of the two legislative systems. It means primarily that Senators are spread much more thinly than Representatives, and are unable (or unwilling) to spend the time or energy to achieve a deep expertise in a relatively narrow area, as House members can and do. Senators are forced to devote their efforts to a wider range of legislative interests, and the greater number of committees and subcommittees means more meetings and hearings, deepening the difference in time commitments and accessibility between legislators in the two bodies, and hence the difference in relative need for additional resource commitment in the legislative area.

The greater number of committee and subcommittee assignments in the Senate also means that the chairing and ranking memberships of subcommittees are not left solely to the most senior members of the body—there are enough to go around for nearly everybody, including freshmen. This, of course, accentuates the difference between House and Senate in the degree of specialization, for a large number of Senators hold several subcommittee chairs over more than a single committee, which increases their need to divide their attention, as well as their limited time, into many legislative fields.

It also means that committee staff resources, which in the House are held by a handful of members, are much more widely distributed in the Senate— nearly every Senator has at least one professional committee staff member at his disposal, directly responsible to him. This provides additional legislative staff resources for Senators to employ. In addition, by breaking up the concentration of the resources which control information on pending legislation away from a handful of committee heads and ranking members, it decreases the importance of these individuals as potential information cues for other Senators.

What we have suggested here is a complex interplay of mutually reinforcing factors, institutional and behavioral, which combine to produce a distinct difference in the way the House and the Senate conduct their legislative affairs. Whether or not the overall outputs from these legislative bodies are identical, the internal decision-making processes and the channeling of available resources are decidedly different in the House of Representatives compared to the Senate. We have suggested that membership size is an important explanatory variable, both directly and indirectly. This fact should be of great importance both to future scholars doing comparative legislative research, and to legislative reformers. Perhaps there is an optimum size for a legislative body, which "maximizes" its decision-making ability, if that is possible.

One final point should be made. Recent reforms in the House of Representatives regarding clerk-hire allowances, subcommittee chairs and dispersal of committee staff resources, along with such external societal factors as the continuing increase in the size of the federal budget, suggest a future trend for the House which will align it more closely with the Senate in its allocation of staff resources for legislative decision-making. The implications of this trend, in both a macro and a micro sense, remain to be studied.

NOTES

1. See, for example, David Truman, *The Congressional Party* (New York: John Wiley, 1959); Aage Clausen, *How Congressmen Decide* (New York: St. Martin's, 1973).

2. See, for example, Arthur G. Stevens, Jr., "Informal Groups and Decision-making in the U.S. House of Representatives," unpublished Ph.D. dissertation, University of Michigan, 1971.

3. See Donald R. Matthews and James A. Stimson, "Decision-making by U.S. Representatives: A Preliminary Model," in Sidney Ulmer, ed., *Political Decision-making* (New York: Van Nostrand Reinhold, 1970).

4. John Kingdon, *Congressmen's Voting Decisions* (New York: Harper & Row, 1973).

5. The full research product is reported in, "Information, Resources and Legislative Decision-making: Some Comparative Perspectives on the U.S. Congress," unpublished Ph.D. dissertation, University of Michigan, 1972.

6. For the House, if at least one full staff position (including two half-time people) were devoted entirely to legislative purposes (gathering legislative information especially, but including also researching and writing bills, sifting co-sponsorship requests, or writing floor speeches), the office was ranked as "high" in terms of a reliance on staff for legislative purposes; if an office devoted some portion of one staff position, but not an entire single position, to these activities, it was ranked as "medium"; if no staff member in an office devoted a substantial amount of time to the legislative activities defined above, the office was ranked "low or none." For the Senate, initially, two full staff positions were required for a "high" reliance on staff for legislative aims. The House definition was used for Table 1.

7. *1973 Congressional Staff Directory,* Charles Brownson, ed., Washington, D.C.

8. *Report of the Secretary of the Senate,* Francis Valeo, and *Report of the Clerk of the House,* W. Pat Jennings (Washington, D.C.: Government Printing Office, 1973).

9. I was unable to obtain reliable data for two Senators. The titles "legislative assistant," "legislative aide," and "research assistant" were used. Both the *Staff Directory* and the *Reports* independently calculate information on Senate and House staffs, and the sources were used to confirm each other; if doubt existed, an individual was not counted. A validity check, using the staff and legislator interviews, was also carried out.

10. Though the Senate data show similar patterns for liberal Republicans, there simply are not enough of them in the House for the data to reflect their comparatively high use of legislative staff resources.

11. For a fuller description of these patterns, see Ornstein, "Information, Resources . . ." chs. 3 and 4.

12. See Richard F. Fenno, Jr., *Congressmen in Committees* (Boston: Little, Brown, 1973), pp. 1-14.

13. Kingdon's respondents confirm this assertion. See Kingdon, *Congressman's Voting Decisions,* ch. 7.

14. Stevens, "Informal Groups," pp. 58-59.

15. Kingdon, *Congressman's Voting Decisions,* p. 196.

16. The likelihood of liberals doing just that has been suggested by Norman J. Ornstein and David W. Rodhe, in "Seniority and Future Power in Congress," in Norman J. Ornstein, ed., *Congress in Change: Evolution and Reform* (New York: Praeger, 1975), pp. 60-71.

17. Ninety-Third Congress data show similar results. See Herbert B. Asher, "Committees and the Norm of Specialization," *The Annals,* Vol. 411 (January 1974), p. 68.

18. It also enhances the role of the staff in scheduling their Senator's days, and in effect influencing the nature of his communications sources. The most vivid published illustration of this point is "A Senator's Day," by James Boyd, in Charles Peters and Timothy Adams, eds., *Inside the System* (New York: Praeger, 1970).

19. John Bibby and Roger Davidson, "The Office of Mike Monroney," *On Capitol Hill* (New York: Praeger, 1970).

20. Asher, "Committees."

21. Neil MacNeil, *Forge of Democracy* (New York: David McKay, 1963), p. 41.

22. As reported in George Calloway, *The Legislative Process in Congress* (New York: Thomas Y. Crowell Company, 1953), p. 543.

23. Herbert B. Asher, "The Learning of Legislative Norms," *American Political Science Review,* Vol. 67 (June 1973), p. 501.

24. Ibid., pp. 508-513.

25. A difference removed, at least on paper, by the 1970 Legislative Reorganization Act. Senate hearings are still much more heavily covered, by predilection of Representatives as well as media.

26. See, for example, Victor Thompson, "Bureaucracy and Innovation," *Administrative Science Quarterly,* Vol. 10 (June 1965); James D. Thompson, ed., *Approaches to Organizational Design* (Pittsburgh: University of Pittsburgh Press, 1966); Homer D. Barnett, *Innovation* (New York: McGraw-Hill, 1953); Edwin Mansfield, "The Speed of Response of Firms to New Techniques," *Quarterly Journal of Economics* (May 1963); S. N. Eisenstadt, *The Political Systems of Empires* (Glencoe: Free Press, 1963); Peter M. Blau, *The Dynamics of Bureaucracy* (Chicago: University of Chicago Press, 1963); and William S. Starbuck, "Organizational Growth and Development," in James D. March, ed., *Handbook of Organizations* (Chicago: Rand McNally, 1965), pp. 451-533.

27. Lewis Froman, "Organizational Theory and the Explanation of Important Characteristics of Congress," *American Political Science Review,* Vol. 62 (June 1968), pp. 518-526.

28. V. Thompson, "Bureaucracy and Innovation"; Mansfield, "The Speed of Response"; and Eisenstadt, *The Political Systems.*

29. Lawrence R. Mohr, "Determinants of Innovation in Organizations," *American Political Science Review,* Vol. 63 (March 1969) esp. pp. 119-122.

30. Of course it should be noted that the total of Senate members and employees is still considerably less than the comparable House total.

31. Institutional jealousies are involved here as well—but House members are satisfied to have an aggregate edge in appropriations, without taking into account their individual-level disadvantage.

THE EVOLUTION OF CALIFORNIA LEGISLATIVE STAFF

RAYMOND DAVIS

Legislatures in the United States and elsewhere, like all organizations, are constantly going through a process of change. The California legislature is no exception, for changes in the legislative environment, the structure of the legislature, and its processes in the last twenty-five years have been substantial. And yet, although we know that legislatures are constantly changing, we know little about why legislatures change, what stages they go through in the process of change, and what the structural responses of legislatures are as they change.[1] One way to understand the process of change is to view it as a process of institutionalization. This approach will serve to introduce this chapter, where my argument will be that legislatures have changed most through the addition of permanent staff structures.

INSTITUTIONALIZATION

The concept of institutionalization is one largely applicable to modern societies and modern institutions (italics added):

> [Institutionalization] asserts that crucial to the conception of modernization is the norm of *voluntary* action, a conception of the self as appropriately and actually manipulator and participant in a wide range of social affairs . . . associated with the universalization of the norm of voluntary action are the ideas of *choice* and *contract,* values that distinguish modern from medieval and classical political philosophy.[2]

Thus, institutionalization assumes patterns of behavior and/or structures which can successfully adapt to new internal and external arrangements. More specifically, political institutionalization is

> the creation and persistence of valued rules, procedures, and patterns of behavior that enable the successful accommodation of new configurations of political claimants and/or demands within a given organization whether it be a party, a legislature, or a state.[3]

The viability of institutions in the political system is crucial to political change which is responsive to public demands. In emerging nations, one of the crucial factors is the establishment of political institutions. How are they created so as to be functioning parts of a larger political system? In systems where institutions are firmly established, the crucial questions about the continued existence of institutions is their ability, as Sisson puts it, to accommodate "new configurations of political claimants."[4]

There has been a good deal of interest recently in the notion of institutionalization, not all of it in basic agreement over a definition. The works of Samuel Huntington[5] and Nelson Polsby[6] are indicators of two major approaches to institutionalization—one a general model, the other an attempt to apply the concept in the U.S. House of Representatives. Huntington sees institutions as "stable, valued, recurring patterns of behavior" and institutionalization as "the process by which organizations and procedures acquire value and stability."[7] The level of institutionalization of any organization is measured by its adaptability, complexity, autonomy, and coherence. Adaptability to Huntington is measured over an extended period of time and is seen by the organization's age and its ability to survive generations of leadership. Complexity is measured by the complexity of goals (and displaced goals) along with structural complexity. Autonomy is "the extent to which political organizations and procedures exist independently of other social groupings and methods of behavior."[8] Coherence is the extent of agreement about the boundaries of the organization and mechanisms for resolving internal disputes.

Nelson Polsby's approach to institutionalization is to apply some notions of it to the U.S. House of Representatives. His measures of institutionalization are: (1) the organization is "well-bounded" or clearly differentiated from its environment; (2) the internal functions of the organization are separated in "some regular and explicit basis"; (3) the organization uses "universalistic rather than particularistic criteria, and automatic rather than discretionary methods for conducting its internal business."[9]

Both approaches offer some indicators of institutionalization of organizations in complicated societies. Huntington suggests a well-developed model for understanding the levels of institutionalization while Polsby describes the series of measures of institutionalization in a legislative body. Both authors, however, are very general in explaining the causes for institutionalization. Huntington, for example, suggests that the longer an organization is in existence, the more institutionalized it becomes.[10] Polsby, in a like manner, argues that the greater the scope of governmental activity, the greater the level of institutionalization.[11] This chapter examines the process of institutionalization in one organization—the California legislature—looking primarily at the structural indicators. More specifically, we will first look at the causes for the institutionalization of the California legislature. Second, we will examine the form that institutionalization took. We will suggest an organizational theory model for understanding the behavior of legislatures through the establishment of staff structures that, as Polsby says, are specialized to political activity.

INSTITUTIONALIZATION AND LEGISLATIVE STAFF

Nelson Polsby's article on the institutionalization of the U.S. House of Representatives has some suggestions for causes of change.

> First, we agree that for the political system to be viable, for it to succeed in performing tasks of authoritative resource allocation, problem solving, conflict settlement, and so on, in behalf of a population of any substantial size, it must be institutionalized. That is to say, organizations must be created and sustained that are specialized to political activity.[12]

Polsby is arguing that for a political system or a legislature to survive, it must become specialized through the establishment of structures that are to perform specific function. In any legislature, there are limits on the degree of specialization of the elected members and on the specialized structures in which they divide themselves (committees). *Thus, it is mostly through the establishment of special structures made up of specialists employed by the legislature or staff that a legislature responds to the tasks asked of it in a complex political setting.*

Legislatures in complex societies must have specialized structures to "service the demands and protect the interests of its constituent groups."[13] Most state legislatures, however, have expected the legislator to be his own counsel, her own investigator—in other words to be his or her own staff. This arrangement has not proved satisfactory for most of the more populous states. The experience of the legislature in California is illustrative of the point. Before 1941, the legislature had always relied upon the governor and the Department of Finance for their information about proposed budgets and their performance. In 1939, the legislature found that changes in the governor's budget and laws passed by the legislature had been "rendered meaningless"[14] by the juggling of funds from one account to another by the governor. The legislature, feeling that they could no longer rely upon the information supplied them by the Department of Finance, established by law a post audit office. The legislation was vetoed by the governor. In 1941, the legislature created its own independent budget office, called the Legislative Analyst, by joint rule.[15] The legislature had relied upon a large and experienced budget staff of the governor to evaluate the proposed budget and to assess its effectiveness after enactment. The legislature had no independent budget information and found itself the tool of the governor. The legislature could not control its sources of information and thus found its budget tasks fraught with uncertainty.

Ostensibly, the establishment of legislative staff structures has been explained as the result of legislative demands for a competent, professional staff to handle the myriad of complex problems that arise from modern, complex societies. The assumption was, and to an extent still remains, that staff were the neutral, apolitical instruments of the members *and* of the legislature as a whole. In addition, the staff were seen in a purely internal role having little or no exchange with the member's or legislature's environment.

A good deal of the literature on organizations is similar in approach to the legislative staff literature. Most of the literature considers staff in organizations as the professional, apolitical instruments of the organization's leaders and their role as almost entirely internal or closed. Thus both areas of literature have assumed the neutrality of legislative staff and its internal-closed function. Recent writings in both areas seem to signal an end to this approach and some suggestions for understanding staff as a part of the organization's politics and in exchange with the organization's environment.[16] Kenneth Kofmehl summed up the redirection in a passage on congressional staff.

> Congress is but a part of our over-all system of government. Consequently, it cannot be considered in isolation as a self-contained entity. Any attempt to describe and appraise its staffing must take into account its relationship with the executive branch, political parties, organized and unorganized interest groups, and other official and unofficial constituents of the governmental system.[17]

The literature on legislative staff reflects a change in the approach to staff. But what do we know about the process of change that has been and still is occurring in state legislatures? More importantly, for the purposes of this chapter, what concepts can we use to help understand the causes for change and the impact of the addition of staff structures in legislatures as part of the process of change? The literature has not addressed itself to the process of change in legislatures, nor has there been any substantial attempt to explain the reasons for change involving staff. One of the reasons for this omission in the literature, I will argue, is the lack of any model of the behavior of legislatures. Note that the word is legislatures, not legislators. The emphasis is on the organization, the behavior of the organization as a whole.

The organizational theory literature reflects a change in the way that writers conceived of organizations, and it is to this that we now shift before discussing the evolution of staff in the California legislature.

ORGANIZATIONAL THEORY MODEL

There are various ways to look at organizations—called theories. One analytical approach, useful for the study of legislative organizations, has been developed by James Thompson.[18] He classifies the approaches to the study of organizations as the rational or "closed strategy" and the uncertain or "open strategy" methods.[19]

Simon[20], March and Simon[21], and Cyert and March[22] provided the integration of the "closed" approach with notions of uncertainty—social setting and the human restraints upon social behavior. Organizations, in order to deal with situations of great complexity, "must develop processes for searching and learning as well as for deciding."[23] Thus, the organization's ability to "decide" is based on approximate information called "satisficing" rather than "maximizing" which depends upon complete information. The writings of Simon and others posit that organizations strive for a rational decision process within constraints which limit the ability of the organization to make rational decisions. Simon comments on the logical extremes in the earlier approaches of organization theory.

> Theories of human behavior tend to go to one or the other of two extremes in their treatments of rationality. At the one extreme we have theories, advanced principally by economists, that attribute to man a very high degree of rationality in his behavior. At the other extreme we have theories, chiefly psychological, that are preoccupied with motivations, emotions, and other aspects of effect in human behavior; and theories, sociological and anthropological that seek to explain human behavior in terms of culture in which it is embedded.[24]

The integration approach is one of emphasis, but to the study of legislatures, the difference is a great one. The integrationist approach of Simon and others offers the groundwork for analysis which is able to combine attempts at rationality with the uncertainty that all organizations must face. The source of uncertainty is wide, as pointed out by Simon, and varies from the emotions of individuals to the organizations' relations with other organizations. For the purposes of structural research on organizations, individual sources of uncertainty are less important than an emphasis on the organizations' environment. Mayer Zald comments about "strategies" for the study of organizations by political scientists.

> When political scientists have made empirical studies of large-scale organizations, they have usually turned to psychology or sociology for their conceptual apparatus. Herbert Simon and his colleagues, for example, have been largely interested in explaining the decisions and perceptions of middle-level managers (March and Simon, Cyert and March). While the phrase "coalition" appears in the index of *A Behavioral Theory of the Firm*, there is little analysis of coalition process, composition, or change in the book. Such analysis is scanty, partly because, for Simon and his colleagues, "coalition" signifies mainly the willingness of an individual to join a firm. More important, however, political process is also neglected in this work simply because the analysis of one decision at a time makes it extremely difficult to locate coalitions, since the finding of stable coalitions depends upon the examination of choices and alliances over time. In part the absence of politics results from restricting the unit of study to hierarchic organizations. Just as nation-states range from monarchies to republics, from totalitarian dictatorships to multiparty democracies, so large organizations range from almost anarchical religious orders to hierarchic extensions of one-man rule, from democratic voluntary associations to loose confederations of giant bureaucracies. Decision theory misses their structural variations.[25]

When studies have been concerned with the "larger" organization and its setting, the tools have been again "general sociological concepts" in which political analysis has played a minor part.

> In this vein Herbert Kaufman has marvelously described the forces molding the geographically dispersed United States Forest Service into a single, homogeneously acting organization. Interestingly enough, however, political science seems to have played little part in his analysis.[26]

One group of organization theorists has attempted to focus on the larger organization and the problems of the organization's environment along with the internal processes. These theorists, centered around Philip Selznick and his students, have an approach which is "goal-oriented, focusing on the external social base of the organization and examining the interdependence of, and the conflicts among, groups—both within and without the organization."[27] Selznick, for example, has written a good deal about the importance of goals and the maintenance of goals by leadership as an insight to understanding of complex organizational change.[28] The Selznick group was essentially a school of general theorists at a time of narrow theory. Their general theory, however, served as a basis for the return to general or macro-organization theory by a host of writers, most of them sociologists with a general approach to the study of organizations which they call the "political-economy model." This model, which encompasses the open-closed strategies for the study of organizations, attempts to understand organizational change in both the context of rational or purposeful terms, and change which is unanticipated.[29]

The Political Economy Model

Recent writing among the sociological school of organization theory, called political economy, has tried to step out of the assumptions of efficiency, adaptability, and the alteration of technology to argue that it is the exchange of products for resources that explain internal and external behavior of organizations. Mayer Zald comments,

> The political-economy approach focuses on proximal internal and external determinants of change. . . . It links change to organizational structure and goals as opposed to leaping from internal problems to leadership decisions; thus it spells out a rather complete causal and contingent chain.[30]

The political economy approach asks us to concentrate on the structure and goals of the organization as an indicator of change. The political-economy model, while it "draws concepts and tools from both political science and economics . . . is intrinsically a sociological approach, stressing the determinative influence upon policy exercised by the organization's social milieu."[31] The political-economy model involves three basic concepts.[32] One, the interaction between the political and economic structures. The political structures are the institutions of government for the allocation of resources by fact of coercive power. The economic structures are developed by the system of producing and exchanging goods. For example, the decisions by a legislature reflect the need for political "goods" by facets of the society and the legislature's need for further resources.

Second, the political-economy model involves not only a free marketplace for exchange but a "normative" concept of the use of the exchange for certain goals. Organizational goals or their normative orientation can be seen through constitutions as evidence of organization purpose. Norton Long has pointed out the importance of the study of community constitutions.[33] A constitution "sometimes refers to a total pattern of organization and the relationship among its parts."[34] Constitutions regulate behavior in four normative sectors. They regulate incentive exchanges, the range of discretion of positions, the "ownership" of the organization, and the collective goals. Thus, the goal process of the political structures is an indicator of the ends desired in the organizational setting. In the realization of goals, the resources of the organization along with the market demand for services from its publics or clients must be taken into consideration in addition to the internal resources and process for the production of "goods."

Third, the political-economy model affords an approach which attempts to understand organization change. Change in organizations through the medium of the political-economy model is significantly different from the usual use of the word in organization theory. Change has been approached as the consequence of adaptation on the effectiveness of the organization,[35] from the viewpoint of individual change[36] and from a normative perspective of change with a particular direction.[37]

The political-economy model offers an analysis of the direction of change. The approach "was originally developed to help explain the direction and processes of organizational change." The P-E perspective in addition, offers some breadth:

> The political-economy approach focuses on proximal internal and external determinants of change; thus it retains focus. . . . Because it assumes that organizational character shapes decision premises, it allows room for both "rational" and "irrational" decision premises to enter into organizational choices; thus it avoids the biases of rationalistic and irrationalistic approaches to organizational change.[38]

But what are the specific areas of interest in the legislative organization to which the political-economy model can be applied? In a design in which he established four categories along two variable lines (contrasting the political and economic structures along vector lines), Zald posits that "the operating power system and the operating economy of an organization are constrained by and contain constitutional norms. We consider the power system the actual means by which decisions are influenced."[39] Zald argues that there is not that much difference between the power and constitutional systems, as he defines them, but there is constant tension in the process of accommodation. Zald defines the constitutional system as the "fundamental normative structure" of an organization and the power system as the "patterned use of social influence in an organization."[40] In addition to the two categories of power and economic systems, Zald adds the dimension of the internal economic environment to make four broad sectors for analysis of organizations.

An example of sector A would be the relationship of the organization with the clients or "publics" of the organization. In the context of the legislature, this area of the political-economy model refers to the structures which deal with the organization's "publics" (i.e., organized groups and constituents). Sector B would include the distribution of power in the organization—assignment to committees and chairs—along with the process of leadership selection. Sector C includes the input to the organization from without in terms of demands in the "marketplace." This would include, in the legislature, the demands for action on the part of the legislature and the processing of those input demands. The last, Sector D, includes such things as division of labor, the use of technologies, processes for processing the incoming demands, incentives, and internal exchange among structures. This chapter will attempt to show the function of legislative staff within a political-economy model. The advantage of this categorization is to emphasize the presence of differing demands both within and outside the organization which require staff in the exchange process.

There are three basic premises abstracted from the organization theory literature that form the political-economy model. First, organizations attempt to accomplish their goals in as rational a manner as possible (the most efficient use of the organization given limited resources and information) which includes attempts to limit the incursion of uncertainty in the organization. Second, organizations, like individuals, have complex sets of goals such as aspirations of power, prestige, security, and the accomplishment of work. The goal of self-interest in terms of maintaining or improving a position is central. Third, organizations undergo structural changes to improve their rationality by limiting impositions from the environment.

THE CALIFORNIA LEGISLATURE

A number of significant yet subtle changes have occurred in the political environment as well as in the structure of the legislature in the past twenty-five years. In the political environment, the most startling change has been in the tremendous population growth along with increasing political and economic complexity. In the more immediate legislative environment, significant changes occurred beginning with constitutional reforms which allowed annual sessions in 1946 up to the passage of Proposition 1-A in 1966, which allowed unlimited sessions of the legislature and increased the pay from $6,000 to $16,000 a year. But to return to the questions that were asked at the beginning of the chapter: What are the causes of change, what are the stages of change, and what is the impact of these changes on the nature of the California Legislature?

External Change

The most significant change in the California Legislature has been the evolution and addition of a series of staff structures. This process of change, it is argued in this chapter, is the result of increasing complexity and, hence, uncertainty.[41] The California Legislature has adapted to the growing complexity through the establishment of staff structures which have specialized tasks. As early as 1913, the legislature established a legislative counsel to aid in bill-drafting and other legal tasks. In addition to the growth of staff, the legislature responded to complexity by requesting changes in the Constitution by the voters to make the legislature a full-time organization.

In less complex societies, where district populations were smaller, and the legislature had a low visibility in the eyes of the public, the legislature had to respond to few demands from interest groups and the general public. With changes in society, there have been changes in the legislature. A growing complexity has required that the legislature take a greater role in governing the interdependence of people. The requests for governance are more complex, as are the variety of requests where the legislature is looked to by a growing number of groups for authoritative decisions. The California Legislature, in the early years, had to deal or "exchange" with only a limited number of interest groups and citizens. As the society became more diversified, the legislature found itself dealing with a much more diverse spectrum of society.

For example, the number of registered lobbyists in Sacramento doubled from the middle 1950s to 1970. What is most important, the type of lobbyist has changed. Whereas the lobbyist of 1950 tended to represent established business interests, new lobbyists tend heavily toward public interest groups, public employees and associations, and special-issue groups. More and more, the legislators find that not only are the established interests represented but also the more unorganized and inarticulate public. In essence, the California Legislature now faces a more diverse environment attempting to influence the distribution of resources. This suggests the first proposition: *The more diversified and complex the society, the more the demand for special-purpose structures and the use of technology by the legislature to resolve conflict at minimum cost with maximum control over the resources and over intrusion from the environment.*

California's legislative history chronicles the establishment of staff structures, starting with the legislative counsel in 1913, as aides for increasingly complex tasks. The legislative counsel was established after the attorney general of the state had complained that the legislature was writing ambiguous legislation and laws which contradicted each other. The glaring need for technical, legal advice was the major cause for the establishment of the counsel. As was mentioned earlier, the Legislative Analyst's office was created in 1941 because of the lack of credibility of the governor's Department of Finance in budget and audit information. Additionally, the legislature has had to develop the technical skills in order to maximize its use of information from counsel, analyst, and the more recently established auditor general.

The evolution of legislative staff has been a part of the legislature's attempt to maximize its control through the internalization of functions crucial to its operation. *Legislative staff have been internalized to improve rationality. If information-gathering is left to structures outside the legislature, there is greater uncertainty and unpredictability.* What is meant by internalization of staff functions?

Every legislature has information available to it. Most legislatures depend upon other individuals and organizations to bring information to them—this is one of the function of lobbyists. Lobbyists are, for most state legislatures in the United States, an informal staff. But to leave that crucial information function to lobbyists is also to leave a good deal of influence and control in their hands. To increase predictability, lessen uncertainty, and maximize the control over information, the California Legislature has "internalized" the staff function with the establishment of their own information gathering and/or channeling staff.

Starting with legal staff (legislative counsel), the legislature has moved to equip itself with budgetary (analyst) and audit (auditor general) staff, and most recently has moved toward committee, personal, research and political party staffs to complement the other staff improvements. This process of internalization of information-gathering and information-channeling structures has altered the exchange relationship of the legislature to lobbyists and other representatives of government and private groups. It does not mean that these other sources of information or influence are not important; it is just that they now find themselves in a competitive position with others to influence a member of the legislature. Additionally, and more important for the members, the legislature is able to get more balance in the information it receives and the influence to which it is subjected. This is reflected in comments from lobbyists, such as, "Some lobbyists would not admit it but the increase in staff in both houses has had a great impact—and that is why so many of them fought it. It makes the game more competitive." But there are factors other than information that the addition of staff brings to the legislature. Another lobbyist comments; "There are changes [with the addition of staff] and you find you are dealing more with the administrative assistants and the consultants and less with the members."

The addition of staff for committees and the members themselves not only internalized their information base but also provided them with some insulation, which has changed the atmosphere.

Now they [lobbyists] have to know what they are talking about. There is really less of an opportunity here today for them to have that much influence because, for very real purposes, there are too many influences at work, too many people, too many varieties of people involved in the process which would make it impossible.

Lobbyists are still a part of the legislative organization just as Barnard argued that clients are part of any organization.[42] Although they are not a part of the formal organization and recent changes have tended to alter their influence, they still perform the important function of advising the legislature of the opinions of an "interested" public. In addition to this information, the lobbyists are an additional source for plotting changes in the environment.

Legislative staff are used by the legislature to buffer it from outside influences which it seeks to avoid or control. Staff attempt to modify or channel the flow of information from the environment. The staff additions which have been made in the last twenty-five years in the California Legislature have not only reflected the demands for sources of information but also have come to be the legislature's "early warning system." Staff in the California Legislature were recruited with two particular roles to perform. Early in the evolution of the legislature, the "professional" role was emphasized in the recruitment of lawyers and budget personnel for the staff of the legislative counsel and legislative analyst offices. The primary role of these two structures was to equip the legislature with the expertise necessary to make legislative decisions. Their use to the legislature was to deal with an informational uncertainty. With the addition of committee, research, personal, and caucus staffs, the role of the personnel became more political than professional. That is to say, the role of the staff became directed more at the political uncertainty that the legislature faced. The two roles are not easily separated. For example, many committee consultants recruited because of their experience and expertise in a policy area also find that their role is one of surveillance of the articulate interests in the policy area to make sure that everyone's interests are registered.

From the experience of the California Legislature, the first staff structures established were information specialists. The establishment of legislative counsels and budget offices was a common trend in many states and in California showed the legislature's need for legal and budgetary expertise. Starting in the 1950s and culminating under the leadership of Speaker Jess Unruh (1961-1969), the legislature's staffing pattern shifted from the technical experts to the political experts. Unruh emphasized the growth of committee and research staffs in the lower house of the California Legislature, the Assembly. These new staff were specialists, but their orientation was more than just to internal areas of expertise. Committee consultants were a liaison with the legislature's environment.[43] A good example of the role of the committee consultant can be seen in the activities of William Kier, consultant to the Senate Natural Resource and Fish and Game committees.

William Kier

Kier is a native Californian who was first employed by state government in the Fish and Game Department in 1959. Trained as a fish biologist, he worked in the Fish and Game Department in evaluating the impact of water development projects on fish and wildlife. Kier was recruited into the upper echelons of the Resources Agency, of which the Fish and Game Department is a part, in an unconventional fashion by Hugo Fisher, Secretary of the Resources Agency under Governor Edmund Brown.

Fisher, a state senator from San Diego for one term (1958-1962), lost his bid for reelection, and was appointed Secretary of the Resources Agency in 1962. When Fisher's attempts to increase the agency's budget to provide increased staff for the Secretary's office was refused by the legislature, he responded by looking to the department in his own agency for "independent, restless types." Kier and several others were mentioned and were recruited as assistants to Fisher. Kier proved to be a valuable resource for Fisher, functioning as technician in many areas—troubleshooter for the agency, speechwriter, resource for both technical and political information, and personal assistant to Fisher. Kier made the transition from a fish biologist to a technical administrator whose major responsibilities lay in the politics of the Resources Agency.

After Governor Brown's defeat and the resignation of Fisher in 1966, Kier returned to the Department of Fish and Game as assistant head of one of the sections within the department. Finding the return to the more technical and narrow aspects of the Fish and Game Department constraining, he applied in early 1967 for the position of consultant to the Senate Natural Resources and Fish and Game committees when the then consultant, Ford B. Ford, took a position as assistant to new Secretary of the Resources Agency Norman Livermore. The other candidates for the job included a more "politico" type—a Republican campaign worker for the Bay Area. Kier was the only candidate with agency experience and although affiliated with the prior Democratic regime, was hired by the two committee chairmen—Robert Lagomarsino and Fred Marler, both Republicans. He started work as the committee consultant on April 1, 1967.

Because of his prior experience, Kier was well acquainted with the major issues that had existed before the legislature's resource-oriented committees in the past years. He was also familiar with the major groups involved in the policy area, in the legislature, private industry, and in state and local government. Because of the freedom afforded by his two chairmen, the lack of any

substantial conflict on the committees, and the fact that controversial legislation often went to other committees, Kier had a free hand in the definition of
his position and his approach to analysis of legislation before the committees.

The first and more formal responsibility of the committee consultant is to
provide the members with an analysis of the legislation pending before the
committee. For most of the consultants in the legislature, the analysis is a
comparatively short compendium of the provisions of the bill, a review of the
issues and conflicting groups, if any, and a comment on ramifications of the
legislation upon existing arrangements such as expenditures and agreements
made in the past by the committee. For committees with heavy bill loads, the
bill analysis responsibility can amount to a large share of the workload of the
consultant, although for the most part, the analysis is perfunctory, involving
time more than the critical abilities of the consultant. Calls to the major
groups, either private or government, offer a profile of the bill's support and
opposition, an item that the members rely upon in order to assess the impact
of their vote on constituents.

The bill load for the Natural Resources and Fish and Game committees of the Senate was comparatively low from 1967 to 1970. The total
number of bills referred to each committee averaged fifty per year. The low
number of bill referrals gave ample time for research on bill analysis. As he
saw the impact of detailed analyses upon the members however, Kier changed
approaches.

> My early bill analyses sometimes ran to one and one-half pages, single
> spaced. Well into the 1967 session I realized they weren't reading the
> things, although I had them sent to the offices two days in advance of
> the hearing. So I revised my style, I became much more graphic. I
> became more brazen in my analysis. At times I almost said that a
> particular bill was a turkey. I think this kind of analysis was more
> accepted by the members and often they hurled my things at the
> witness, which occasionally embarrassed me if they would refer to me.

Kier's comment indicates a change toward a more concise, major-issue
approach to the bill analyses with a reliance of the members upon technical
information. A complicated bill analysis is, for the most part, not useful to
the members. The "old hands" know the issues and the participants. The
newer members may read the long analysis until they realize that they cannot
afford to spend all that time. The members with a stake in the bill will use the
analysis for ammunition. For most of the members, the function of the bill
analysis is to acquaint them as quickly as possible with the major provisions
of the bill and the conflicts and conflicting groups involved.

On the Natural Resources and Game and Fish committees, the details of
bargaining were taken care of by the consultant and the interested parties to

the conflict. Members became involved when they had a particular interest. Numerous times when the committee was hearing a bill and some disagreement was aired concerning a technical point, the chairman would hold the bill over for a week or two with instructions to the consultant to get together with the concerned parties and work out an agreeable compromise amendment. If the problem was just on technical language to which the committee had agreed in principle, the instructions to the consultant would be to prepare amendments and process them through the legislative counsel's office to ensure their legal accuracy.

The other major area of responsibility of the committee consultant on the two conservation committees of the Senate was to stay current with what was happening in the Resources Agency, related departments, and in conservation in general. The committee consultant would call or write the departments or interest groups on behalf of the chairman. He requested opinions about pending or possible legislation and information on specific questions. Kier spent much of his working time in telephone or personal communication with interested parties over possible and/or pending legislation. The communication was not usually initiated by Kier but more often by lobbyists or representatives of executive departments who often would seek out his opinion on policy or legislation in order to eliminate the possibility of committee opposition to legislation.

Lobbyists. As a routine part of the job, the consultant would check with lobbyists concerning legislation before the committee. In most instances, the lobbyist checks in with the committee consultant when the legislation that he is interested in is in the draft stage, or at the latest, when it is referred to the committee. It is an integral part of the lobbyist's responsibility to communicate with the members and the consultant before the legislation is introduced, to ward off the possibility of opposition. Lobbyists not only serve as a resource for the legislators, they staff the staff. The committee consultant's office is most often the crossroads for those interested in or having business with the legislation before the committee. For some lobbyists, the consultant represents access to the chair and members of the committee. In the words of one consultant, "The less artful lobbyists and the John Qs come beseeching the consultant, while the more skillful simply advise him of the outcome of discussions already concluded with the chairman ... and the most skillful never have to mess with the consultant at all."

A large part of the consultant's communication over policies and legislation deals with lobbyists from the departments of state government. These lobbyists seek out the consultant over proposed policies or legislation. The contact initiated by the consultant is usually of two types—the consultant is seeking information on some matter of interest to him- or herself or the chairperson or as a result of a telephone call or note from one of the members concerning a constituent letter which they have forwarded to the consultant for the drafting of a reply.

In Kier's case, his knowledge of the Resources Agency and the personnel enabled him to call upon employees who did not speak for the Agency but who, because of the friendship with Kier, talked frankly to him about events or conflicts within the departments. Kier would go over to the resources building every couple of months to browse through the building seeking out old friends with no avowed purpose other than informal conversation. Other social occasions would serve the same purpose. Lunch in the cafeteria of the resources building usually meant running into old friends, which attracted a wide cross-section from the department.

A good deal of the communication with lobbyists or other private individuals takes place in social situations. Lobby groups sponsor dinners for the committee staff, take them to lunch, or just buy a drink and a few minutes' conversation. Kier would attend some of the social occasions to further some policy that he had in mind, to gather some support for legislation, or to listen to what was going on. Some of these social gatherings, especially after a few years' attendance, prove to be barren as information-gathering devices. Others bring together new faces concerning new topics and can be useful either as new information sources or as platforms to try out some new ideas for legislation by the chairman.

The numerous state commissions and boards in conservation areas required a good deal of attention by the consultant. In Kier's policy area, the numerous state officials and unofficial boards and commissions—ranging from the State Lands Commission to the State Water Resources Control Board—are always making decisions which have the potential to affect the legislature. For example, the oil well blowout near Santa Barbara in 1969 occurred in the district of the chairman of the Senate Natural Resources Committee. The oil-drilling regulations of the State Lands Commission, which controls off-shore state lands, was thus of great interest to Kier and his chairman.

Kier, if he could not attend the board or commission meeting, received copies of the meeting reports, which he pored over in detail. Kier's responsibility for information extended to the federal level. He ordered and read a broad variety of federal government and congressional reports which affected California's policies or funding in the resource arena. One of the pieces of legislation to come out of the committee, the 1968 California Waterway Act, was an act to supplement the federal Wild Rivers Program but extended to marshes and estuaries in California. The legislation built upon the federal legislation to include water areas of importance to maintenance of wildlife and open space.

The Waterway Act is an example of the interaction that occurs around a consultant when a major piece of legislation is introduced. Part of Kier's responsibility, although self-determined, was to conceive at least one major piece of legislation per year to establish the credentials of his chairman as an innovator in the resources-environment arena. The 1968 act (actually initiated in 1965 by another state senator who had since been defeated) was dusted off, updated, and introduced in 1968 under the authorship of Senator Lagomarsino. The bill, which faced a good deal of opposition in the past, had smooth sailing before the committees of the two houses mainly because of the preparation work by Kier. Over the course of three months, he contacted and ironed out major opposition to the bill by private groups and the state Resources Agency. Kier comments:

> We started out by putting in a spot bill. We didn't hear a word about the bill, except from some imaginative conservationists who read into the bill certain possibilities. In the first week of May we brought it out—we held a press conference to announce the intention. The next day I got a call from Larry Kiml of the Chamber of Commerce. He said some of his boys had some problems and told me to get a pencil to mark up the bill. I told him that as far as I was concerned the bill was letter perfect. Kiml told me I would lose the bill in its present form and I wouldn't know where the opposition came from. I asked him what he would suggest. The next day there were twelve guys in my office representing the full spectrum of land and water interests. I listened to their problems and I explained our intentions. We got a lot of things resolved. I said that every man who had problems with the bill—his concern would get full attention. But if anyone had a problem and didn't tell me and opposed the bill later, he and I would be through. This was good business on my part. Kiml acted as a clearinghouse for drafts and redrafts. I received all sorts of suggestions, all sorts of scribbled ideas and so forth. And we worked it out to the satisfaction of everybody. None of the objections really created any problems.

The proposal of legislation on behalf of the chairman of the committee requires that the consultant identify the various views of the concurring and opposing groups and deal with them. Often this process demands an alteration of the bill but in other cases, such as with the 1968 bill, the opposition is less substantial and more procedural. The lobbyists want to display to themselves and their constituents that they have access to the legislative decisions.

The members. The members of the legislature make demands on a staffer's time once his or her expertise is established.

Two types of member communication came to Kier. One involved requests to answer constituent mail on a question in his policy area. For the most part, these types of questions were not complicated, usually a student requesting information. A second kind of communication involved member requests for technical information about proposed legislation or a problem that had come to the member's attention. These two types of information requests were high-priority items for the staff members. Although employed by the committee chairman, Kier—like most consultants—felt an obligation to serve all the members. Good service might win a needed vote in the future or a friend when leadership changes came about.

Other legislative staff. A number of issues that are proposed in or are referred to the committee are of concern to other committees in the Senate or Assembly.

Issues before the Natural Resources and Fish and Game committees of the Senate also surfaced in the Senate Water Committee, the Assembly Water Committee, the Assembly Natural Resources Committee, the Senate Finance Committee, and the Assembly Ways and Means Committee. The staff members of these committees were often in communication with Kier. They wanted to know what the possible actions of the committee would be on certain legislation. Kier, in turn, called other consultants about possible legislation. Other committee consultants, with different perspectives on the legislative environment, are often good sources for indications of change. Much of the conflict over resources policy in California is between water interests as expressed by the Department of Water Resources and the more general environmental interests, represented variously by the Department of Fish and Game and by private conservation lobby groups. The consultants for the two water committees, one with experience in the Department of Water Resources, serve as good bases of information for what is going on in the department. More formal attempts at gaining information would often only result in perfunctory replies.

The general public. Most of the interaction with the general public is handled by the personal staff of the members. The consultants are referred some of the constituent mail. Assembly consultants for the most part do more constituent work than their counterparts in the Senate. Primarily, consultants in both houses deal with the more articulate groups immediately in or around the legislature. There are two situations which are exceptions to this rule. Kier from time to time would get a public reaction to legislation which would be addressed directly to him, rather than to a member. At other times, he would seek out private individuals for support of legislation.

There are certain issues before the legislature which excite the general public into involvement in the legislative process. In early 1969, the oil spill in Santa Barbara resulted in much public concern expressed to the legislators and staff. Also in 1969, the issue of regulation of growth in the San Francisco Bay area through the establishment of the Bay Conservation and Development Commission (BCDC) received great public interest. It was articulated by the formation of interest groups which gathered petitions, published ads in the newspapers, and publicly expressed their displeasure with certain members of the legislature. These rare incidents of intense public interest in a policy issue mean a good deal of involvement with the interested public by the consultant.

Kier's function as a committee consultant was twofold. One, he brought to the Senate a technical and political background which familiarized him with the issues and problems in the resources-environment policy area. This background enabled him to adapt quickly to the legislative system and recognize and understand problems which confronted the committee in the form of legislation. Two, Kier brought a knowledge of the major groups articulate in the policy area—both public and private—and thus gave to the legislative committee a good "radarscope" of the groups and individuals interested in the activities of the legislature. Both functions enable the legislature to respond better to the issues that it confronts in the form of legislation and to estimate and control the "concerned" public's involvement in the legislative process.

The function of legislative staff is to regularize environmental influences and to adapt to and anticipate change which cannot be buffered or controlled. The committee and personal staff of the legislature, when influences from the environment are impossible to buffer, attempt to regularize or channel these influences. For example, in both the Assembly and the Senate, a common practice is to hire a person from the member's district as an administrative assistant. Problems, complaints, and requests for favors can then be channeled through the local representative of the member. In addition, having a representative in the district is a means whereby the member could use his or her assistant to deal with problems or give advice regarding changes occurring. This is especially important to a member as election time comes near, as it did for one member of the Senate in 1969.

For a number of years prior to 1969, one of the growing issues in the Bay Area of Northern California focused on regional regulation of the San Francisco Bay. All land restrictions were in the hands of local government which had no integrated policy toward the development of the lands adjacent to the Bay and the filling in of low-lying marsh lands. Several conservation groups brought the issue to the state legislature asking for a regional government equipped with powers to regulate development and land filling. It was a new issue for the legislature, which was unsure of the concern on the local level for regional government but sure of the opposition of the business groups tied to development. Several members of the Assembly polled their districts on the issue through a mailer paid by the legislature and found a surprising amount of support for the regional government concept. Senator Richard Dolwig of San Mateo County, just to the south of San Francisco, opposed the legislation establishing the regional agency to be known as the Bay Conservation and Development Commission (BCDC). Close to lobbyists and reluctant to use the personal staff that other members of the Senate had already established, Dolwig did not see the issue as particularly salient as far as his district was concerned. After he publicly announced his position against the BCDC bill, several groups in San Mateo County garnered over 75,000 signatures on a petition in support of the bill and asked Dolwig to reconsider. He did and later announced that he was not a candidate for reelection. The senator elected the following November was a staunch supporter of BCDC.

The access of some organization in the legislature's environment is related to the legislature's dependence on that organization for resources. Access thus varies with the legislature's need for resources.

The California Legislature, in the past, depended greatly upon other organizations for resources—information, money for campaigns, and the rest. As the legislature has changed in the last twenty-five years, so has its dependence. Through the addition of staff, the legislature has increased the resources available to the membership within the organization and decreased the reliance upon outside resources. Tables 1 and 2 chronicle the changes in the member's district offices in both houses of the legislature over a seven-year period. The figures show the significant increase in emphasis upon local staff, especially in the Senate, where staffing was more decentralized. In the Assembly, staff tended to be more centralized in committees and research organizations. Tables 3 and 4 show some of the broad growth trends in both houses of the legislature for general staff. In overall expenditures, the tremendous growth of staff can be seen.

TABLE 1
GROWTH—ASSEMBLY DISTRICT OFFICE AND ADMINISTRATIVE STAFF

	DISTRICT OFFICE STAFF		
	Total	Women[a]	Monthly Costs[b]
October 1963	187	123	$64,851.76
October 1966	229	159	70,745.00
October 1968	232	161	66,133.23
October 1970	245	171	77,538.38

a. This category, referring almost always to secretarial and clerical help, is one used by the State Controller's office.

b. Includes both monthly and semi-monthly salaried persons.

TABLE 2
GROWTH—SENATE DISTRICT OFFICE AND ADMINISTRATIVE STAFF

	DISTRICT OFFICE STAFF		Total monthly salaries
	Total	Women	
October 1963	57	42	$26,404.56
October 1966	66	33	45,806.00
October 1968	147	86	57,137.63
October 1970	196	121	95,271.15

TABLE 3
GROWTH—ASSEMBLY EMPLOYEES

	Steno	Desk[a]	Others[b]	Total
1953	77	18	23	118
1955	105	21	20	146
1957	118	21	33	172
1959	125	22	46	193
1961	128	22	33	203
1963	151	23	75	249
1965	179	24	95	298
1967	180	23	102	302
1969	205	24	120	347[c]

a. Desk refers to employees who work on the floor of the house and help administer the business of the legislature while in session.

b. Includes administrative assistant, consultants, and sergeants-at-arms.

c. *Handbook of the California Legislature, 1953-69.* The legislative handbook figures do not represent all of the assembly employees. The figures give some indications of change.

TABLE 4
GROWTH—SENATE EMPLOYEES

	Steno	Desk	Other[a]	Total
1953	57	23	12	91
1955	62	20	22	104
1957	67	28	17	112
1959	67	25	32	124
1961	70	27	57	154
1963	86	28	64	178
1965	93	24	70	187
1967	120	17	79	216
1969	119	17	101	231[b]

a. Includes administrative assistant, consultants, and sergeants-at-arms.

b. *Handbook of the California Legislature, 1953-69.* The handbook figures do not represent all of the Senate employees but give some indicators of change.

TABLE 5

	Assembly	Senate
Staff Salaries		
1955-1957	$997,505.90	$403,980.39
Staff Salaries		
1972-1973	$8,208,313.61	$5,228,803.22
Per Diem for		
Staff 1955-1957	$980.75	$9,888.75
1972-1973	$231,453.14	$29,230.85
District Office		
Cost 1970-1971	$391,989.78	$324,453.42
1972-1973	$474,715.00	$394,248.28

The costs of elections and/or campaigning and the reliance upon outside organizations to contribute resources are greatly reduced by the addition of staffing structures on the district level. Thus, the addition of staff has attempted to limit the uncertainty that the legislature faces by its reliance upon other organizations and at the same time improve its ability to control or channel exchanges with the environment.

The change in the legislature's technology has also been marked. Technology is defined in Perrow's terms as "a means of transforming raw materials (human, symbolic, or material) into desirable goods and services.[44] In terms of the California Legislature, technology refers to the delivery of "goods" to constituents, or the ability to communicate with the public. The goals of the legislature in changing their communication technology have been to gain greater and more reliable ways to gauge the mood of the public and improve the capabilities of the legislature to communicate with the public. The primary "technology" used by the legislature to accomplish these two tasks is through specialized staff such as local district staff and the addition of public relations specialists within office staffs. In addition, the legislature has attempted to communicate directly with its public to both seek their opinions and to deliver information. The manner for this direct communication is called the "mailer."

Because of the size of Assembly and Senate districts (249,414 and 498,828 respectively) and the competition for name recognition, both houses of the legislature instituted in the middle 1960s mailed news releases and questionnaires as a way of disseminating information and surveying their publics. This system allowed each member of the Assembly and the Senate to mail a letter of his or her own design to each voter in the district. The mailer could vary from an advertisement of the member's accomplishments during the last session to a detailed questionnaire concerning the voter's opinions on questions before the legislature or of importance to an upcoming election. The system used for the mailed questionnaires allowed the member to know the area of the district from which the response came. This allowed an analysis of opinions by locale—a very useful tool for member's districts that were large or heterogeneous. The mailers in 1968 cost the Senate approximately $700,000 to $1,000,000. In 1967, the cost to the Assembly was approximately $1.2 million. In addition, the cost of general postage in the Senate rose from $236,250 in 1968-1969 to $469,500 in 1969-1970. In the Assembly, the cost of postage rose from $233,054 in 1963-1965 to $502,617 for 1968-1969.[45]

Technology and the addition of staff to employ technology has vastly improved the California Legislature's members' ability to survey their environment—manage or channel uncertainty and anticipate change.

The more that the legislature depends upon specialists, the more that any access to the legislature is tied to an organization's ability to perform a specialized function. The specialized function is tied to one or two factors. One, the organization can provide scarce expert information in a specialized area and two, the organization's size and resources offer an infrastructure which the legislature does not have itself. An example of the latter point is the political party which provides an infrastructure for a campaign organization. Recent additions of staff represent moves to compensate for specialization in both areas mentioned above. Offices of research in both the Senate and the Assembly have moved to hire specialists in areas such as education finance and health care to provide the legislature with its own expert information. The addition of caucus and committee staff has been to compensate for the reliance of the legislature upon the lobby and political party organizations. In both instances, the legislature has moved to internalize those functions of specialists which add to the legislature's control of its environment.

It should be mentioned that the addition of staff does not end the legislature's dependence on other organizations for crucial functions. What it does mean is that the legislature is no longer completely tied to other organizations and their resources. For example, the use of the mailer is a way to limit the organization's dependence upon the news media. It does not end dependence, but it provides an alternative to newspapers, radio, and television as the only means of communication. In addition, the use of the mailer assured the member of the "quality" of the information when delivered. The communication does not have to pass through revisions before it reaches the public. It is a form of direct communication—at state expense on the member's terms.

The legislature attempts to maximize its resources in dealing with its environment. One way of accomplishing this is to exchange with organizations which "aggregate" diverse interests. It is not difficult to understand why the California Legislature or other state legislatures exchange extensively with lobbyists. The lobbyists represent a cheap form of exchange with a diverse constituency. As Almond comments, there are three different "publics" with which a legislature must deal: the general, the attentive, and the articulate.[46] Most of the public fits the category of general. The more attentive they become, the more the legislature exchanges with them. In addition, the more articulate the public, the more organized they are and thus the more the legislature maximizes by dealing with their representatives or lobbyists.

By dealing with representatives of "aggregating" organizations, legislatures encourage the formation of large organizations which cut across diverse environments. By dealing with these organizations, legislatures lessen the costs of dealing with the general public. In California, the legislature has encouraged the formation of "public" organizations such as the County

Supervisors Association of California, the League of California Cities, and the California State Employees Association so as to be able to deal with one organization rather than with myriad groups.

The various staffs of the legislature function as facilitators with groups that are organized and articulate. The district staff of the members are there to deal with the organized and articulate interests in the member's district. The committee staff deal directly with lobbyists who are affected by the legislature's action in a specific policy area. Even the establishment of political party staffs shows the legislature's concern with maximizing relations with the political parties and the articulate within the political parties. In effect, the staff of the California Legislature have become "buffers" for the legislature itself. They are the arm of the legislature which maximizes their resources by dealing with the articulate and attentive public, leaving the legislature's dealing with the general public to the technology of the "mailers."

The more homogeneous the legislature's environment, the more that staff tend to be "surveillance" in nature. Where the environment is heterogeneous and subject to change, the staff tend to become "search"-oriented in addition to surveillance. In states where there is great stability and the political, social, and economic environment is slow to change, the legislative staff tends to be reactive in nature—reporting changes in the environment as they occur. Even the internal, professional staff involved in legal, budget, or audit work tend to be reactive in nature, reacting to changes in the law or the governor's budget, or to money misspent. In environments which are heterogeneous or diverse and/or in a constant state of change, surveillance is not enough to survive. Problems which require action (symbolic or tangible) on the part of the legislature in a complex setting must be more than reactive; there must be some anticipation of problems—or at least some anticipation of the type of response that the legislature or its spokesmen are going to take. The search function involves not only the research of problems coming before the legislature but also the seeking out of innovative approaches to problems which have not yet arisen or those which have not yet been articulated by an organization.

The need for a search as well as a surveillance function in the California Legislature is most evident in the area of taxation and finance. To react to complaints from various articulate and attentive groups is not to solve long-range problems associated with public school finance. Under the leadership of Speaker Jess Unruh, the Assembly Office of Research became a resource for the study of possible solutions to a variety of problems in public school and other finance areas. The continuity of the legislature depended upon its ability to not only react to problems but, to an extent, foresee them. In the California Legislature, by the late 1950s, the time had come to plan.

It should be mentioned that from time to time the California Legislature has found issues which are considered zero-sum—that is, in the words of one state legislator, "no win." The issue can be so volatile that the legislature considers any action as not in its best interest. In a situation like this, the legislature passes the responsibility for action elsewhere. The most used process is the public referendum—let the people decide. Using democratic rhetoric, the legislature announces that the issue is so important that the people should vote and decide it themselves. The more heterogeneous the environment, the more the possibility that issues will be raised which are complex and thus require an increased "search" function in addition to "surveillance" on the part of staff.

In a complex and heterogeneous environment, legislature seek formal information-gathering staff structures which reflect a wide section of the environment. The informal information-gathering system provided to the legislature by lobbyists does not mirror the entire political environment. The lobbyists offer a profile of only a portion—that of major interest groups. In a complex society where the legislature becomes important to many different sectors of the society, the legislature must respond by enlarging its sources of information. An example of this orientation in the California Legislature is seen not only in the addition of new staff, but in their locale. The staffs for the members, especially in the Senate, are located to a great extent in the district. In the large senatorial districts, as many as three district offices were maintained. From interviews with many of these local staff, it becomes apparent that their job is more than to sit awaiting the public. They see their role as exploring problems which do not come through ordinary channels —that is, are not brought by representatives of organized groups. Not that staff are ready to jump into any and all controversy at the local level, but rather they can make their senator or Assemly member aware of changes.

So far in this discussion of the function of staff in the California Legislature I have talked of the role of staff in interaction with the environment, but have not made explicit the reciprocity or exchange involved. *In a complex environment, the legislature's dependence upon staff is exchanged for access and influence.* Just as lobbyists had and still do have influence in exchange for their services, the newer staff structures are also allowed access. In addition, staff which interact with the environment also exchange information for access and influence by groups in the environment. To be more specific, part of the role of the committee consultant is to regularly interact with the articulate, attentive, and general public affected by the actions of his or her committee. The surveillance role also means that those surveyed require access in exchange for their aggregating function. This exchange relationship creates a system relationship—the more staff, the more input and thus complexity for the legislature. One of the problems of the great increase in staffing in the California Legislature was the abundance of suggestions for change, more than the members wanted to handle.

Internal Change

Hitherto, this chapter has emphasized the legislature's exchanges with its environment. The central theme has been the search and surveillance nature of legislative staff. I would like to turn now to the internal function of staff and its relationship to changes occurring there.

Legislatures, in a complex environment, decentralize the decision-making apparatus into committees which act in tandem. State legislatures in the United States vary in the degree of decentralization. The indicator of decentralization is the amount of authority delegated to the leadership groups. In California, the Assembly vests a comparatively great amount of power in the speaker, while in the Senate power is more widely dispersed to the president pro tem and four others who make up the Rules Committee. In both houses, however, the major tasks—and hence, the power—have been delegated to committees.

The staff structures of the California Legislature are likewise decentralized in what may be called a "cluster" rather than a hierarchical system. Some staff are responsible to committee heads, some to the members themselves, some to the leadership, and some to the party leadership. In the California experience, this decentralization, in addition to being a result of increasing equalization brought about by reapportionment, seniority, and other factors, is the legislature's attempt to deal with greater uncertainty. The decentralization of staff is, in essence, the specialization of members *and* staff by designing staff to serve specific interests in the legislature's environment. Strong leadership is sacrificed in order to emphasize adaptability through the decentralization of staff, and to establish "fiefdoms" of legislator expertise and power. In order to have the flexibility for staff structures that have both search and surveillance functions, decentralization of power is mandatory.

There is also another reason for the decentralization of staff in legislatures. Staff perform a necessary function for the legislature faced with complex environments. In exchange for their functions, the legislature affords them independence and access to legislative decision-making. The amount of independence and access is related to the staff's crucial role with the environment. In the California Legislature, the greatest amount of independence and access is given to committee and research staff. Legal, budget, audit, and member staff have correspondingly less, given their more constricted position, which requires less flexibility. The greater the uncertainty that the legislature faces, the more it depends upon staff and thus the more that staff, both internal and external, have influence.

Although staff are given independence and access, some limits are imposed. In the decentralized system of the California Legislature, staff are expected to be loyal to their immediate superior and to the house. Staff are expected to have input into decision-making but that input is not expected to be in conflict with input from legislators. For those internal staff and lobbyists who take sides, being on the winning side is paramount to survival.

Staff in legislatures also provide a curious function for the efficiency rating of the organization. Legislatures, as organizations, are not easily given to being evaluated in terms of quantitative efficiency. For example, an efficient legislature may be the one that does not enact legislation, if the criterion of efficiency is the quality of legislation passed. But that standard is a difficult one to sell to the public and a difficult one for the public to easily digest. So instead of attempting to exhibit efficiency in terms of quality, legislatures resort to the same tactic as other organizations—they quantify everything that they do. Thus, the number of bills introduced and passed, number of days in session, and the number of committee meetings become standards of efficiency. And it is the staff that provide the input for legislation and general business that supports the standard. In essence, the legislature attempts to put efficiency in lay terms.

A press release of the Joint Committee on Rules substantiates the point.

In 1966 the voters of California approved Proposition 1-A, telling the legislature to work full time, and without the constraint of time limits on the sessions.

This is the fifth year under those rule changes and the Joint Rules Committee has decided this is an appropriate time to examine our operations. . . . Especially we are concerned with finding ways to make the best possible use of the time and talents of the 120 men and women in the Assembly and Senate who have been sent here by the voters in their district.

More than 5,200 pieces of legislation were introduced this year, and there is no reason to expect that workload to decrease significantly in the future. Consequently, we must search new ways to improve our operation before we become hopelessly bogged down by the volume of work.[47]

As one committee staff put it, "The responsibility of committee staff is to come up with proposed legislation to make your man look good—preferably in some area of expertise."

Search, Surveillance, and Resource Acquisition

The California Legislature has two task requirements: One, the legislature must organize itself, establish auxiliary structures to aid in the performance of tasks, and in general attempt to make the decision-making process as rational as possible for the members. Two, because of the environmental orientation of its task, the legislature must deal with the uncertainty that comes from a universal political environment where access to the organization is potentially open to every member of the society.

The central argument about the changes in the legislative organization in California is that the addition of staff structures since the establishment of annual sessions in 1946 has been to enable the legislature to better deal with its environment and improve the rationality of the internal organization. These changes are generalized as follows: *The function of legislative staff in the legislature is to perform "problematic search" for the rational reaction of the organization to change. It also is intended to perform the function of "opportunistic surveillance" of the organization's environment.*

The evolution of the staff structures of the California Legislature followed a trend of internalization of functions which the legislature deemed crucial. These functions, if left to external organizations, could affect the ability of the organization to control the flow of external information. As the legislature approached becoming a full-time, year-round organization, the staff structures took on technical staff to do the research for the "search" function. At the same time, the growth of committee staff in the Assembly and personal staffs of the members in the Senate shows the emphasis on the "surveillance" function. These latter staffs were created to survey the attentive and articulate groups in the legislature's immediate environment along with the general environment, the member's constituents.

The interviews with the various staff members of the legislature add credence to the last proposition. The more environmentally oriented staff— the administrative assistants—describe their activities in broad surveillance terms. Such activities as monitoring of district newspapers, dealing with constituent complaints, maintaining relations with attentive and/or articulate groups in the district, cultivating and offering leadership to the political party point toward substantiation of the "surveillance" thesis. Additional empirical data are provided by the short analysis of one consultant's activities over the course of one year and the application of the two categories to his tasks. Kier's major responsibilities were as an interactor with "articulate" groups in his policy arena and as a resource for technical information gained by a number of years' experience in a state agency.

The recruitment of "professionals" in policy areas for committee consultants serves not only the technical information needs of the legislature but also brings a familiarity with the major interests in a policy area. The professional staff is recruited not only for its technical qualifications or potential but also to interact and communicate with the major elements of the committee's environment. The responsibility is to deal with problems before they arise and to bring disparate groups together in support of legislation which the committee leader and the committee prefer. The more "political" staff show functional characteristics which correspond to the "professional" staff, but with a different orientation. The administrative assistant to the member, or the consultant who has been recruited from the member's office or district has a technical knowledge of the major political elements of the district. The number of staff in some members' offices allows a division of labor. Staff in the district are thus oriented to the constituent environment in the district, whereas the staff in the member's office in Sacramento are oriented toward the immediate environment of the legislature. The two functions are not distinct, but the emphasis gives some idea of the major responsibilities of the two types of staffs.

"Problematic search" and "opportunistic surveillance" can be interpreted as staff functions which react to change from outside the organization, rather than implement change. This concept is especially appropriate in an organization such as the legislature, which is so environmentally oriented. Constitutional requirements and the tradition of open access of the legislature hold in the establishment of the "reactive" role. Part of the role of the legislature is as an ombudsman for the general public—reacting to complaints from various citizens. In a decentralized legislature with a plural leadership structure, the ability of the legislature to initiate change is limited.

But the addition of staff structures such as those in the California Legislature institutionalizes a more positive approach to the initiation of public policy. Both the "search" and the "surveillance" functions are designed to elicit resources from elements of the environment (inputs) with which the legislature must exchange in order to survive. The input varies from the inflow of information about the nature of the member's constituency to the internal staff's input of innovative ideas concerning the solution of complex problems. The uncertainty of the legislative environment in conjunction with attempts to improve the rationality of the internal organization have led to the establishment of staff structures designed to enable the legislature to cope with change. The staff structures and their broad functions of "search" and "surveillance" involve more than a legislature attempting to manipulate its environment and close off its decision-making to the outside. Policy innovations and change are also possible.

The legislature lives in an environment increasingly marked by other organizations which have concentrated material and personnel resources. With the complex legislative environment, the exchanges required of the legislature for support are numerous. The more complex the environment and the more the organization's need for input to carry out its role, the more the necessity for exchanges. In reaction to the growing complexity and the need for resources, the legislature has established staff structures to "administer" exchanges with elements of the environment and internalize functions, which in the past were left to the environment. The bargaining position is also improved by the addition of both technical and political experts, thus improving the ability of the legislature to recognize and adapt to change in the environment.

NOTES

1. Students of politics have been less concerned recently with institutions and more concerned with behavior and process. However, in modern societies which have to deal with complexity and rapid change, legislative structures have come to occupy central positions in decision-making. Legislatures, like other organizations, have reflected the complexity of society in their own structures. The focus on these crucial institutions, then, would appear warranted.

2. Richard Sisson, "Comparative Legislative Institutionalization: A Theoretical Exploration," in Allan Kornberg, ed., *Legislatures in Comparative Perspective* (New York: David McKay, 1973), pp. 19-20.

3. Ibid., p. 19.

4. Ibid.

5. Samuel P. Huntington, *Political Order in Changing Society* (New Haven: Yale University Press, 1969).

6. Nelson Polsby, "The Institutionalization of the U.S. House of Representatives," *American Political Science Review,* Vol. 62 (March 1968), pp. 144-168.

7. Huntington, *Political Order in Changing Societies,* p. 12.

8. Ibid., p. 22.

9. Polsby, "The Institutionalization of the U.S. House," p. 145.

10. Huntington, *Political Order in Changing Societies,* pp. 13-14.

11. Polsby, "The Institutionalization of the U.S. House," pp. 164-166.

12. Ibid., p. 144.

13. Loc. cit.

14. D. Jay Doubleday, *Legislative Review of the Budget in California* (Berkeley: Institute of Governmental Studies, University of California, 1967), p. 38.

15. The legislative analyst was given statutory authority in 1951.

16. On legislatures and legislative staff, see Warren H. Butler, "Administering Congress: The Role of Staff," *Public Administration Review,* Vol. 26 (March 1966), pp. 3-13; David Price, "Professionals and 'Entrepreneurs': Staff Orientation and Policy Making on Three Senate Committees," *Journal of Politics,* Vol. 33 (May 1971), pp. 316-336; and Edward Schneier, "The Intelligence of Congress: Information and Public Policy Patterns," *Annals of the American Academy of Political and Social Sciences,* Vol. 388 (March 1970), pp. 14-24. On organizations, see James D. Thompson, *Organizations in Action* (New York: McGraw-Hill, 1967) and Mayer Zald, "Political Economy," in Mayer Zald, ed., *Power in Organizations* (Nashville: Vanderbilt University Press, 1970).

17. Kenneth Kofmehl, *Professional Staffs of Congress* (West Lafayette, Indiana: Purdue Research Foundation, 1962), pp. 5-6.

18. Thompson, *Organizations in Action.*

19. The theory of Frederick Winslow Taylor and Luther Gulick and Lyndall Urwick was based on the rationality of the organization or at least upon the ability of the organization to control or "close" its boundaries. The open approach of such people as

Philip Selznick accepts, as given, the uncertainty of conflict in the organization and the unpredictability of the organization's environment from which the organization must gain its resources. See F. W. Taylor, *The Principles of Scientific Management* (New York: Harper & Row, 1947); Luther Gulick and Lyndall Urwick, eds., *Papers on the Science of Administration* (New York: Institute of Public Administration, 1937); and Philip Selznick, *TVA and the Grass Roots* (Evanston, Ill.: Row, Peterson, 1949).

20. Herbert A. Simon, *Administrative Behavior* (New York: Macmillan, 1957).

21. James March and Herbert A. Simon, *Organizations* (New York: John Wiley, 1958).

22. Richard M. Cyert and James G. March, *A Behavioral Theory of the Firm* (Englewood Cliffs, N.J.: Prentice-Hall, 1963).

23. Thompson, *Organizations in Action,* p. 9.

24. Herbert A. Simon, *Models of Man* (New York: John Wiley, 1956), p. 1.

25. Mayer Zald, *Organization Change* (Chicago: University of Chicago Press, 1970), p. 14.

26. Ibid., p. 19.

27. Ibid., p. 15.

28. Charles Perrow has followed a similar approach in an article which argues that the center of power in organizations changes as the goals of the organization shift. In a later book, Perrow constructs a broader model for the study of organizations from this combination of the open and closed strategies. See Charles Perrow, "The Analysis of Goals in Complex Organizations," *American Sociological Review,* Vol. 26 (December 1961), pp. 854-866.

29. Current P-E theorists have a long intellectual heritage. A good deal of groundwork had been done by prior scholars including William Gore. Gore's "heuristic model" showed some of the theoretical bent which was later to become the P-E model with an organic macro-structural organization; Gore's approach is much like Simon's in that the focal point is the organizational decision rather than structures. However, Gore represents something of a transition in that he points out the politics of organizations along with the marketplace in which they exist. See William Gore, *Administrative Decision-Making: A Heuristic Model* (New York: John Wiley, 1964).

30. Zald, "Political Economy," p. 222.

31. James R. Wood, *Protestant Enforcement or Racial Integration Policy: A Sociological Study in the Political Economy of Organizations* (unpublished Ph.D. dissertation, Vanderbilt University, 1967), p. 53.

32. See John Thibaut and Harold Kelly, *The Social Psychology of Groups* (New York: John Wiley, 1959); George Homans, *Social Behavior: Its Elementary Forms* (New York: Harcourt, Brace & World, 1961); and Peter Blau, *Exchange and Power in Social Life* (New York: John Wiley, 1964).

33. Norton Long, *The Polity* (Chicago: Rand McNally, 1962).

34. Zald, "Political Economy," pp. 225-226.

35. Robert H. Guest, *Organizational Change: The Effect of Successful Leadership* (Homewood, Ill.: Irwin-Dorsey, 1962).

36. Floyd C. Mann and L. R. Hoffman, *Automation and the Worker: A Case Study in the Power Plants* (New York: Holt, Rinehart & Winston, 1960).

37. Warren Bennis, *Changing Organizations* (Boston: McGraw-Hill, 1966).

38. Zald, "Political Economy," p. 222.

39. Ibid., p. 229.

40. Ibid., pp. 225 and 229.

41. We cannot with certainty suggest that environmental complexity is conclusively

the cause for the growth of staff in the California Legislature. What can be said is that staff have grown significantly and, to a large degree, their responsibilities lie in dealing with the legislature's environment.

42. Chester I. Barnard, *The Functions of the Executive* (Cambridge, Mass.: Harvard University Press, 1938).

43. It is interesting to note that under the leadership of Jess Unruh in the Assembly, the emphasis was on committee and research staffs. Under the more decentralized leadership in the Senate, the staffing patterns were more toward staff for individual members. Committee and research staff also developed, but on a smaller scale.

44. Charles Perrow, *Organizational Analysis* (Belmont, Calif.: Wadsworth, 1970), p. 75.

45. The years are not the same for the Senate and the Assembly because of different accounting procedures used by the two houses. Some years total postage was more discernable than others. Legislative accounting in California is a lesson in obviation.

46. Gabriel Almond, *The American People and Foreign Policy* (New York: Praeger, 1950).

47. *Sacramento Bee,* November 25, 1971.

LEGISLATIVE STAFFING PATTERNS IN DEVELOPING COUNTRIES: PROBLEMS AND PROSPECTS

ABDO I. BAAKLINI

In the last few years, several non-Western legislatures witnessed organized attempts at legislative reforms. What differentiates these attempts from their predecessors is that, rather than concentrating on constitutional and electoral changes, they have concentrated on structural and procedural changes in the way legislatures carry out whatever functions they are engaged in. These reform attempts vary from one setting to another. However, a common thread unites them. We shall discuss only one aspect of these reforms— namely, the attempt to provide legislatures with a professional staff that would enable them to perform their function in a technological society in the midst of large-scale government involvement in developmental efforts. Specifically, the experiences of Brazil, Costa Rica, and Lebanon will be the subject of our discussion.

THE STRUCTURE AND IDEOLOGY OF LEGISLATIVE REFORM IN DEVELOPING COUNTRIES

Brazil, Costa Rica, and Lebanon have recently been engaged in comprehensive legislative reforms that include procedural and structural changes. These

AUTHOR'S NOTE: This is a revised version of a paper presented at the annual conference of the American Society for Public Administration, Los Angeles, April 1973. The author would like to thank the Comparative Development Studies Center of the State University of New York at Albany and its Director, James J. Heaphey, for the financial help in undertaking research. The conclusions and ideas expressed in this paper are, however, the sole responsibility of the author.

reforms call for the introduction of new machinery and equipment such as a computer in Brazil, the compilation and indexing of all recent legislation in Costa Rica, and other innovations. A salient feature of these reforms is the provision of a professional legislative staff to help the institution in its work. In the case of the Brazilian Senate, over forty professional staff members were added to the Advisory Department, while in the Brazilian House of Deputies a similar number of professional staff was added to the Legislative Department. In Costa Rica, a new department, the Technical Department, was established, headed by a director who worked directly with the president of the legislature and chairmen of committees under the administrative supervision of the director general of the legislative staff. Eight professional staff members have been recruited to this department. In Lebanon, a bill was introduced and approved providing for a study and research center at the directorate level working with the president and the leadership committee of the Chamber.

Justification for Reform

In all the above cases, the stress was on the legislator's need to have the necessary information for rational policy choices. A review of how these changes were brought about and the functions with which the staff was entrusted will help identify the emerging legislative staff patterns in some developing countries and the problems and prospects they pose for the legislative institution.

Legislative reforms in the United States were characterized by incrementalism and political overtones. Legislative reforms were justified in terms of redressing the imbalance between the executive and the legislature or enabling the legislature to exercise its oversight function. In many cases, they took the form of a partisan struggle. Although the rhetoric of reform was efficiency and more rational policy decisions, the actual reforms took certain political variables into consideration. Professional legislative staff members were normally selected with full consideration of their political allegiance. The power to appoint, transfer, promote, and dismiss the staff was reserved for the legislative leadership. Legislative leaders and staff members were at least partially aware of the political role played by the staff and, therefore, took proper provision to elaborate the "rules of the game" within which the staff may operate. In other words, professional legislative staff members were aware that they served at the pleasure of the political leadership, and that in the final analysis they were judged by the extent to which they contributed to the strengthening and promotion of the values, goals, and objectives of that leadership.

In the three countries under discussion, the process and goals of providing the legislature with a professional staff seemed to follow a different pattern. Extreme caution was taken to ensure that the body entrusted with the study of reform and the adoption of recommendations was nonpolitical, nonpartisan, and unbiased. In the Brazilian Senate, a bipartisan committee of prominent senators, assisted by a committee of experts, was entrusted with the reform. In Costa Rica, a committee headed by a member of one of the minority parties was established.[1] In Lebanon, the Bureau of the Parliament,[2] assisted by an advisory committee of prominent civil servants from the executive branch,[3] supervised the legislative reforms. In all cases, the criteria for appointment to the committees were not political allegiance but technical ability and skill in administrative, legal, and legislative matters. The work of these committees was open and public. They were charged with providing the legislature with the most rational administrative set-up. Compared to legislative reform attempts in the United States, where reform efforts usually were evaluated in terms of their impact on the distribution of power among the leadership and the members of the legislature, the legislative reforms in Brazil, Costa Rica, and Lebanon were characterized by a deliberate attempt to provide these institutions with rational and efficient administration. There was also little discussion of the impact of these reforms on the power of the legislative bureaucracy vis-à-vis the legislators.

The legislative reforms in Brazil, Costa Rica, and Lebanon were not justified as a means to increase the political power of the legislature vis-à-vis the executive. Nor were they interpreted as a means of increasing the power of one political group over another in the legislature. Rather, reform was justified in terms of allowing the legislature to acquire an increased rationality in making policy choices. As Deputy Saborio Alvarado of Costa Rica said, the aim of the legislative reform was the "modernizing of our system and turning it into an efficient legislative chamber so it may help it meet what modern needs demand of a developing country like Costa Rica."[4]

It was this need to participate in and contribute to the development effort that provided the justification for legislative reform. Deputy Solano Chacon, also from Costa Rica, was more explicit in his advocacy for reform. According to Chacon, the act of legislation is a transcendental act, requiring the incorporation of many skills and specialties; therefore, no legislative committee can ever cope with all the complexities regardless of the qualification of its members. "Hence the need to change the system. The modern science of legislation indicates that the text of the laws must come out of specialized units, out of committees dedicated to the drafting of bills, their defense, etc."[5]

It is very interesting to note that the act of legislation, rather than being viewed as a compromise or struggle among different interests and values in which each party tries to maximize its interest, is viewed by Deputy Chacon as a "transcendental act" played in accordance with scientific laws which are determined rationally.

Brazilian reformers also justified their work in terms of being "able to attend to the process of development."[6] The Lebanese enabling legislation provided the same justification:

> It is important within the context of the reorganization of the chamber to examine the relationship of the deputy with the administrative and staff machinery that assists him so he may benefit the most. It should be noticed that the legal, economic, and cultural matters in this age have reached a high degree of complexity beyond the ability of the individual to comprehend it without the necessary help. . . . How is it possible for the institution to develop itself so it may catch up with the new wave which is science, so democracy may be realized through science?[7]

The rationale for legislative reforms seems to ignore the political nature of the legislative process and consequently the nature of the staff that would adequately meet those needs. The apparent attempt to minimize the role of the legislative staff to the mere provision of "objective" information to the legislature in order for the latter to reach "rational-scientific" decisions may be based on a number of considerations with which advocates of legislative reforms in each country had to contend.

In the first place, under the impact of the literature on modernization and development, the political and intellectual leaders of many developing countries are skeptical of political decisions as being corrupt, immoral, and inferior to "scientific," "objective" decisions. Through their admiration of the technological and scientific wonders that were achieved in some of the developing countries, the political and intellectual leaders of developing countries came to believe that if development were to be achieved, all decisions including policy choices need to be reached "scientifically" and "objectively."[8] Hence, the stress on the legislature's need for "scientific" and "objective" information and the concomitant role that the staff was envisioned to play.

A second reason for the trend to provide the legislature with "neutral," "objective" staff, as opposed to a staff sensitive to the political needs of the various groups in the legislature, had to do with the relationship between the executive and the legislature in those countries. In the case of Brazil, for example, although a presidential system of government, the legislature avoided giving the appearance of bolstering its staff capacities for the purpose of confronting the executive. A "neutral" staff, therefore, was more acceptable to the executive since its function was conceived to enhance the rational decision-making process of the legislative institutions. Executives, dominated by bureaucratic elites, as is the case in Brazil, are more likely to tolerate the development of the legislative institution along bureaucratic lines rather than along political lines. Furthermore, legislative leaders in the three countries felt that by acquiring neutral staff they would be able to legitimize their choices to the executive and to the general public on the basis of the "objectivity" and the "scientific" nature of their information. A new legitimacy for the legislature to participate in basic policy choices, therefore, was created on the same foundation as that used by the executive.

Finally the resort to a "neutral" legislative staff was a means to meet the needs of the minority and opposition parties more than the majority or government parties. Through their intimate work relationship, the members of the majority party, especially in Costa Rica and Brazil, have better access to executive information than opposition or minority parties. Therefore, the opposition and minority parties were in favor of a "neutral" staff that would be independent of control by the majority party or the executive. In fact, the overwhelming majority of the members of the opposition party in Brazil reported that their first recourse for getting information was the legislative staff, while more than fifty percent of the deputies from the majority party resorted to the executive to obtain their information.[9]

Patterns of Legislative Staffing

Since the policy role of the legislative staff has been consciously recognized in the United States (if not in the political science literature, at least in practice), several measures have been taken to contain and control it. Majority-minority staffing, staffing for leadership, staffing for individual members, committee staffing, temporary appointments, lack of tenure and a variety of other institutional and procedural devices were devised to keep the staff members in line. The pattern of legislative staffing in developing countries seems to encourage a strong policy role for the staff in spite of the safeguards that are usually institutionalized.

In the three countries examined, professional staff have been organized in central units to serve the whole legislature. The staff reports directly to the president or to an administrative tenured officer under him, and, therefore, is protected from the political control of various legislative leaders, representatives of minority parties, parties in the opposition, or even chairmen of committees. To ensure the political independence of the staff, elaborate procedures embodied in writing the internal rules of each legislature were devised. The advisory units were centralized to ease their supervision by a director, who acts as a shield against political influence. Administratively, the director is responsible to a director general and eventually to the president of the legislature. The director of the advisory department is responsible for drawing up the work agenda for his department, including work priorities. Each legislator is entitled to the professional service of these advisory units.

However, such services are restricted to official legislative business. In other words, priority is given to services that are of a general institutional nature. Research associated with private, member-sponsored bills or with constituency-related issues is considered private or personal in nature and, therefore, discouraged. The use of the staff to aid a legislator in identifying problems relevant to his political success is not considered legitimate. The needs of the legislator for a staff to identify and alert him to negative situations he should avoid or to positive opportunities that he should capitalize upon are discouraged as being corrupt and partisan. Thus, to ensure their political neutrality, legislative staff units were limited in areas that could strengthen the legislator, and strengthened in areas that could contribute to the institution, such as the collection, control, and dissemination of information that will constitute the basis of decision-making.

Another procedural device to ensure the neutrality of legislative staff is the immunities granted them in developing countries as regular civil servants (even when they enjoy separate personnel law, as in Brazil, Costa Rica, and, to a certain extent, Lebanon). Thus, recruitment, promotion, demotion, transfer, and dismissal have to follow the civil service merit laws. In other words, there is very narrow latitude in appointment or dismissal. Once a staff member is appointed, it is unlikely that he or she will be dismissed except for a major violation. The civil service laws provide the legislative staff with a guarantee of lifetime employment.

Against this background of staff careerism and permanence stands the strikingly high rate of turnover among the legislators and legislative leadership and the atmosphere of insecurity within which they have to survive. In Costa Rica, members of parliament are not eligible for reelection. This means that every four years a completely new legislature is empowered. Once elected, it has to contend with an established professional staff which undoubtedly knows more about the business of legislation than most legislators. In Lebanon, while the rate of new entrants to the legislature each year is less than thirty-three percent, the fact remains that the leadership of the legislature as well as the members and chairmen of committees have to be elected annually by the general membership of the legislature. In other words, there is no seniority system in committee appointment or in leadership positions. Brazil is also characterized by a high degree of new entrants (over fifty percent) to the legislature and a biannual selection of legislative leaders and committee members.

The dependence of legislators on one source of information, the absence of other sources of research and information (e.g., lobbyists, research institutions, university-sponsored research), the career security of the staff and the high turnover among legislators, legislative leadership, and legislative offices undoubtedly contribute to a strong staff.

While the hierarchical nature of the staff organizations in the three legislatures imposes an administrative control over the legislative professional staff, similar to the bureaucratic control in the executive departments, nonetheless this seems to fall short of the political control and responsiveness needed by an institution engaged in the choice of values. Legislators' needs are not restricted to "objective" information, but to information and data that tend to support their values and their political orientations. A "neutral" staff obviously cannot tailor its research to fit such particular needs.

Role Perception of Legislative Staff in Developing Countries

American legislative staff's perception of their roles have been shaped by the prevailing theories in the public service. Thus, the politics-administration dichotomy or the principles of the scientific management movement stressing the difference between factual choices and value choices have had an impact in defining the role of a staffer.[10] Although in recent years the reverence given to political decisions has been on the decline, the momentum of the American system has sustained a respectable place for political decisions. Students who adhere to the politics-administration dichotomy or fact-value distinction have been able to develop a respect and appreciation for political decisions. The realm of politics has been legitimized in the literature of constitutional theory, political philosophy, and public administration. When it became apparent that the politics-administration dichotomy did not portray the realities of administrative behavior, a new literature on the public interest and the role of the civil servant in serving this interest appeared. Once it was recognized that bureaucracies are engaged in policy choices, a whole literature appeared justifying that role and advocating ethical, moral, and structural constraints on how that role is to be played, how success is to be measured, and what system of accountability needs to be installed. In other words, when theories of public administration could no longer sustain a separate and distinct domain for political decisions, a whole body of literature circumscribing how the political role was to be played came into existence. It is important to note that the new literature did not attempt to deny the political domain but tried to extend it to areas previously thought to fall outside it. Within the context of the new literature, policy decisions became no longer the prerogatives of elected bodies, but also of appointed officers. In this schema, politics was not demoted but became a pervasive phenomenon influencing both choices of value alternatives as well as what was previously thought to be value-free choices. If anything, it helped to sensitize the "expert" or "professional" to the value content of his choices and recommendations. Bargaining and compromise, long the domain of legislatures, were extended to include the decision-making process in the bureaucracy, including the so-called "objective" professional decisions.

This orientation in the literature undoubtedly left its impact on the attitudes of the "experts" and their "scientific" values, vis-à-vis the political values. Balutis' study of the New York State Legislature revealed that the overwhelming majority of the legislative staff are aware of and appreciate the political environment within which they live.[11] In a similar study on the norms of congressional staffers, Patterson found that staff members tend to adopt the goal orientations dominant among members of the committee, that they do not press their own policy but rather try to be sensitive to limitations on their own conclusions and proposals, and that they usually have a high sense of loyalty to their committee head and try to enhance his prestige and interest.[12] He also found that they defer to congresspeople, which was illustrated by statements of the sort that staff members must "be on tap, and not on top," that they must not "try to run the show," and that "you must remember that staff is staff and members are members."[13]

In brief, both the theory of administrative behavior which defines the role of an "expert" as well as the norms within which the legislative staff in the United States works have placed some limitations on the power and the policy role they may play. If these limitations are taken with the structural and procedural limitations discussed in the previous section, the legislative staff is found to be under some control in terms of the role they may legitimately play.

What are the "rules of the game" defining the relationship of staff to legislators in developing countries? Little systematic research exists on this subject. However, the author's intensive interaction with legislative staff over the past four years can be utilized for a preliminary assessment.

I previously have argued that the literature on development has destroyed whatever deference was left for the political domain.[14] By stressing efficiency, productivity, modernization, and other related goals, the literature on development paid little attention to how things are done and more to the fact that they are done in the quickest way. Development became a job to be done in the shortest possible time. The "expert," the "specialist," became the hero; the politician became the villain standing in the way of development. Politics (to development theorists) is a negative attribute that should be eliminated. Even when positively conceived, it was thought to be a leisurely activity that only people from "developed" countries could afford. The center of the political system became the planning board, suitably located to ensure its immunity from the political process. The question then became how to avoid the political process in order to achieve developmental objectives.

Within this atmosphere, it is only natural to expect a conflict between political values and "scientific" values. Professional legislative staffers who normally associate with the "scientific" perspective are likely to feel that they are more qualified by the nature of their training to make policy choices than the elected members of parliament, who may lack high academic achievement.

A recent conversation with a legislative staff member may help illustrate this point. He stated that fifteen percent of the legislative body within which he worked is composed of university professors, intellectuals, and leaders of their profession (doctors, lawyers, or engineers), whom he and his staff colleagues respect and identify with. Another thirty-five percent of the legislators are looked upon as capable of being educated, and, therefore, staffers are willing to spend time explaining the alternatives of a policy choice to them and are willing to try to persuade them with regard to a particular issue. The remaining fifty percent are incapable of being educated, and, therefore, the staff tries not to waste any time arguing with them. It is not important whether the situation actually corresponds to this perception. What is important is the way the legislators are viewed by the staff. Those who are respected are those whom the staff thinks share their "scientific" attitude; others are educable and, therefore, can be "scientific"; the rest are hopeless and, therefore, should be ignored.

Another legislative staff member who is unusually sensitive to the political dimension of decision-making had this to say in justifying the need for professional staffing (italics added):

> The main characteristic of legislators is the temporary nature of their term in office. The turnover is approximately 60%. . . . In general, they [legislators] do not have an overall view of national problems or the functions and powers of the legislature. Since they devote little time to the functional activities of their House, it is vital that there be a professional legislative staff whose knowledge and skills are totally devoted to the legislature. The work in a political assembly is special and the staff must be capable, discerning, bright, dynamic, public-spirited, independent, and discrete. They should be able to assist the new members who do not know the history of particular issues, their repercussions for the country, the workings of the legislative process, and various parliamentary by-laws. *The legislature continues because of the existence of a permanent, experienced, non-partisan staff with a knowledge of parliamentary rules and traditions and dedicated to the institution.* [15]

The image of the staffer as savior and redeemer of the legislative institution cannot be conceded despite the disclaimer that all the above activities are to be performed under the direction and upon the request of the legislators.

In a book by a former member of the Lebanese legislative staff, the author makes his distrust of politicians and political decisions apparent. He goes so far as to recommend that the agenda for parliamentary committee meetings or floor debate be determined by the staff rather than by the president or leadership committee since the staffers are more "objective" than the members of parliament.[16]

Development ideologies, structural and procedural variables (discussed in previous section), and the fact that the legislative staffers in developing countries are career people with a greater sense of permanence than the legislators whom they serve may all contribute to the failure to realize the intended consequences of professional staffs. In the absence of a set of norms defining the relationship of staff to legislators and the legislature, staffers may be oriented negatively toward both legislators and the process of policy choice. This may contribute either to the undermining of the legislative process or, more likely, to the loss of influence on the part of the staff units, since legislators would tend to avoid consulting with a hostile staff that owes no allegiance to them.

LEGISLATIVE STAFFING: PROBLEMS AND PROSPECTS

Norman Meller, one of the first scholars to draw attention to the role played by legislative service agencies, argued that whether the staff agencies perform the role of assembling data, weighing data, or taking definitive action, they are actually engaged in influencing the outcome of policy decisions.[17] Furthermore, when legislative staff performs its functions with a view of the legislator as a "statesman," the legislator's actual needs as a political animal which has to survive politically if he is ever to have a chance to act as a statesman, is usually sacrificed. Specifically, a legislator who needs to relate to the interests of his or her constituency and to various pressure groups if (s)he is to be reelected will be neglected.

The legislator's needs in relating to his or her constituency are considerably different from the needs as a statesman. Legislative staff can meet some of the needs of the legislator as a politician if the staff is properly oriented and structured. Legislative staff may perform a variety of functions that are not only related to the legislator in his capacity as a statesman but also in his or her capacity as a politician who needs to be reelected.

In contrast, the newly created staff units in the three legislatures under discussion are structured and oriented to play a different role. Legislative staffers are likely to view the legislator's needs as those of a statesman, at one extreme, or those of someone who needs to be educated, at the other. In both cases, staff are likely to confuse their roles and to provide the legislator with information and advice he does not need. Such a role may contribute to a growing alienation between the staff and the legislators, leading to loss of confidence and consequently to the forfeiture of the goals which the staff units were originally designed to achieve.

The dilemma posed in the previous discussion, while it is acutely manifested in developing countries, is by no means restricted to those countries. Attempts at legislative staff reforms in developed countries, in Europe and in the United States at the state and national level, have had to contend with a number of questions related to the relationship between strengthening the legislative staff and strengthening the legislature.[18] If professional legislative staffing leads to an increase in the amount of information available to legislature, then what is the relationship between increased information and legislative effectiveness?[19] To whom should information be provided, to the rank-and-file legislator or to the legislative leadership? If the purpose of legislative development is to enable the legislature to exercise effective control and review of the programs of the executive, then which is more effective, strengthening the legislative leadership or strengthening the individual legislator? Furthermore, if one of the rationales for the importance of legislatures in the development process is that they normally bring to the decision-making process factual and value components that do not exist in the executive, then are we not, through the provision of professional legislative staff, destroying this unique contribution of legislatures by standardizing and professionalizing information and values?

And, finally, if one of the major contributions of legislatures is their integrative functions through constituency service,[20] what kinds of staffing patterns would maximize the integrative function of a legislature without minimizing its overall policy function? Thus, a central staff in the capitol may help the legislator to play a more effective role vis-à-vis the central government, a role that may consume all his time as a legislator. However, being a full-time statesman in the capital would reduce his effectiveness as a representative of his constituency vis-à-vis the national government.

On the other hand, to strengthen his integrative function, a legislator may find it necessary to strengthen his staff in the field. If he is to exercise any meaningful control over the information provided by his field staff, he himself has to increase his presence in the field. His presence in the field may strengthen his integrative function, but it would weaken his policy function vis-à-vis the national government. Furthermore, a legislator who is rarely present in the capitol has less clout with the bureaucracy which he is supposed to oversee. If anything, legislators who leave the capital and reside in their constituencies leave an important policy vacuum that is normally filled by legislative leadership and central legislative staff.

Recently, it has been suggested that the intensity of the issues associated with legislative staff reforms are less a reflection of the difficulties of these issues and more a result of social science neglect (especially by public administration) of the needs of the legislature as an institution. Baaklini and Heaphey have argued that behavioralist, theory-oriented social science research has failed to understand or to appreciate the visions and the needs of the political actors and the institutions within which they act.[21] Worthley, in a comprehensive survey of the literature in the field of public administration in the United States, found that the literature can be characterized not by benign neglect but by total neglect—combined with a hostility against legislative institutions. He suggested that public administration has much to contribute to the study of legislatures and legislative development and, therefore, issued a call for public administrators to be involved in legislative studies.[22] Mosher et al., in their official report to the Senate Watergate Committee, recommended a strong legislature to exercise its oversight function effectively.[23]

Undoubtedly, the above developments are steps in the right direction. A focus on legislative staff development and legislative needs is overdue. The contribution of public administration to legislative studies undoubtedly would shed some light on some of the questions raised above. It would help clarify the advantages and disadvantages of various legislative staffing patterns.[24] It would help determine what information legislators need and how to obtain, organize, and present such information. More important, however, is the ability of departments of public administration to imbue legislative staff members not only with technical information, but also with political values and dilemmas of the legislature.

While public administration and other social sciences may help shed light on some of the issues of legislative development, they are unlikely to resolve the inherent conflict between bureaucratic values characteristic of executive or legislative bureaucracies and political values of an institution such as a legislature. Weber's admiration of the superiority of a legal-rational bureaucracy to all other forms of organization was conditioned on the existence of effect political control of that bureaucracy through a legislature.[25] To exercise such control, the legislature is now asked to build and strengthen its own bureaucracy. One can legitimately ask, then, how can the legislature, while preserving its present political characteristics, control its own bureaucracy? How can a legislature preserve its openness, representativeness, and collegial nature and yet control a bureaucracy that tends more and more to be permanent and career-oriented, elitist, secretive, and hierarchical in nature?

In executive bureaucracies, the specialists and the experts were controlled through an organizational system characterized by a hierarchical system of authority, an elaborate communication system, an extensive program to help individuals develop organizational identification, and a notion of efficiency as a yardstick to measure the appropriateness of various alternatives of action.[26] Experts and professionals were relieved, at least theoretically, from the determination of values. The organization has, hierarchically through its leadership, determined what values are to be sought.[27]

This, however, is not the case in the legislature, where the system of authority is diffuse and contradictory. Communication is erratic, contradictory, and incomplete, a system of organizational identification is yet to be developed, and a criterion of efficiency is lacking. Moreover, while experts and professionals in organizations can be relieved of the responsibility to choose among conflicting values, experts and professionals in legislatures are in the midst of the process of choosing among conflicting values. If determination of the premises of decisions is tantamount to determining the outcome of decisions,[28] then undoubtedly the experts and the professionals in the legislature will have a great deal to say in determining the premises of decisions both factually and in terms of values.

A great deal has been written on how legislative staffers are submerging[29] or should submerge[30] their value judgments, leaving the value choices to the individual legislators. Nonetheless, these observations or recommendations ignore the main findings and recommendations of the organizational psychology literature. Authors such as Argyris,[31] McGregor,[32] and Maslow[33] have suggested that individuals in organizations have a need for self-actualization, that unless that need is satisfied the contribution of the individuals is impaired, and that organizations should be designed to promote the satisfaction of those needs.[34] One of the needs that individuals need to satisfy is the realization of their value and of what they believe in. Through the structural and procedural characteristics of most legislatures, the staffers have ample opportunity to see that their needs are satisfied and will most likely seek to do so. Both as staffers and as citizens, they feel it is their right and their obligation to shape what they conceive to be right and just.

In his famous last article, "Politics as a Vocation," Max Weber epitomized the tragic fate of the political leader in societies characterized by bureaucratic organizations. He is the last hope that is destined to be vanquished by the legal-rational organizations. Any proposal aimed at legislative staff development (including the professionalization of the legislative staff), therefore, should be evaluated in terms of its impact on the demise of the Don Quixotes of our political system, the legislators and their institution.

SUMMARY

Efforts at legislative development in the three countries under study stress the creation of a professional staff as a means of strengthening the legislature in its role of making rational policy choices. This chapter has argued that if the intended objective is to be realized, the creation of these staff units needs to be evaluated in terms of their impact on legislative power and legislative effectiveness. If conceived as isolated instances of merely providing the appropriate kind of professionals and technicians, they may end up either weakening the institution which they were supposed to strengthen, or they may be rejected and dismissed as failures. In the countries discussed, the doctrine of legislative staffing which is needed to define and legitimate their role is lacking. It was also argued that the available legitimating doctrine is inimical to the legislative process since the realm of politics in the literature on development has been downgraded and dismissed. Due to these deficiencies in the institutional variables and due to inherent contradictions between political legislative values and bureaucratic administrative values, the attempt to professionalize legislative staffing may prove to be a two-edged sword. In the process of strengthening the information available to legislators, professional staffing may also influence the value and factual premises of legislative decisions, thus undermining the unique contribution of the institution to the decision-making process.

NOTES

1. The committee was composed of the following deputies: Monge Alvarez, Lacle Castro, Leiva Runnebaum, Saborio Alvarado, and Solano Chacon.

2. The bureau of the chamber is composed of the following members of the chamber elected individually by secret ballot by the members of the chamber: the president, vice president, two secretaries, and two questeurs.

3. The proposal to establish the Research and Studies Center came from Mr. Bishara Mnassa and Mr. Mahdi Sadek, staff members of the Lebanese Parliament.

4. From minutes of the ordinary meetings of the Costa Rican National Assembly, No. 52, September 7, 1971.

5. Ibid.

6. Eduardo Pereira, "Legislative Reform in Brazil," unpublished paper presented at the annual meeting of the Society for International Development, San Jose, Costa Rica, 1973, pp. 12-13.

7. From a draft bill to the Lebanese Chamber of Deputies.

8. For a discussion of the impact of development ideologies on the political realm in developing countries, see Abdo I. Baaklini, "Comparative Public Administration: The Persistence of an Ideology," *Journal of Comparative Administration,* Vol. 5 (May 1973), pp. 109-124.

9. From interviews conducted by the author in November 1973 in Brazilia with over seventy-five deputies from both parties.

10. See Herbert A. Simon, *Administrative Behavior* (New York: Free Press, 1957).

11. See Alan P. Balutis, "Professional Staffing in the New York State Legislature: An Exploratory Study" (unpublished Ph.D. dissertation, State University of New York at Albany, 1973), pp. 80-82.

12. Samuel C. Patterson, "The Professional Staffs of Congressional Committees," *Administrative Science Quarterly,* Vol. 15 (March 1970), pp. 29-30.

13. Ibid.

14. From a written statement by one of the staff members of the legislatures under study.

15. Ibid.

16. Antoine Arej, *Lubnan: As-sultan al-ama* (Lebanon: The Public Authorities) (Beirut: Badron Press, 1963), pp. 147-154.

17. Norman Meller, "The Policy Position of Legislative Service Agencies," *Western Political Quarterly,* Vol. 5 (March 1952), pp. 109-123.

18. Citizens Conference on State Legislatures, *Compilation of Recommendations Pertaining to Legislative Improvement in the Fifty States* (Kansas City, Mo.: Conference, April 1967); Milton Gwirtzman, "The Bloated Branch," *New York Times Magazine* (November 10, 1974), pp. 30-31+; and John C. Wahlke, "Organization and Procedure," pp. 126-153 in Alexander Heard, ed., *State Legislatures in American Politics* (Englewood Cliffs, N.J.: Prentice-Hall, 1966).

19. Charles R. Dechert, "Availability of Information for Congressional Operations," in Alfred de Grazia, ed., *Congress: The First Branch of Government* (Garden City, N.Y.: Doubleday Anchor, 1967); and Warren Weaver, Jr., *Both Your Houses: The Truth About Congress* (New York: Praeger, 1972).

20. Albert Eldridge, *Legislatures and Integration in Pluralistic Societies* (Durham, N.C.: Duke University Press, forthcoming).

21. Abdo I. Baaklini and James J. Heaphey, "Legislative Institution-Building in Brazil, Costa Rica and Lebanon," *Sage Professional Papers in Administration and Policy Studies* (Beverly Hills: Sage, forthcoming).

22. John Worthley, *Public Administration and Legislative Management* (Chicago: Nelson-Hull, forthcoming).

23. Frederick C. Mosher et al., *Watergate: Implications for Responsible Government* (New York: Basic Books, 1974).

24. James A. Robinson, "Staffing the Legislature," in Allan Kornberg and Lloyd D. Musolf, eds., *Legislatures in Developmental Perspective* (Durham, N.C.: Duke University Press, 1970).

25. Reinhard Bendix, *Max Weber: An Intellectual Portrait* (Garden City, N.Y.: Doubleday Anchor, 1962).

26. Simon, *Administrative Behavior.*

27. Philip Selznick, *Leadership in Administration* (New York: Harper & Row, 1957).

28. Simon, *Administrative Behavior.*

29. Alan P. Balutis, "Policy-Making in the New York State Legislature: The Role of the Staff," unpublished paper presented at the annual meeting of the New York State Political Science Association, Albany, March 29-30, 1973; Patterson, "Professional Staffs."

30. Worthley, *Public Administration.*

31. Chris Argyris, *Personality and Organization* (New York: Harper & Row, 1957).

32. Douglas McGregor, *The Human Side of Enterprise* (New York: McGraw-Hill, 1960).

33. Abraham H. Maslow, *Motivation and Personality* (New York: Harper & Row, 1964).

34. Warren Bennis, *Changing Organizations* (New York: McGraw-Hill, 1966).

ABOUT THE AUTHORS

H. OWEN PORTER, an Assistant Professor of Political Science at the University of Virginia, received his doctorate from the University of Michigan. He has authored several papers on the information needs of state legislators and is presently conducting a study of legislative committee membership turnover in twenty states.

SUSAN WEBB HAMMOND teaches at American University. She received her B.A. from Bryn Mawr, her M.A. and Ph.D. from Johns Hopkins, and also studied as a Fulbright Scholar at Cambridge University. She has worked as a congressional staff assistant and written professionally on Congress.

MICHAEL A. WORMAN, an Associate Professor of Political Science at Elizabethtown College, was a Florida State University Fellow in 1966 and a World Law Fund Fellow that same year. Mr. Worman was one of the first group of students chosen to be a Florida Legislative Staff Intern when that program was instituted in 1968. He has also served as an administrative assistant in the Florida House of Representatives.

HARRISON W. FOX, Jr., received his Ph.D. from American University and currently serves as Director of Legislation and Research for U.S. Senator Bill Brock. He has written extensively on congressional reform and legislative oversight of the executive branch.

NORMAN J. ORNSTEIN is an Assistant Professor in the Department of Politics at the Catholic University of America. He received his doctorate from the University of Michigan and has authored several articles on Congress. He is the editor of *Congress in Change: Evolution and Reform*, recently published by Praeger.

RAYMOND G. DAVIS, an Assistant Professor of Political Science at the University of Kansas, completed his Ph.D. at the University of California (Davis) in 1972. He has served as an intern with the California State Senate and is currently serving as a NASPAA Public Administration Fellow with the Bureau of Community Health Services in HEW.

ABDO I. BAAKLINI currently is an Assistant Professor of Comparative and Development Studies at the State University of New York at Albany and Associate Director of the Comparative Development Studies Center at that school. He has written extensively on problems of political and administrative development in developing nations and is the author of *Legislatures and Political Development: Lebanon 1842-1972,* forthcoming from Duke University Press.

JAMES J. HEAPHEY is Professor of Public Administration and Director of the Comparative Development Studies Center, State University of New York at Albany. He is the author of *Spatial Dimensions of Development Administration* and of numerous articles in professional journals. He is currently directing a worldwide research project on the role of legislatures in development, in addition to conducting several research projects on organizational aspects of American state legislatures.

ALAN P. BALUTIS is Assistant Professor of Political Science at the State University of New York at Buffalo. He received his doctorate from the State University of New York at Albany, where he was co-director of the New York State Senate Intern Program and Project Officer of the Comparative Development Studies Center. He is currently serving as a 1975-1976 NASPAA Public Administration Fellow.

INDEX

Advisory Commission in Intergovernmental Relations, 23
Alabama, 109, 110
Almond, Gabriel, 213
Alvarado, Saborio, 225
Anonymity. (See legislative staff, norm of)
Argyris, Chris, 235
Armbrister, Trevor, 78
Asher, Herbert B., 179, 183

Baaklini, Abdo I., 13, 234
Bailey, Stephen K., 103, 104
Balutis, Alan, 230
Barnard, Chester, 9, 12, 202
Bentley, Arthur, 20
Bibby, John F., 4
Brazil, legislative reform in, 223-226; legislative staff in, 224-229, 232, 235-236; majority party in, 227-228
Brydges, Earl, 30, 110
Burns, John, 29

California, effect of legislative staffing in, 31-32; institutionalization of, legislature, 191, 193; legislation in, 42; legislative modernization in, 29, 31; legislative sources of information in, 47, 49; legislative staff in, 199-212, 214-219
Chacon, Solano, 225
Church, Frank, 159
Citizens Conference on State Legislatures, 25, 29, 34, 108, 109, 110, 134
Cochrane, James, 30
Committees, Czarism on, 4; decline in power of, 32; standing, 4, 23, 24, 42, 44, 51, 64, 109, 171, 177, 179
Connecticut, 49, 53-54, 109, 180
Costa Rica, legislative reforms in, 223-226; legislative staff in, 224-225, 227-229, 232, 235-236; majority party in, 227, 228
Cyert, Richard M., 195, 196

Data, horizontal collection of, 5; pollution of, 5; vertical collection of, 5
Davidson, Roger, 179
Decision-making, as policy process, 14, 224, 226, 229; collective, 9, 13-14; complexity of, 27; democratic, 29; legislative, 56, 148, 167, 177, 187; patterns of legislative, 176-188; rational, 3, 5, 39, 195, 218, 226; scientific, 8, 226; technical, 28
Dolwig, Richard, 209

Eagleton Institute of Politics, 29, 32
Eidenberg, Eugene, 28
Eisenstadt, S. N., 185
Evans, Rowland, Jr., 139
Executive staff, 11, 28, 48, 50, 157, 234; comparison to legislative staff. (See legislative staff, comparison to executive staff)

Fenno, Richard F., Jr., 172
Florida, 42, 87, 89, 90, 93, 101
Fox, Harrison, 25, 140
Francis, Wayne, 54

Griffiths, Martha, 180
Gross, Bertrand, 104

Hammond, Susan, 25, 140
Heaphey, James, 234
Hevesi, Alan, 115
Huitt, Ralph K., 113
Huntington, Samuel, 192-193

Idaho, 109
Illinois, 29, 42
Information, application of, 26, 45, 124; collegial, 46, 50, 56; difficulty in acquiring, 40, 41, 42-43, 52; exchange of, 149, 215, 57 n 14; factual, 55; formal-informal channels of, 44; gathering of, in Senate and House, 173-176,